IMAGES
of America

STRATHAM

IMAGES
of America

STRATHAM

Helen LaFave

ARCADIA
PUBLISHING

ISBN 978-0-7385-8754-7

Published by Arcadia Publishing
Charleston, South Carolina

Printed in the United States of America

Library of Congress Catalog Card Number: 98-87320

For all general information contact Arcadia Publishing at:
Telephone 843-853-2070
Fax 843-853-0044
E-Mail sales@arcadiapublishing.com
For customer service and orders:
Toll-Free 1-888-313-2665

Visit us on the Internet at www.arcadiapublishing.com

This book is dedicated to my mother and father,
Nancy and Donald LaFave.

Contents

ACKNOWLEDGMENTS

Conducting research, writing, and preparing this book has been a privilege. I am indebted to so many people who took the time to speak with me and answer my questions, sometimes repeatedly. Their knowledge and memories are the core of this work and I appreciate their assistance. Of course, any and all errors are entirely mine.

My appreciation is extended to Carol Aten, Earl and Margaret Barker, Evelyn Barker, Gerry and Betty Batchelder, Bob and Marge Berry, Lucy Chapman Bume, Olive Calef, Lester Carbonneau, Helen Chase, Lucy Hutton Cushman, Marjorie Parkman Goodrich, Betty Wentworth Henneberry, John Hutton, Beatrice Knibbs, Dorothy O'Leary, Barbara and Graeme Mann, Lorraine Stuart Merrill, Nancy Merrill, David and Elizabeth Noyes, Ruth Paul, Mildred Parker, George and Katherine Peabody, Nan Pearson, Martha Peabody Pidgeon, Caroline Saltonstall Robinson, Postmaster Jim Rolston, Barbara Scamman, Doug and Stella Scamman, James Scamman Jr., James Scamman Sr., Jody Scamman, Cameron and Joan Sewell, Teddie Higgins Smith, Walter Smyk, Margaret Pearson Tate, Matt Thomas, Violet McLane Winch, Flossie Wiggin, Jean Cottrell Wiggin, Peter Wiggin, Beatrice Scamman Wolf, and the entire Stratham Historical Society.

The photographs are taken from several collections. Throughout the text, images are followed with these photograph credits: Stratham Historical Society (SHS.); Betty Batchelder (BB.); Bob and Marge Berry (B and MB.); Lucy Chapman Bume (LB.); Helen Chase (HC.); Lucy Hutton Cushman (LC.); Charles and Katherine Peabody (C and KP.); Caroline Saltonstall Robinson (CR.); Jim Rolston (JR.); Doug and Stella Scamman (D and SS.); Cameron and Joan Sewell (C and JS.); Teddie Higgins Smith (TS.); Ernest and Eleanor Wiggin (E and EW.); and Violet McLane Winch (VW.).

INTRODUCTION

Stratham, with its rolling hills and some of the best farmland in the state, was one of the first settled areas in New Hampshire. From its earliest settler, Thomas Wiggin in 1631, through the 1960s Stratham was primarily an agricultural mainstay of the region. Known for extensive poultry and dairy operations as well as orchards and truck farms (which eventually supplied East Coast cities as well as international markets), the land has blessed the people of Stratham.

Besides farmers, others have enjoyed the beauty of the town. John Mason, of the original Mason patents with rights to New England in the 17th century, declared that he would build his baronial seat in Stratham. Of course he never did, but his appreciation of the land was similar to that of the Folsom family, who built country houses on Heights Road in the 19th century. These gracious estates boast commanding valley views.

Since the 1960s, Stratham has rapidly developed from the rural truck farming breadbasket (or rather the fruit, egg, milk, and vegetable basket) of most of its history into a suburban enclave with quick access to major roadways. Although farms still exist, particularly organic farms, Stratham is now a town of homes of people who work elsewhere. Many of the old farmsteads are professional offices and the land has been subdivided to build more housing. Even so, grand homes continue to be built to take advantage of the natural beauty as well as the easy access to the town.

It is easy to look at the town and see how it has changed, especially in the past 30 years. Before 1965 Stratham was still primarily the farming community it had been for centuries, with the land being farmed by many of the same families, including the Wiggin, Barker, Berry, Chapman, Chase, Gowen, Jewell, Parkman, Pearson, Scamman, and Scammon families. If you look for this old Stratham, you will find it.

You may also be surprised at another old Stratham you might discover. In addition and complementary to the agricultural enterprises, Stratham has a tradition of non-agricultural commerce. From the taverns on Kings Hyway serving traveling colonists, to mills, retail establishments, auction houses, and even a resort hotel, this other Stratham thrived and helped make the town a vital community.

In addition to the variety of work that made the community, there was a vibrant social life. At one point there were Baptist, Christian, and Congregationalist churches in town which supported numerous youth and adult programs. There were plays, parties, and dances at the town hall. There were libraries long before the Wiggin Memorial Library was built. The Grange and 4H involved farmers and their children for decades. There was a men's baseball team for decades. There were celebrations of the town bicentennial, the founding of Stratham Hill Park, Memorial and Independence Day, and the annual Old Home Day. The entire community came together for clubs, programs, parties, and events both large and small. Although many of the community organizations are gone, many survive and new ones continually emerge. Stratham has long been a hotbed of community activity.

Schools were established early on; indeed, the need for nearby schooling and churches was the primary reason for granting the town charter in 1716. First there were two, then four one-room schoolhouses. From the 18th to the mid-20th century, Stratham children were educated close to home. When public high schools were established in Exeter and Portsmouth in the 19th century, Stratham students attended.

All these endeavors, from farming and commerce to churches, schools, and entertainment, come together to make a vibrant community. Although much has changed over the centuries, these critical elements remain and old and new Stratham families benefit from a lively, growing community.

This book concentrates from the late 19th through the mid-20th century to correlate with the availability of photographs and the time prior to the suburban growth. The views of the community as it was and as we can still see around us are a powerful testament to the people of Stratham. They were blessed with good land and made a truly commendable community.

—Helen LaFave
June 1998

One

Bicentennial 1916

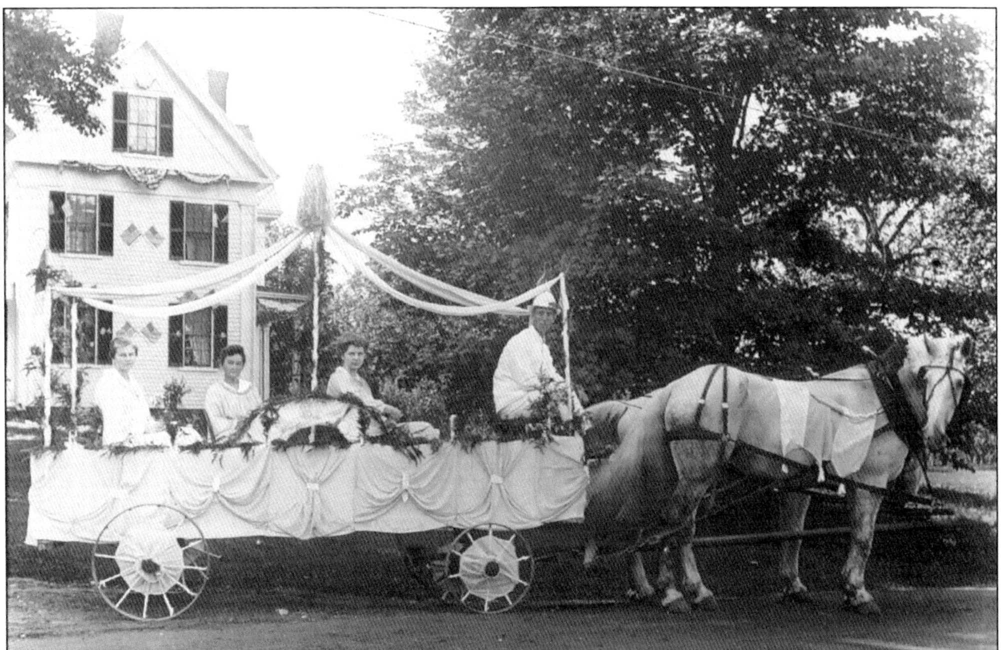

Arthur Jewell drives the three graces, also known as Myrtle Brewster Stockbridge, Ruth Hubbard Brewster, and Nellie Wentworth West. They are in front of 148 Portsmouth Avenue across from the town hall during the bicentennial parade. (SHS.)

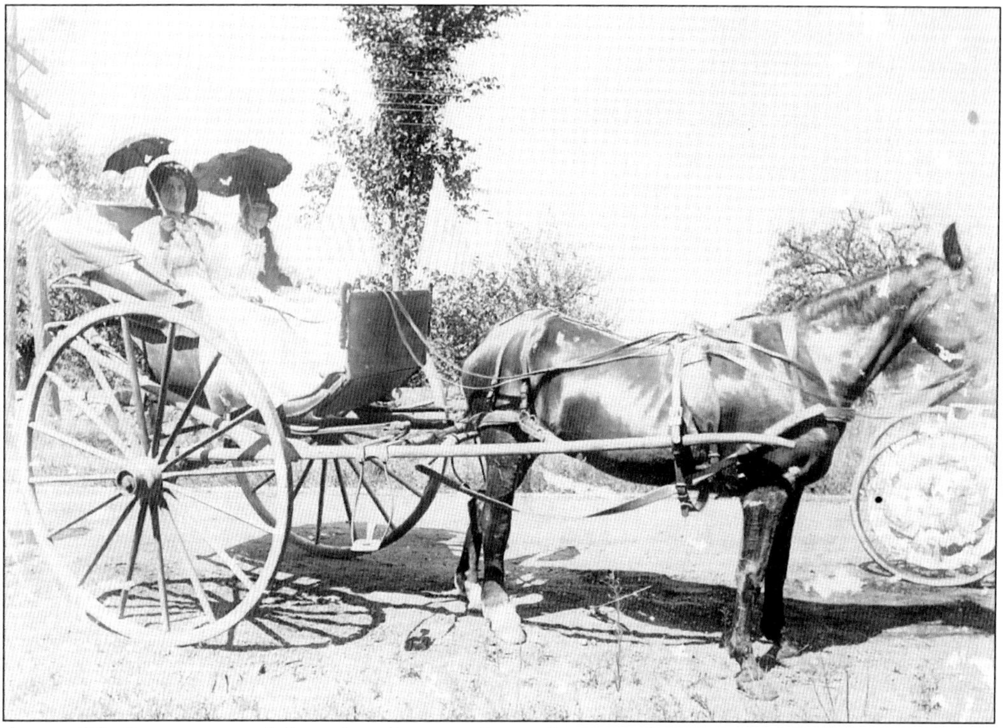

Annie W. Scammon and friend with parasols at the 1916 bicentennial celebration. Annie Scammon was a pillar of the community for many years. (SHS.)

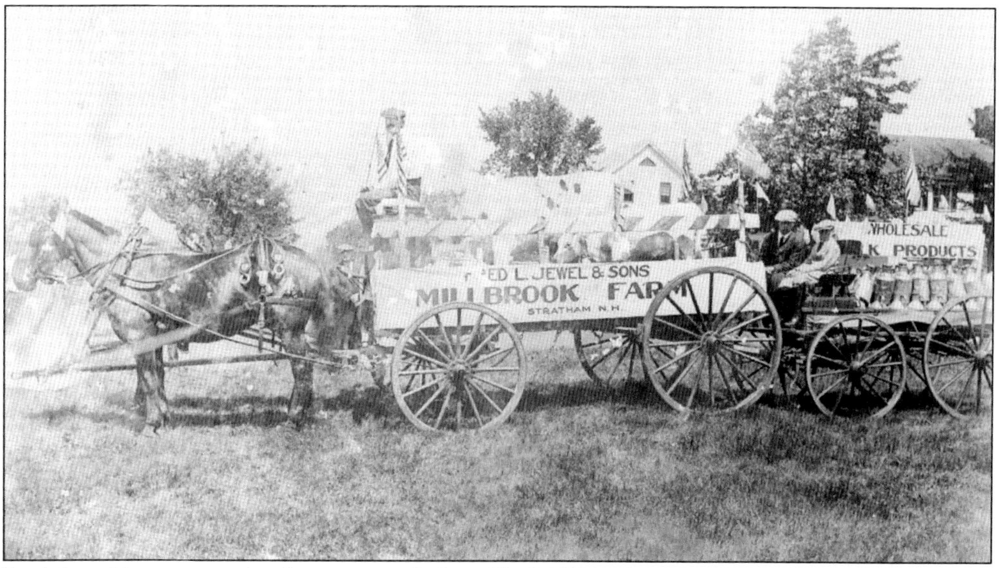

Fred Jewell's cart at the bicentennial. Jewell's Millbrook Farm, near the intersection of Winnicutt and Union Roads, was a prosperous truck farm supplying vegetables locally and to Portsmouth, Boston, and Manchester. (SHS.)

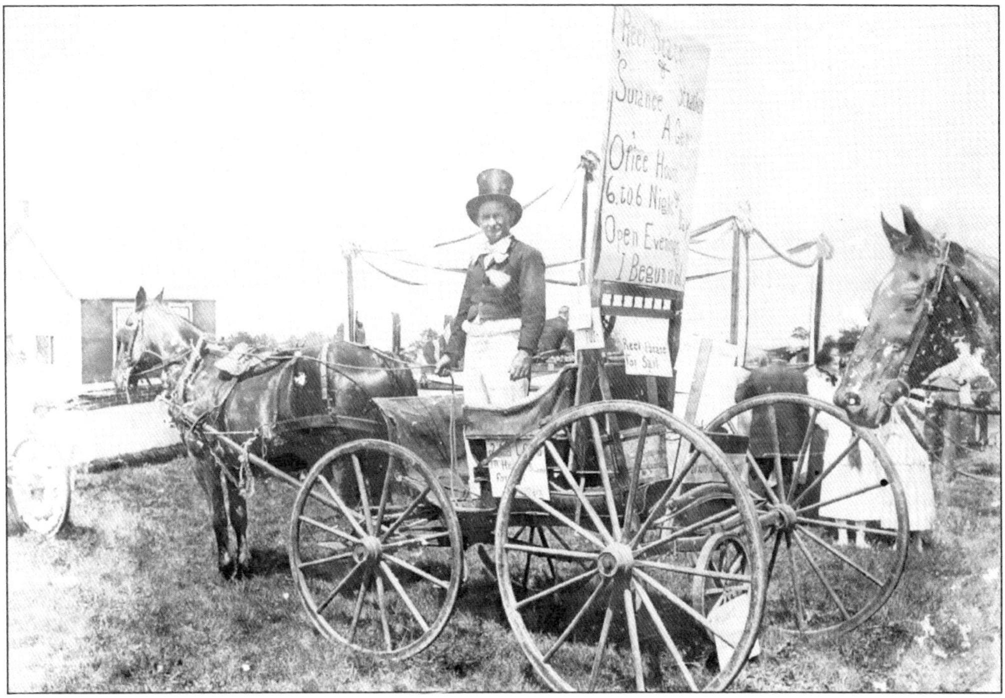

An interesting manner of advertising real estate services at the 1916 bicentennial parade. (SHS.)

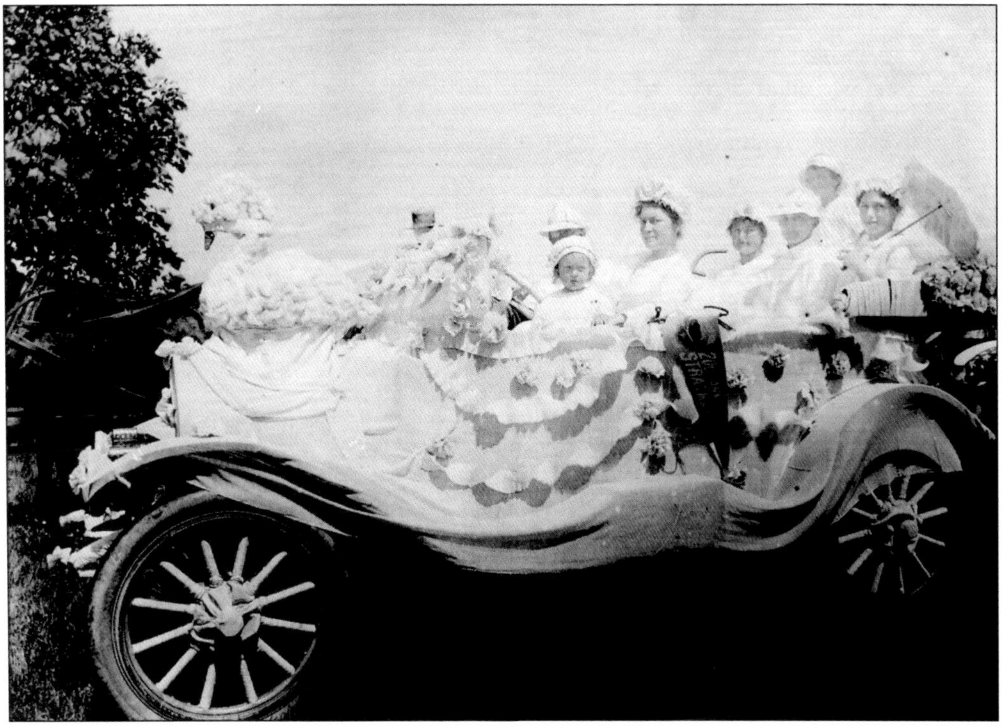

The parade on August 16, 1916. It was a grand celebration of the bicentennial of the founding of the town. In the rear, Bertha Stickney Parks holds a parasol. (SHS.)

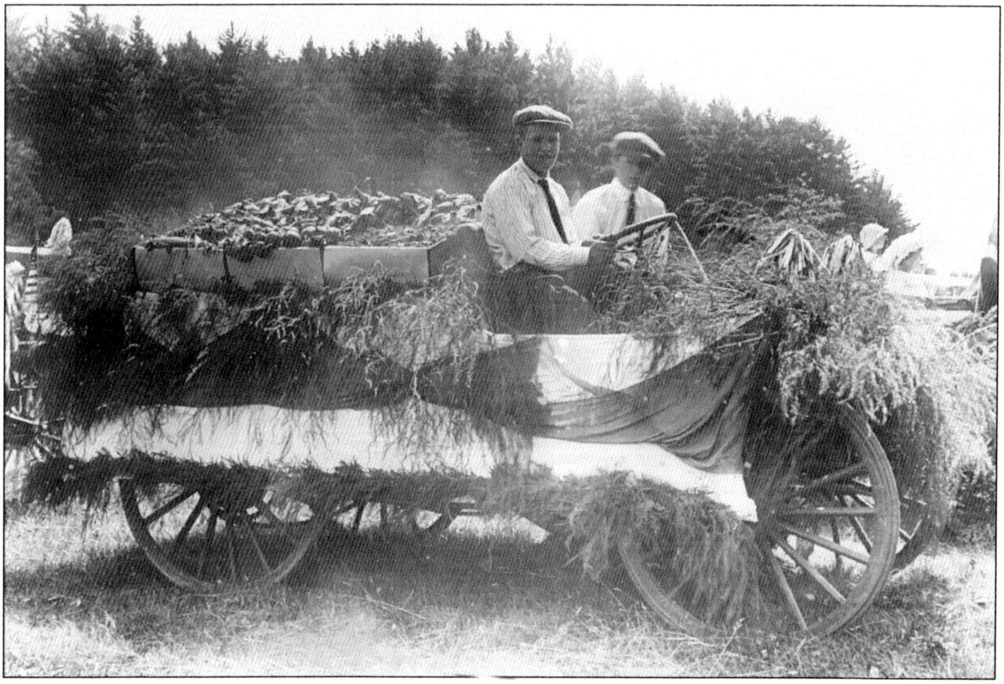

The 1916 parade. It was a 4-mile route from the Plains School (on what is now Heights Road), down Portsmouth Avenue, past the viewing stand at the Wiggin Memorial Library, and ending at Stratham Hill Park. (SHS.)

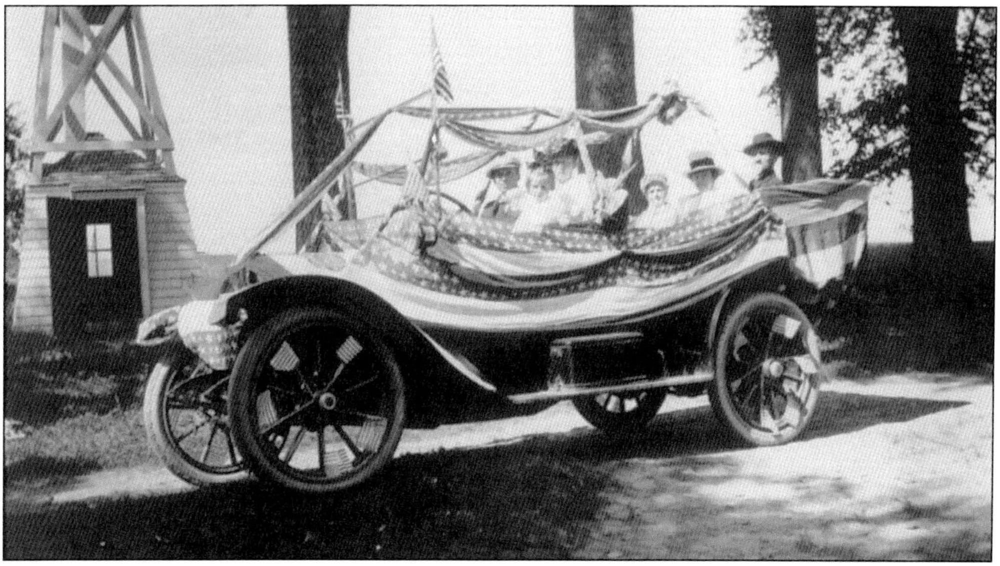

The Pearson Family car decked out for the bicentennial. Frank, Grace, and Georgiana Pearson are in front, while Samuel Pearson, Lena Pearson Low, and Georgiana H. Pearson are in back. Frank Pearson was the president of the bicentennial day events. He was extremely active in town affairs. (SHS.)

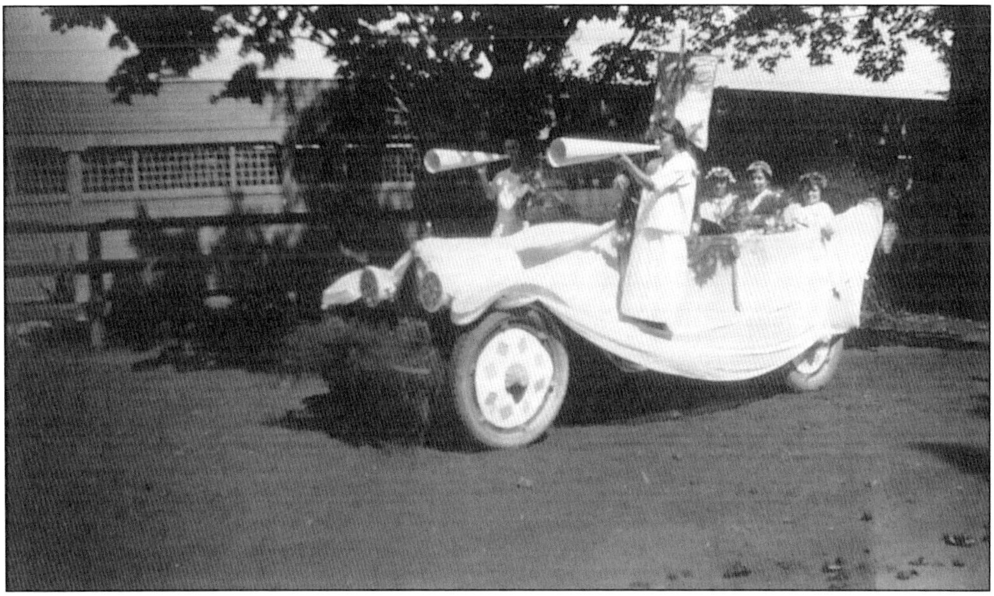

A float at the bicentennial Myrna Cooper, among others. (SHS.)

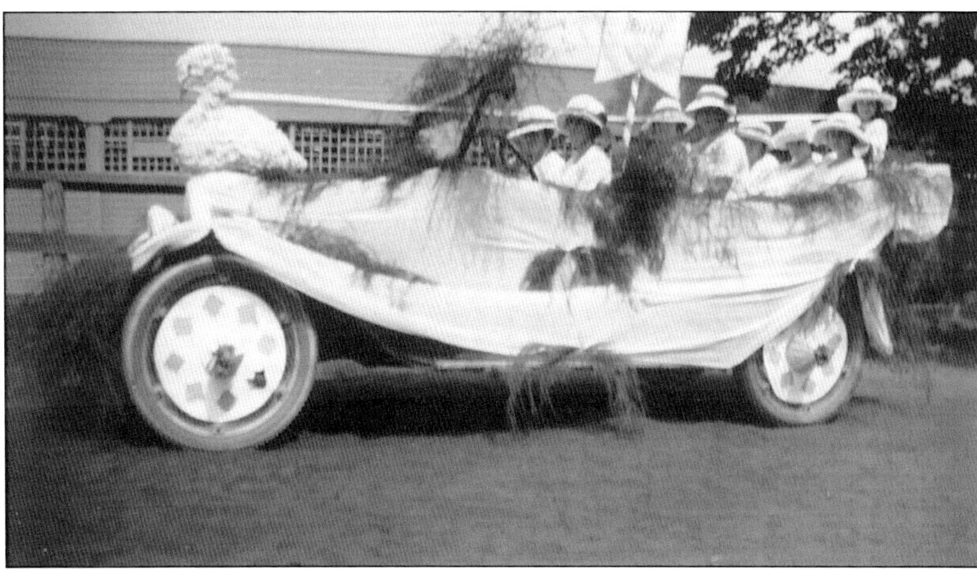

Another Grange car float. Clearly much effort was extended upon decoration, especially the tires. (SHS.)

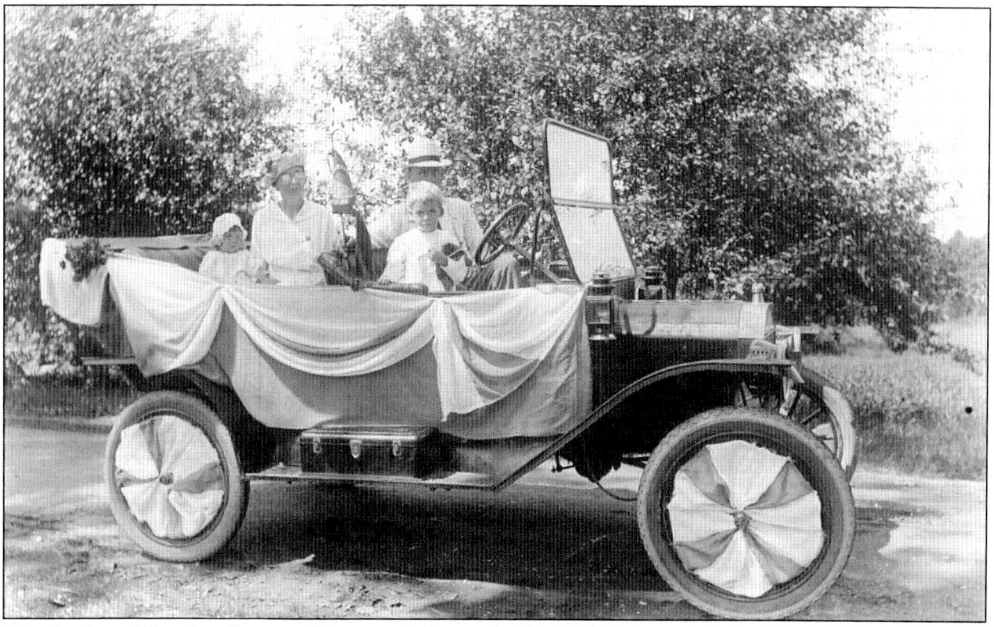

Marshall and Bertha Gowen Chase and their children Florence and Harold about to leave the Chase Farm at 114 Bunker Hill Avenue for the parade. (HC.)

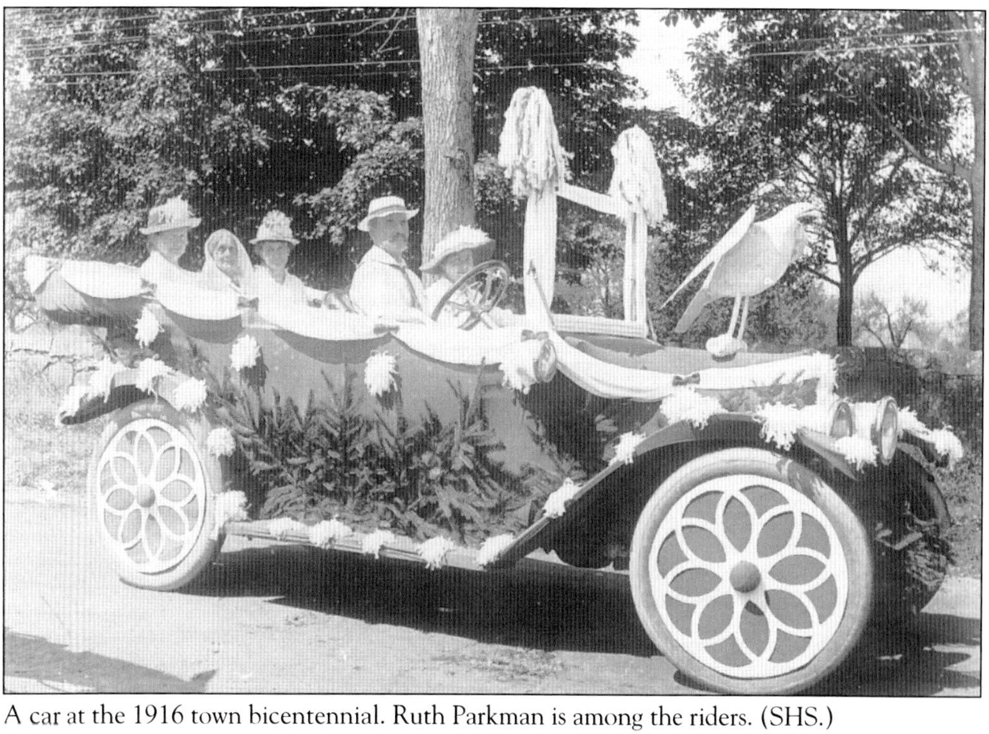

A car at the 1916 town bicentennial. Ruth Parkman is among the riders. (SHS.)

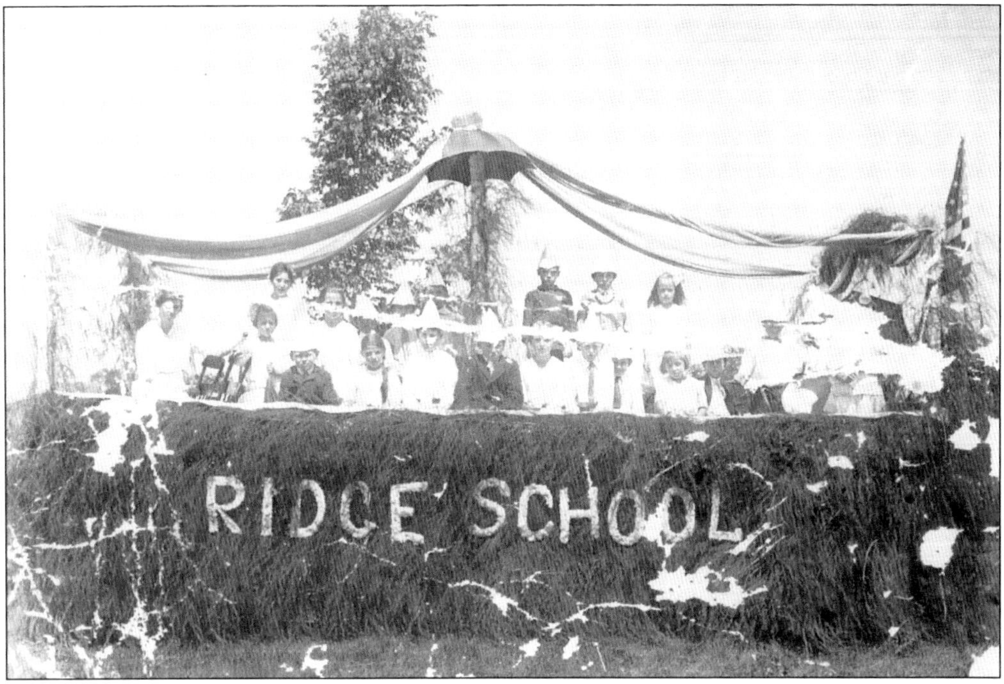

One of the school floats at the bicentennial. Each of the four school divisions sponsored a float. The Ridge School, Division 1, float held Miss de Rochement and students including F. Wentworth, Ruth Crafts, Dorothy Pearson, Arthur Brewster, Florence Wentworth, Lois Robinson, Margaret Pearson, Abbie Caverely, and Lawrence Scammon. (SHS.)

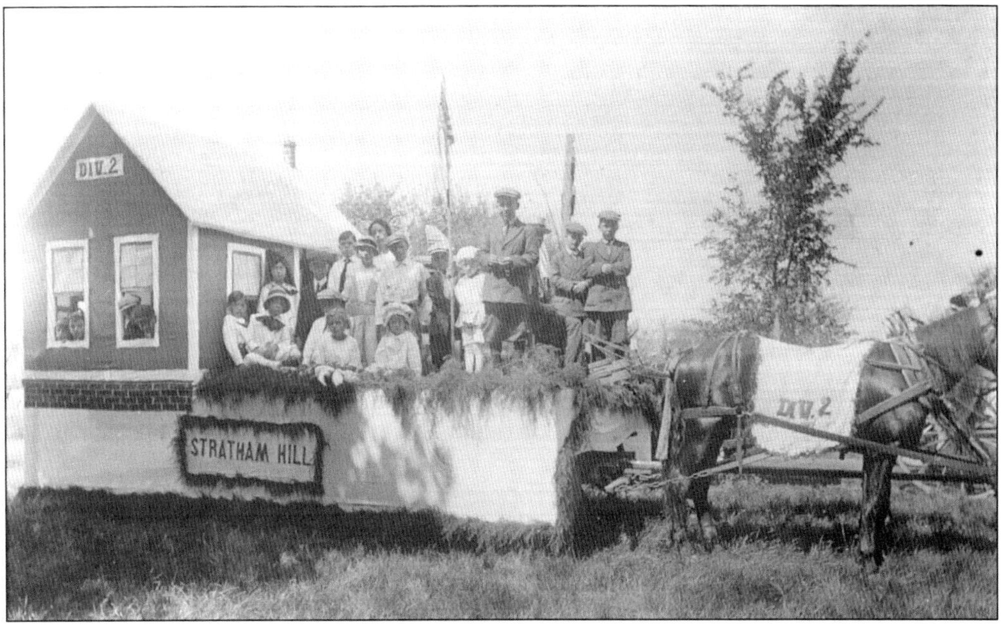

Miss Smith and her students from the Division 2, Stratham Hill (or Lower End) School, on their bicentennial float. Included here are Henry Jewell in the hat, Velma Syphers, Wesley Lane, Murray ?, Avis Lane, ? Morse, W. Bond, Fred Wiggin, and the twins Elmer and Earl Wiggin. (SHS.)

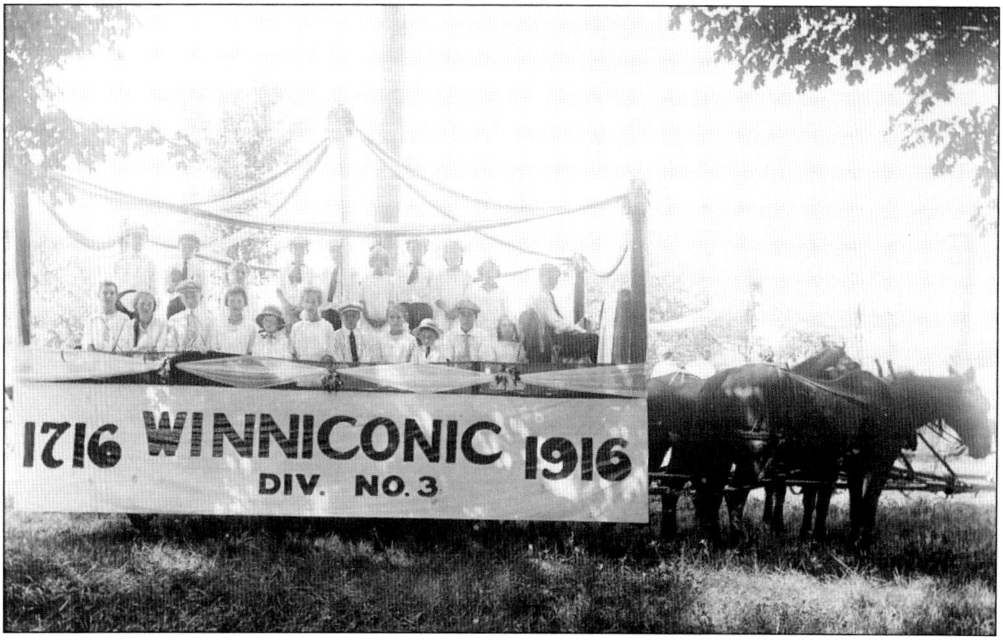

The Division 3, Winnicutt or Winniconic School, float with Jim Piper, Blanche Jenness, Leon West, Carmen Barker, and Nelson Barker, among others. (SHS.)

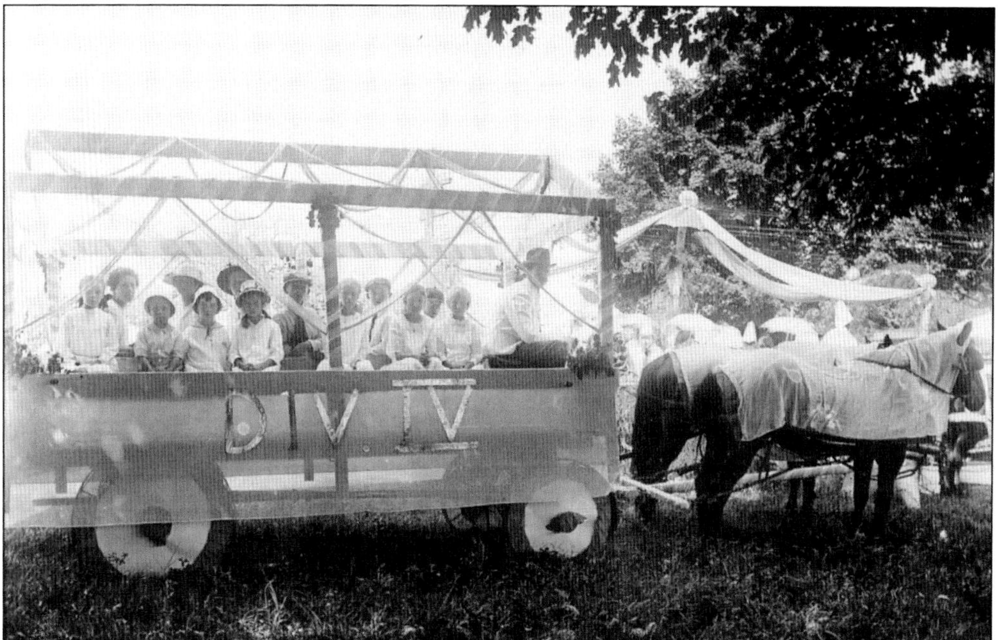

George Gowen (driving) and the Division 4 school float for the Plains School. The Ridge School float is in the background. (SHS.)

Two

Town Institutions

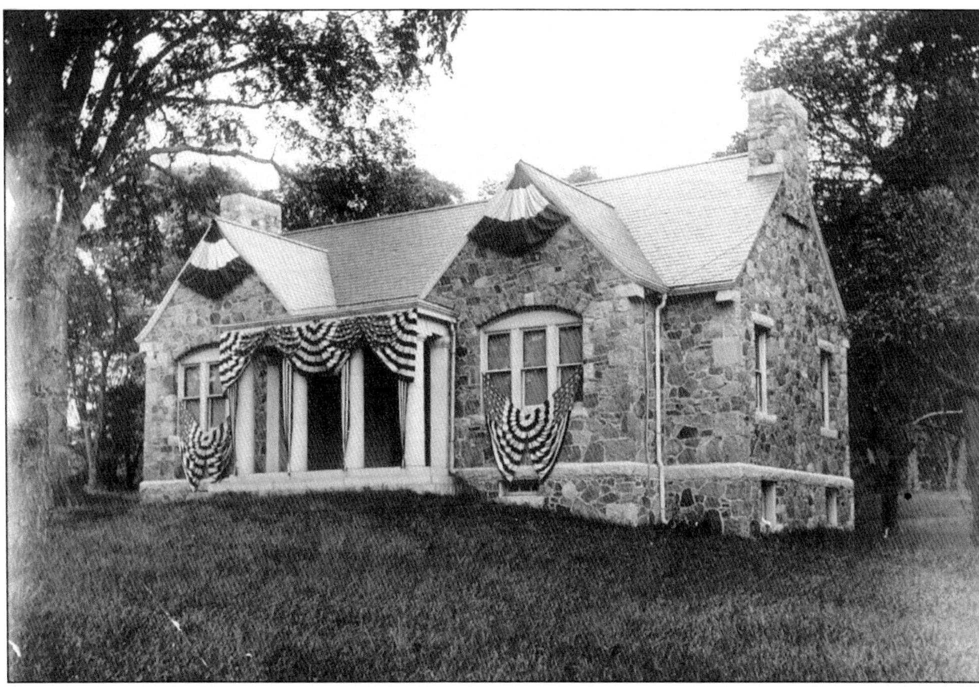

The Wiggin Memorial Library building, built in 1911 from a bequest from Emma and George Wiggin. The Wiggins wanted to give students a beautiful place to study in a prominent area of town. This building, located on the corner of Winnicutt and Portsmouth Avenue, housed the thriving library for nearly 75 years. The columns and steps are made of granite from Deer Island, Maine, and the building is a registered historical landmark. It now houses the Stratham Historical Society. Here it is decorated for Memorial or Independence Day. (SHS.)

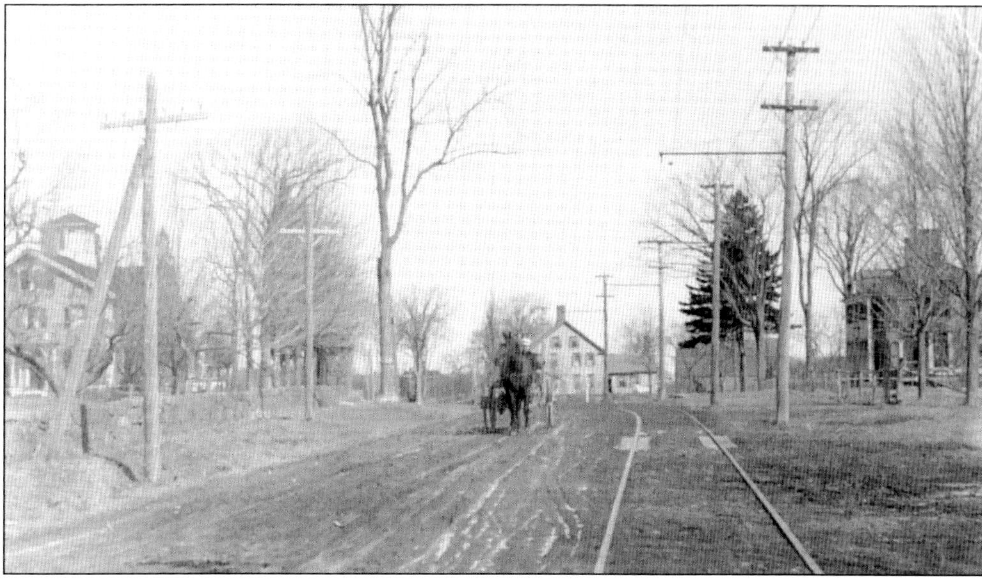

The trolley tracks on Portsmouth Avenue headed toward Portsmouth at the corner of Bunker Hill Avenue, formerly known as Rocky Hill Road. On the left is the Raeder House, now burned, at the corner of Raeder Drive. In the center is the Spencer House on Portsmouth Avenue, which also burned and on the right is the Bartlett/Cushman House on the corner of Bunker Hill Avenue. (SHS.)

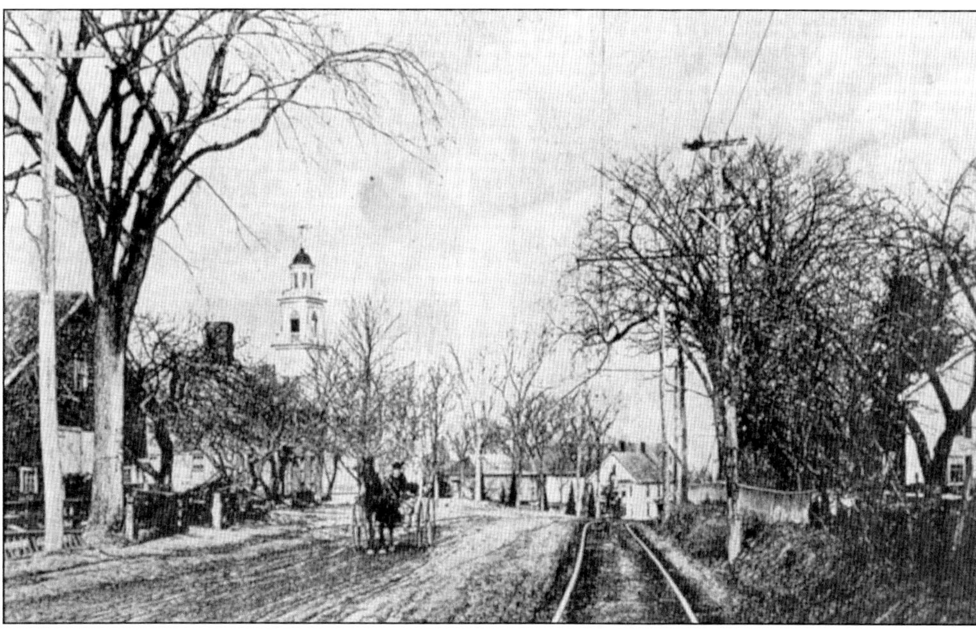

A horse and carriage adjacent to trolley tracks on Portsmouth Avenue in 1907. At that point, Emery Lane was part of Portsmouth Avenue; this view is of the Emery Lane section of Portsmouth Avenue. On the left is 12 Emery Lane (J. Fred Emery's house), the Congregational church steeple, 2 Emery Lane, and 7 Emery Lane on the right. (D and SS.)

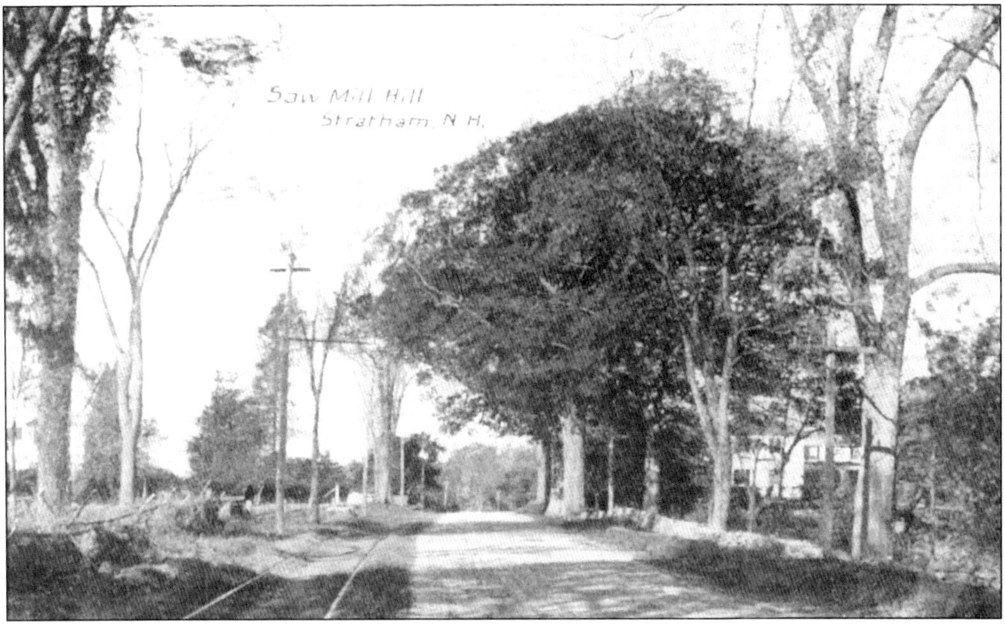

Sawmill Hill. There was a sawmill on Mill Pond where the center of the traffic circle is now. The Stockbridge House is on the right and the Samuel Lane House that sits in the center of the traffic circle now is on the left. Carl Stockbridge ran the gas station until the early 1950s; since then the small stucco station has been a site for the New Hampshire Society for the Prevention of Cruelty to Animals and a shop for a variety of retail establishments. (D and SS.)

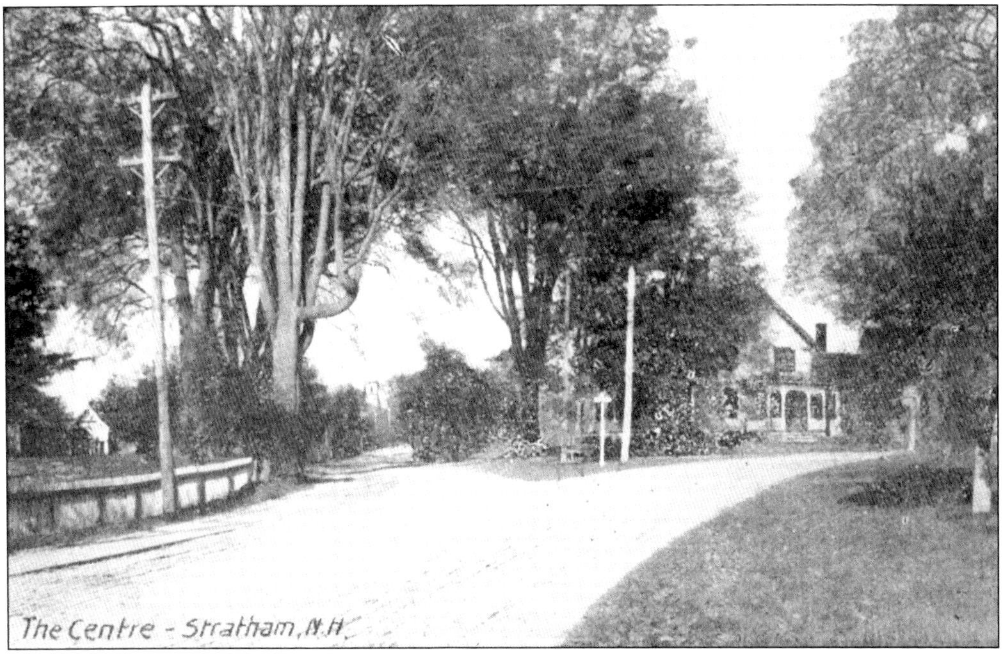

The intersection of Portsmouth Avenue and Winnicutt Road before paving and straightening the road. The Baptist church steeple is visible in the distance; this building was moved to Meetinghouse Hill and is now the Reverend Charles A. Parker Parish Hall. In the center is Odell's house with the store attached, which was later a boarding house. (SHS.)

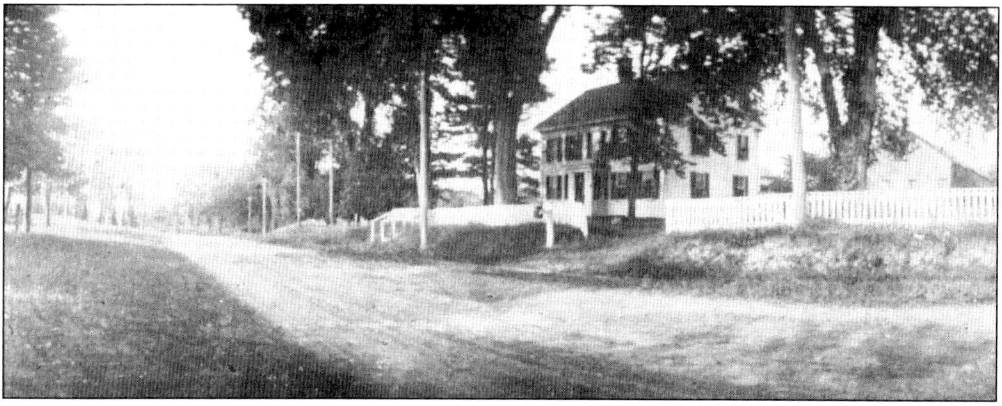

The house at 7 Emery Lane, across from the church. This was the home of Elizabeth Baker, a history teacher in the early 20th century at the Robinson Seminary, the public high school for girls, in Exeter. (SHS.)

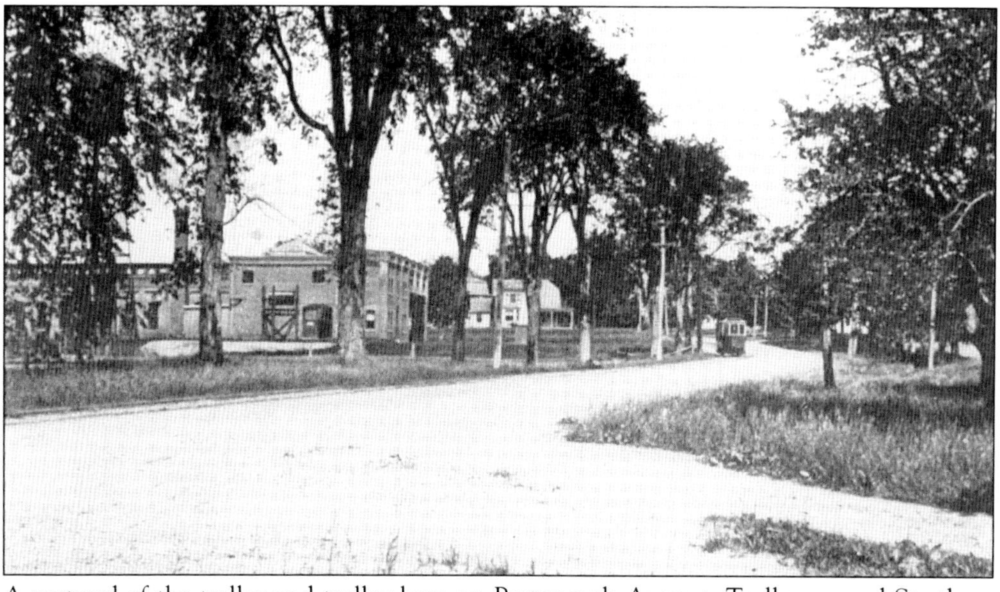

A postcard of the trolley and trolley barn on Portsmouth Avenue. Trolleys served Stratham from 1902 to 1913. The barn, which burned in 1966, was on the circle at the current site of Cadieux Furniture, 145 Portsmouth Avenue. A blacksmith used the barn after the trolley went out of business. Later there was an upstairs apartment occupied by Charlie and Marion Jewell Brown, when Charlie maintained the town road machinery. Cadieux's occupied the building before it burned and rebuilt on the same spot. (SHS.)

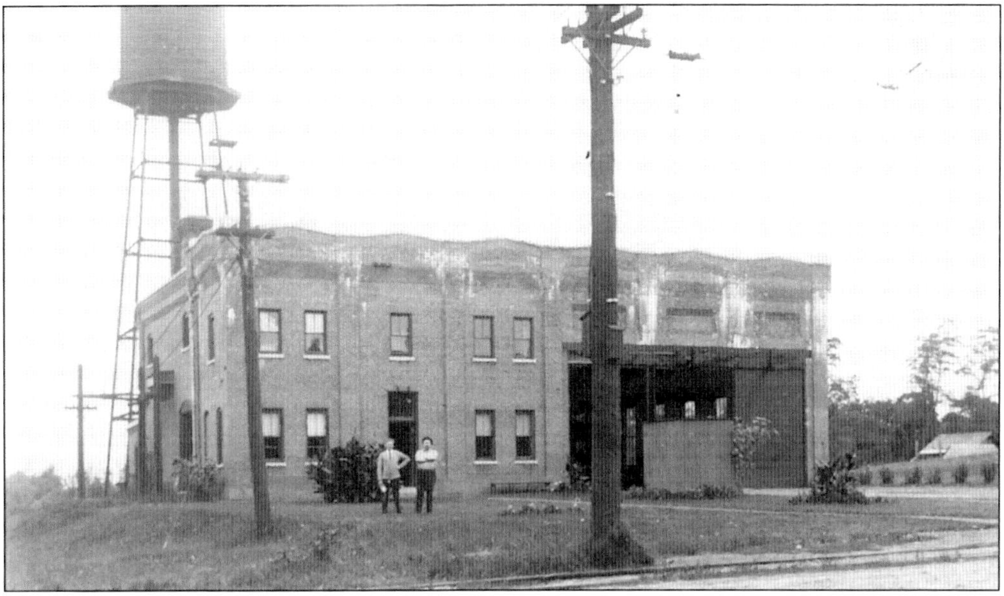

Another view of the trolley barn and the water tower on Portsmouth Avenue. (SHS.)

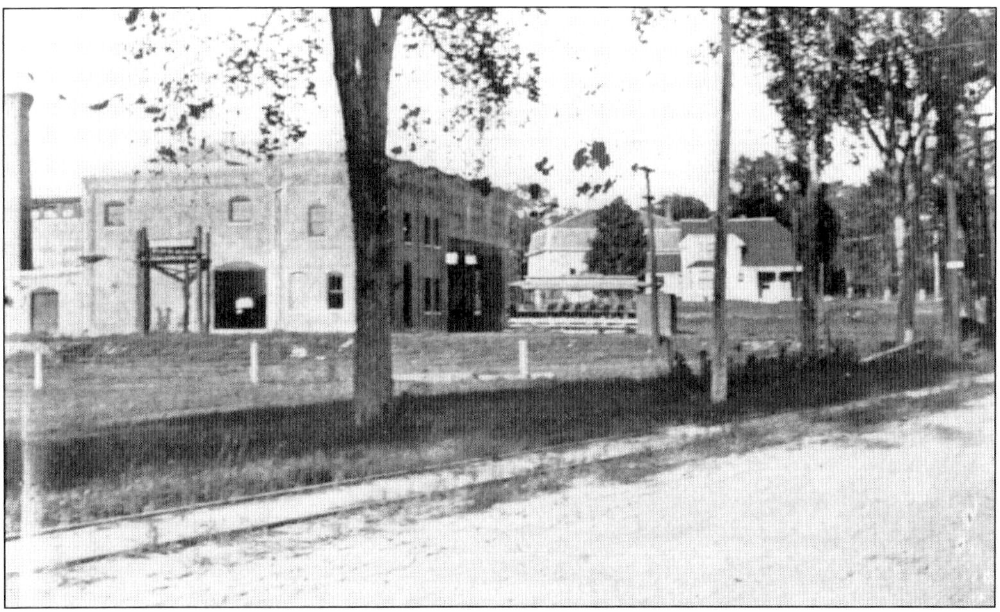

The trolley car barn on Portsmouth Avenue with a view of the town hall and the village market. (D and SS.)

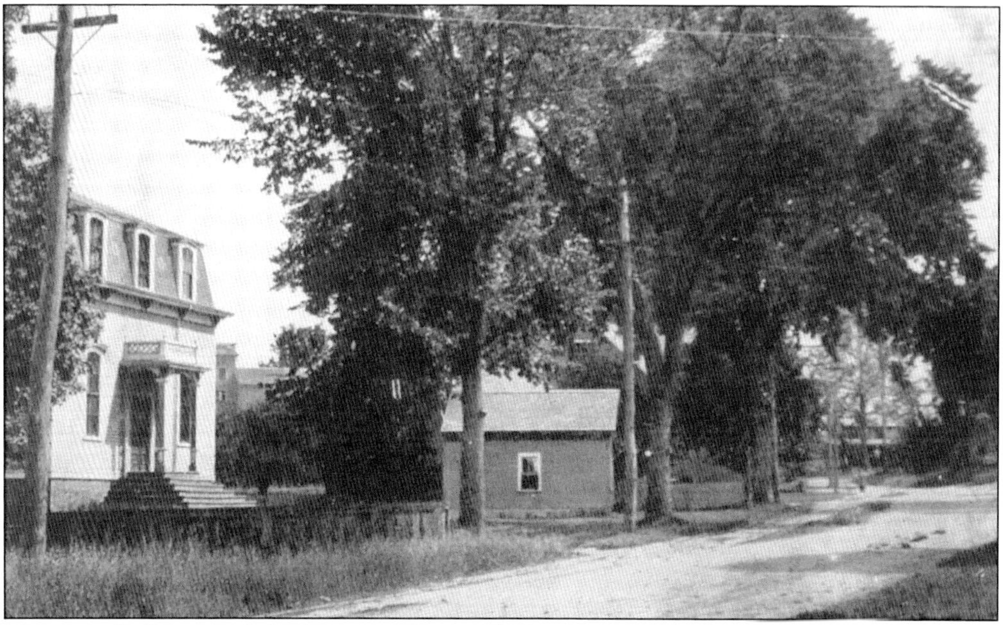

The town hall on the left, the post office in the center, and the Elms, a resort hotel, visible through the trees. (D and SS.)

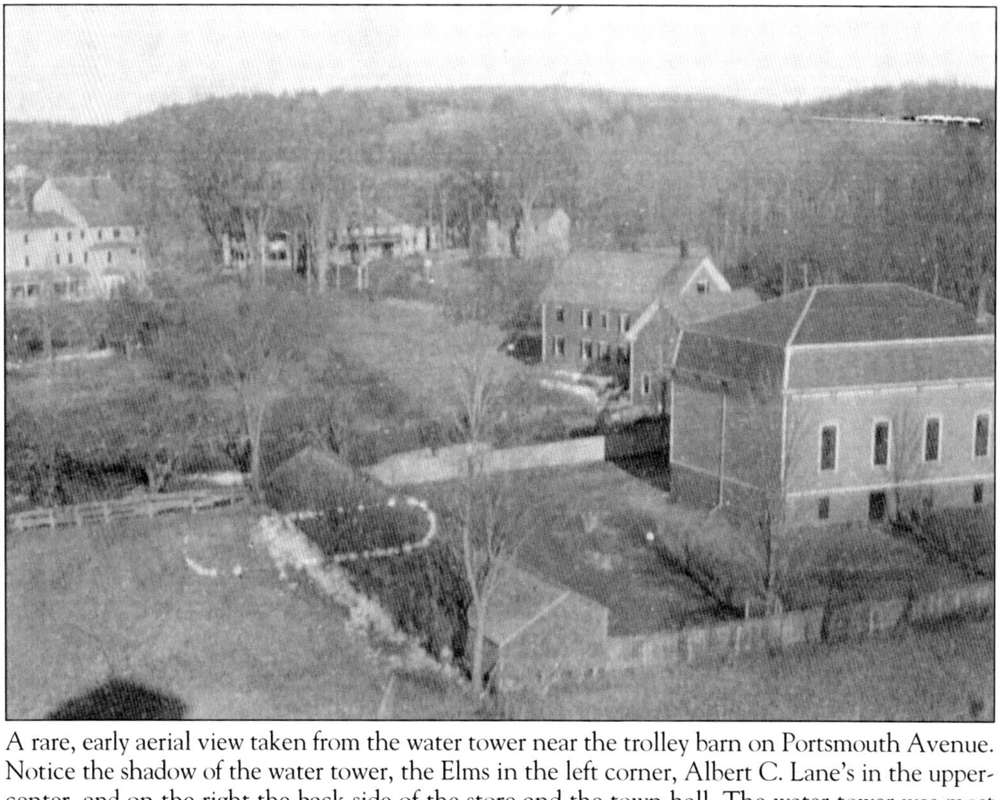

A rare, early aerial view taken from the water tower near the trolley barn on Portsmouth Avenue. Notice the shadow of the water tower, the Elms in the left corner, Albert C. Lane's in the upper-center, and on the right the back side of the store and the town hall. The water tower was most likely pumped by a windmill and gravity fed, and was used to wash the trolleys. (SHS.)

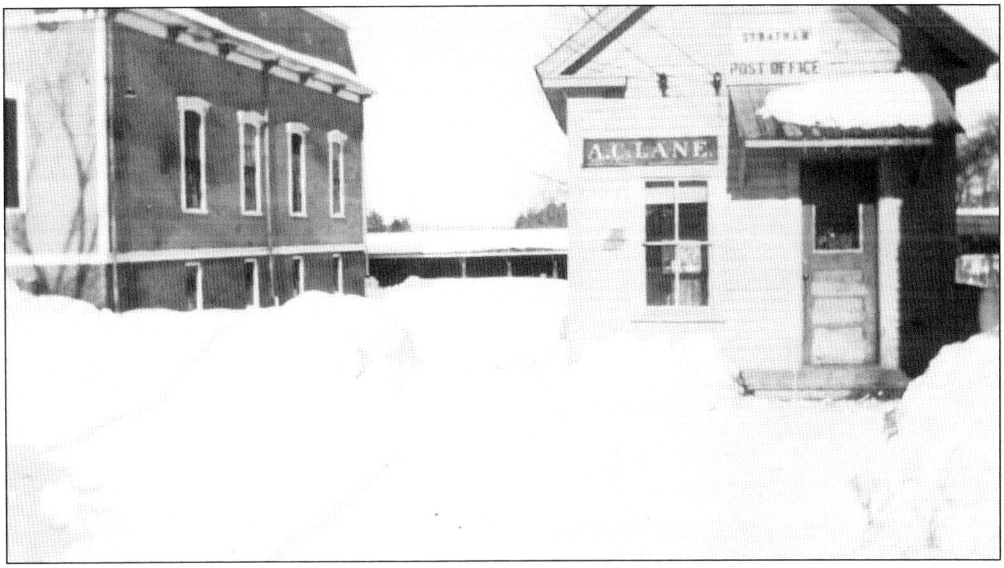

The old post office on Portsmouth Avenue near the town hall. Mail would arrive by train at the station on Depot Road twice daily. People would visit the post office to pick up their mail in times before rural free delivery began. Albert C. Lane was the longtime postmaster in town who published a number of postcard views and was also a descendant of Samuel Lane, the famous diarist. The fire department was in the sheds behind the town hall. In 1956 the sheds burned down. (SHS.)

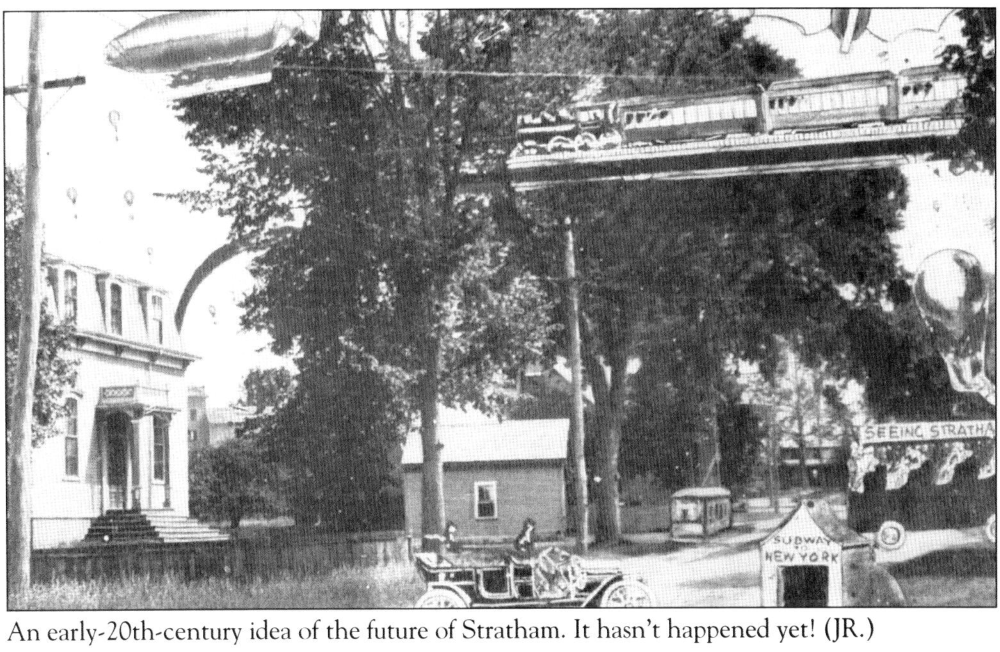

An early-20th-century idea of the future of Stratham. It hasn't happened yet! (JR.)

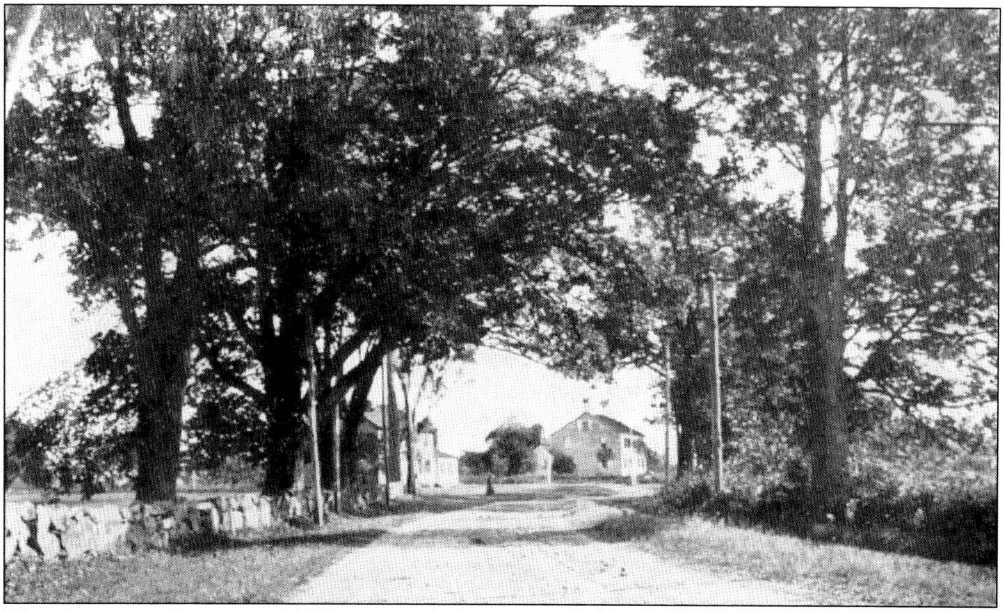

The Kenniston Tavern at 245 Portsmouth Avenue and the corner of Depot Road. This was an early public house on the first road built, King's Hyway, connecting the coast with inland areas. During the Revolutionary War, King's Hyway was changed to Main Road. It is now known as Portsmouth Avenue. This building is on the registry of national historic sites. (SHS.)

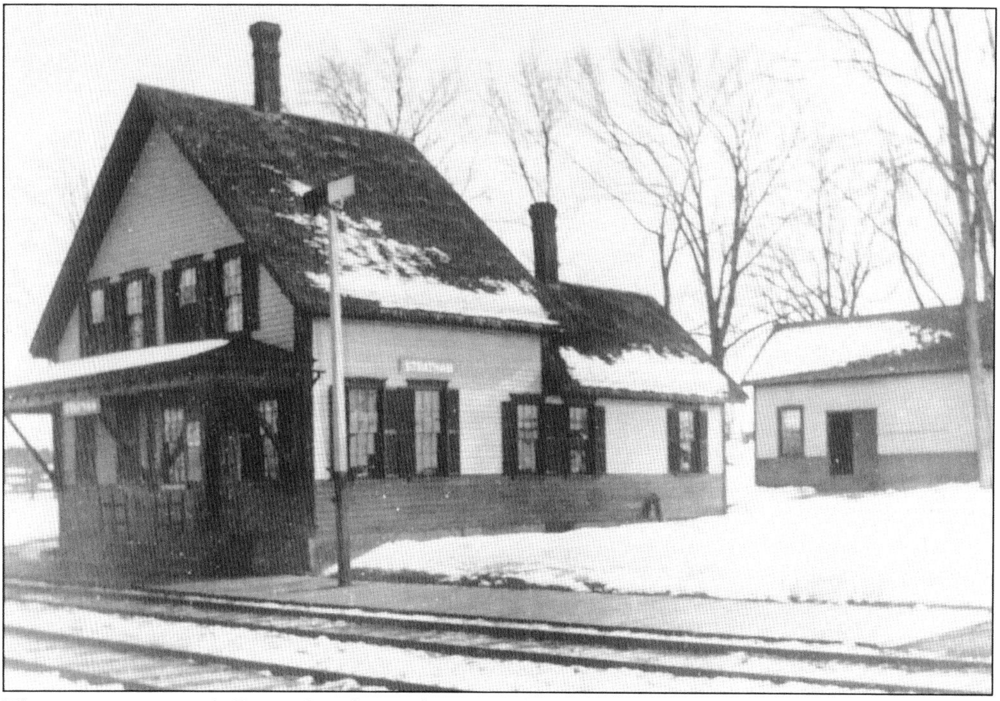

The train station at 69 Depot Road near the Greenland town line. The Concord and Portsmouth Railroad served Stratham from 1849 to 1954, when passenger service was discontinued. The depot, built in 1870 and operated until 1942, at one point housed a postal substation. It is now a private residence. (SHS.)

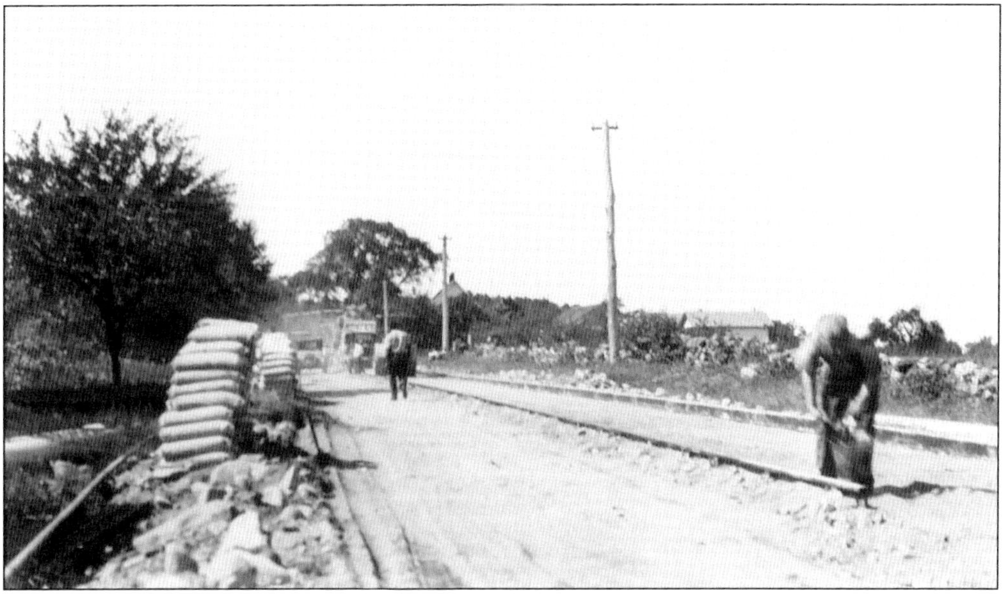

Laying molds for cement for the paving of Portsmouth Avenue in 1929. (D and SS.)

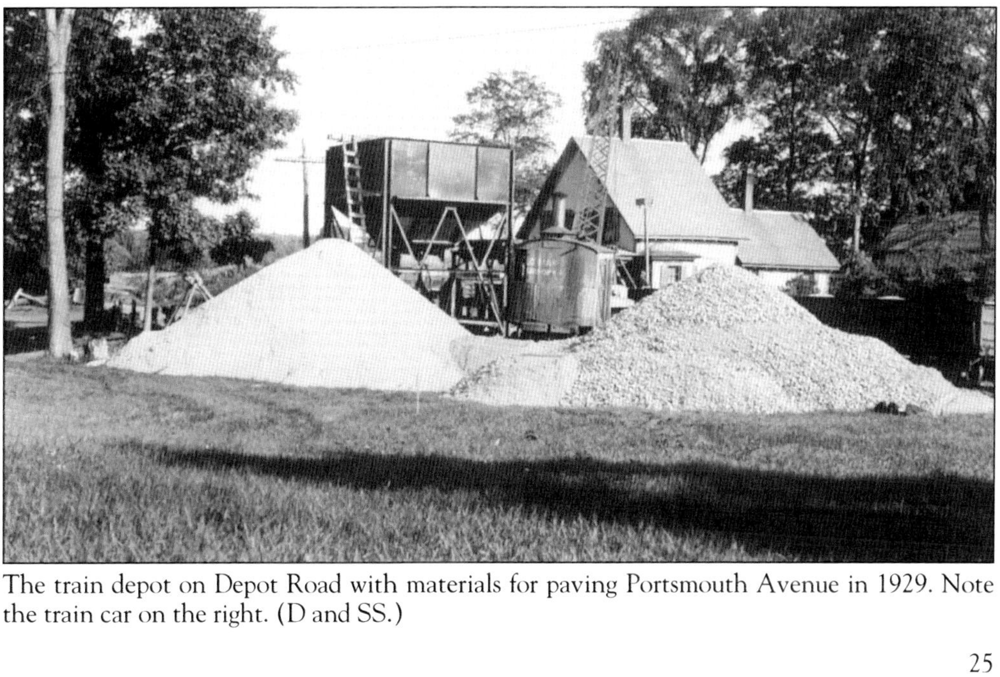

The train depot on Depot Road with materials for paving Portsmouth Avenue in 1929. Note the train car on the right. (D and SS.)

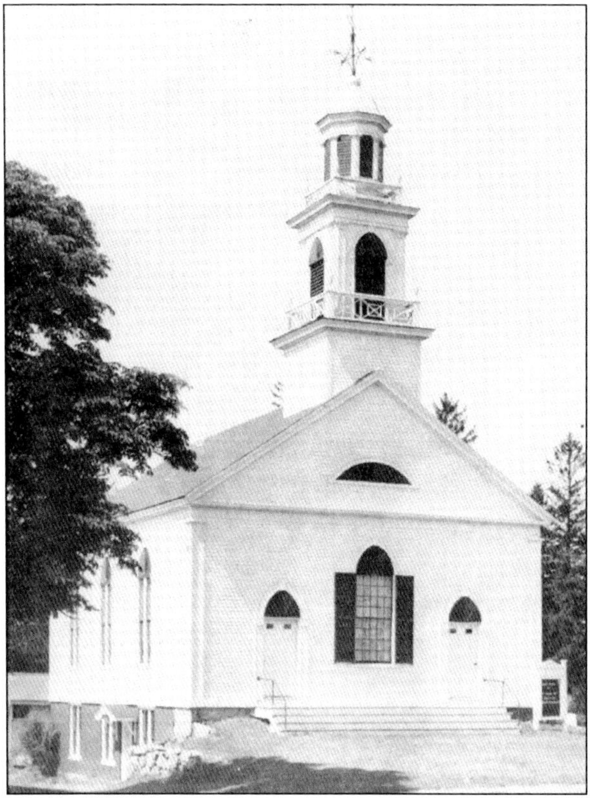

The Congregational church on Emery Lane. (HC.)

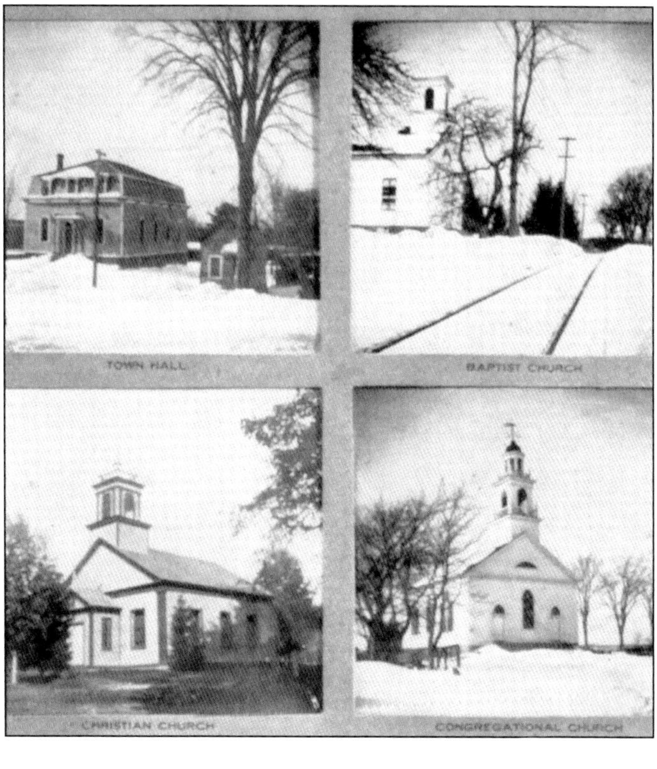

A postcard with views of four public buildings: the town hall on Portsmouth Avenue, the Baptist church on Portsmouth Avenue near the cemetery, the Christian church on Portsmouth Avenue across from the town hall, and the Congregational church on Emery Lane. The Christian church had no heat and was only used in the summer. In 1982 the Baptist church building was moved adjacent to the Congregational church on Meetinghouse Hill on Emery Lane and is known as the Parker Parish Hall, in honor of the minister of the Baptist church. The town hall was built in the 1870s and sold in the 1980s. (SHS.)

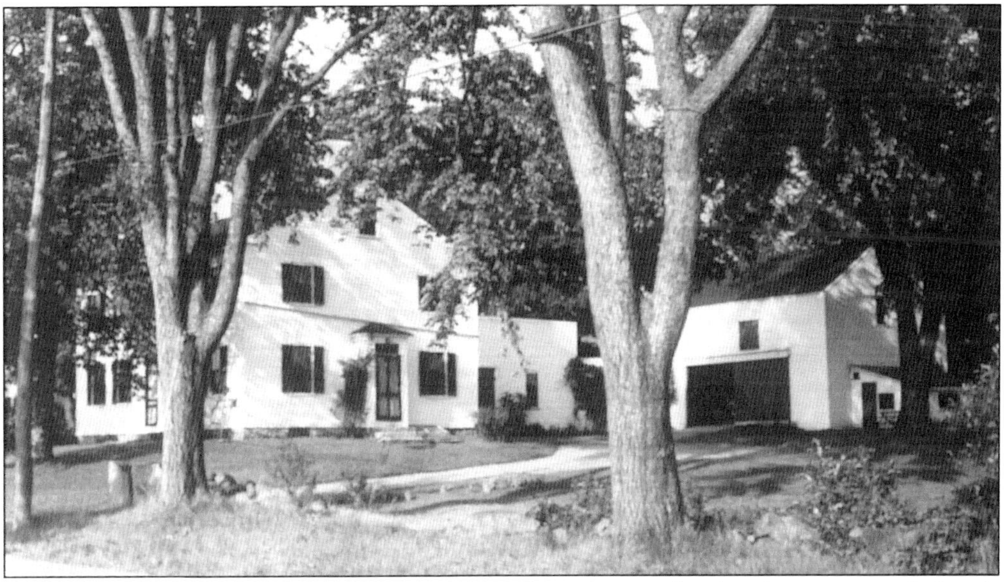

The old parsonage at 94 Portsmouth Avenue. The ministers for the Congregational church lived here. (SHS.)

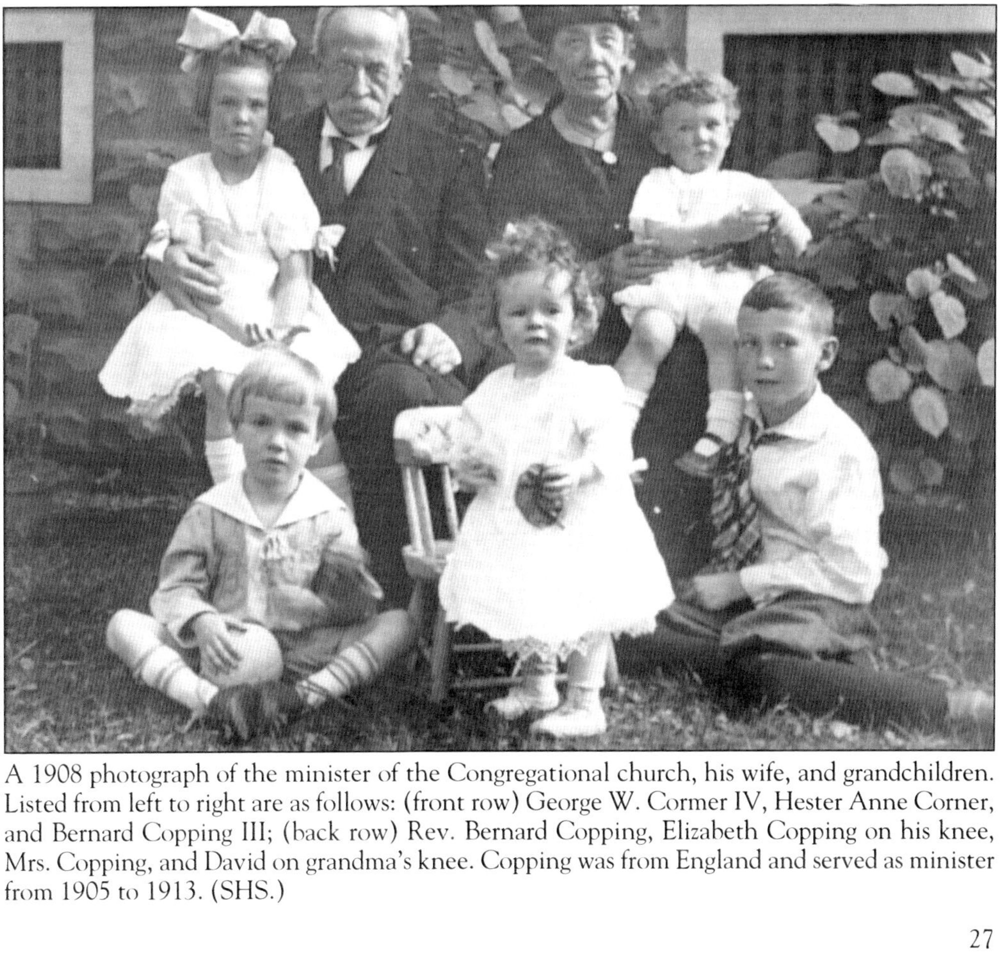

A 1908 photograph of the minister of the Congregational church, his wife, and grandchildren. Listed from left to right are as follows: (front row) George W. Cormer IV, Hester Anne Corner, and Bernard Copping III; (back row) Rev. Bernard Copping, Elizabeth Copping on his knee, Mrs. Copping, and David on grandma's knee. Copping was from England and served as minister from 1905 to 1913. (SHS.)

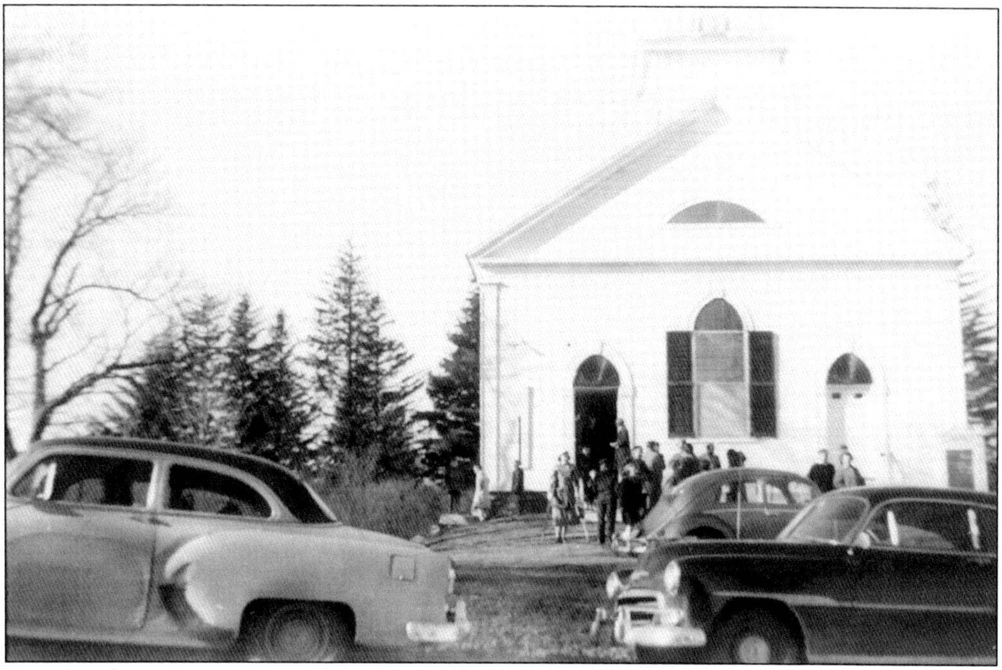

The Stratham Community Church on Emery Lane, *c.* 1949–52. The building dates from 1837. (SHS.)

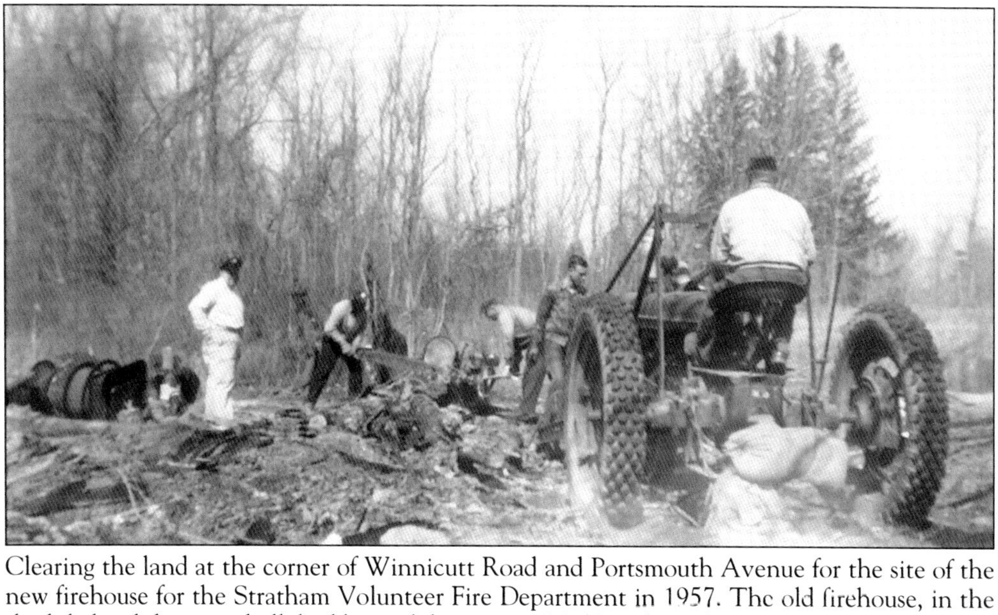

Clearing the land at the corner of Winnicutt Road and Portsmouth Avenue for the site of the new firehouse for the Stratham Volunteer Fire Department in 1957. The old firehouse, in the sheds behind the town hall, had burned down in 1956. (E and EW.)

Three

Schools

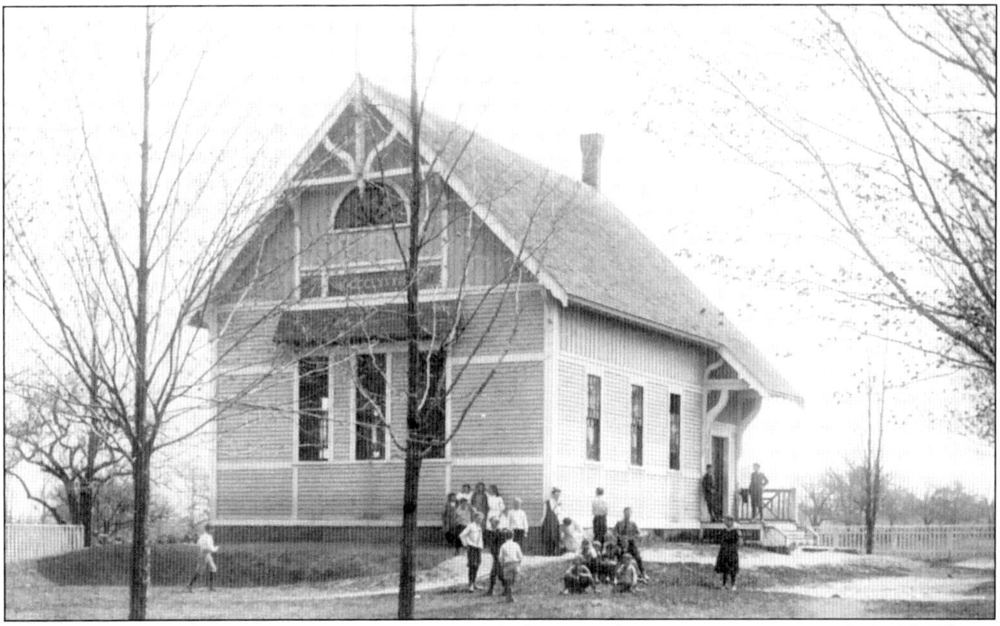

The Ridge School, Division 1, at 78 Portsmouth Avenue during recess time *c.* 1910–20. There were originally two, and eventually four, one-room schoolhouses built in population centers throughout town so that students could walk to school. Since building the multi-classroom Stratham Memorial School in the early 1950s, this building has, at various times, served as a private residence, a group home for children, and a business. (SHS.)

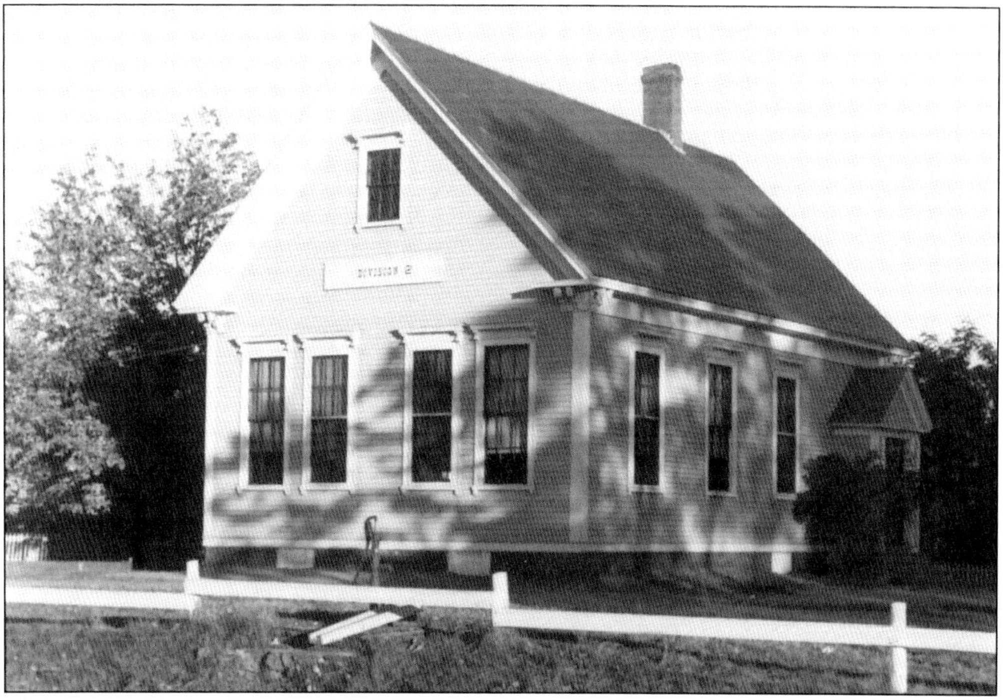

The Division 2, Stratham Hill School, at 240 Portsmouth Avenue in 1940. Notice the water pump in front of the building. (SHS.)

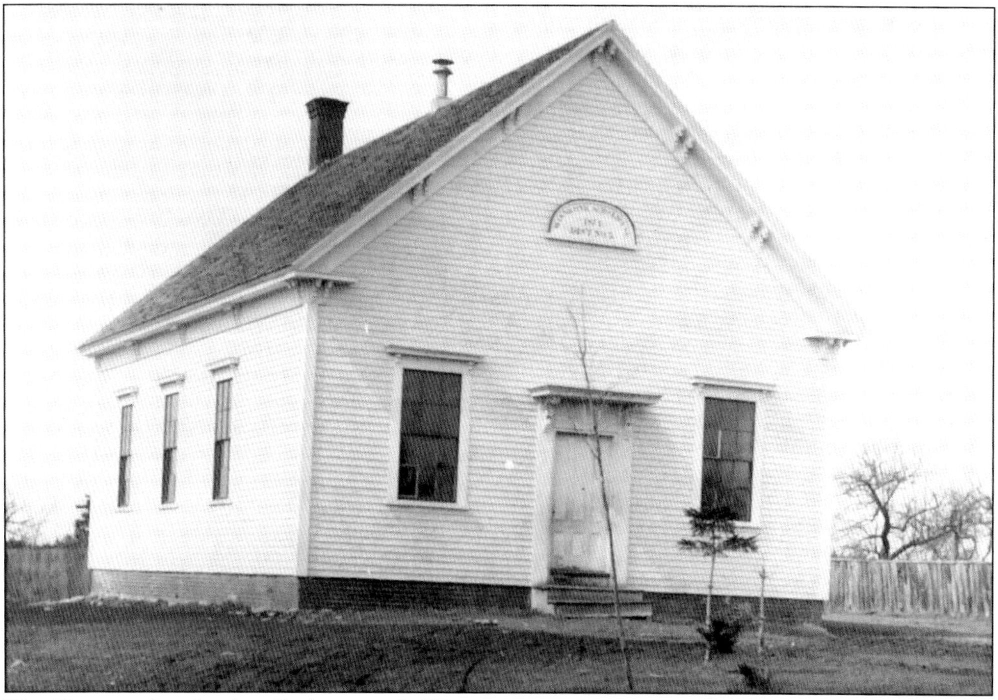

The Division 3 school, called variously Winnicutt or Winniconic, at 6 Barker Road. Built in 1835 as one of the four original one-room schoolhouses and rebuilt in 1875, it has long been a private residence. (SHS.)

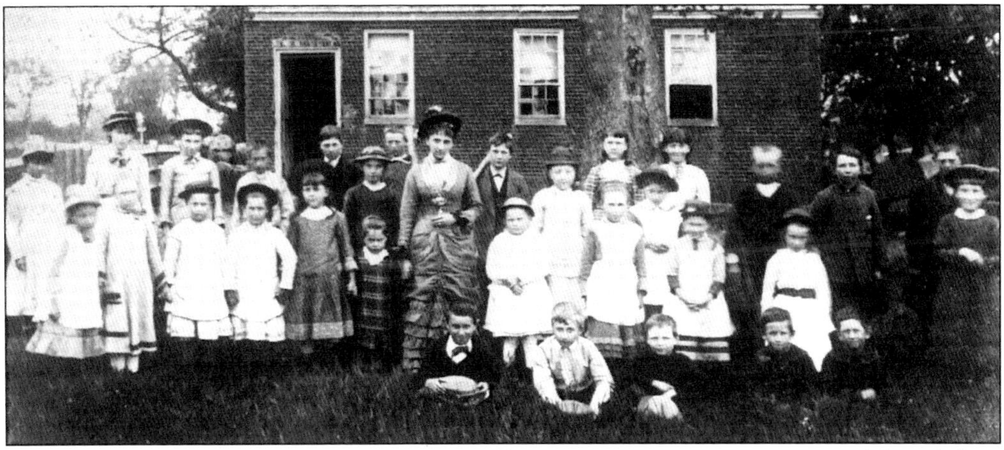

The first school in Stratham, the brick schoolhouse, Division 1, in 1881. Listed from left to right are as follows: (front row) Albert Peabody, Fred Emery, Herbert Fogg, Fred Robinson, and Frank Robinson; (middle row) Lizzie Wiggin, Alice Abbott, Myra Rundlett, Minnie Rundlett, Mattie Healey, Mary Deau, Ella Deau (holding teacher's hand), Miss Eleanor Wiggin (teacher), Mabel Fogg, Lizzie Abbott, Sadie Peabody, Mary Thompson, Grace Peabody, Margie Stuart, and Nellie Smart; (back row) Annie Parkman, Emma Deau, Annie Smart, Frank Brewster, Lewis Fogg, Will Parkman, Frank Tuttle, Alice Healey, Katie Keefe, Charles Parkman, Fred Hodgeden, and George Bowley. (SHS.)

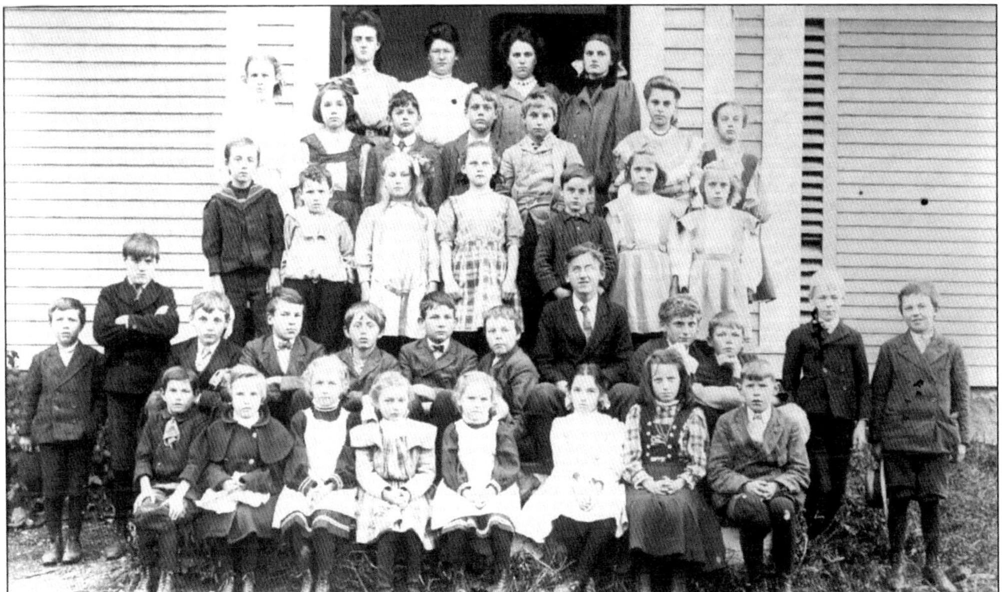

Molly Flynn's class in the late 19th century. Listed from left to right are as follows: (bottom row) Archie Chapman, Eleanor Hall, Cynthia Wentworth, Mary Chase, and Sadie Haley; (second row) Otto Syphers, Vernon Dow, Phillip Gregory, Harold Syphers, Archie Craig, Lauris Godfrey, and Alden Syphers; (third row) George Hodgeden, Johnny Haley, Mary Gregory, Ruth Godfrey, Pearley Wentworth, Vera Cottrill, and Leah Cottrill; (fourth row) Myrtle Beals, Doris Littlefield, John Chapman, Morris Cottrill, Norman Gregory, Ethel Proctor, and Myra Jewell; (fifth row) Eva Butler, Molly Flynn (teacher), Florence Chadbourne, and Edith Lane. (SHS.)

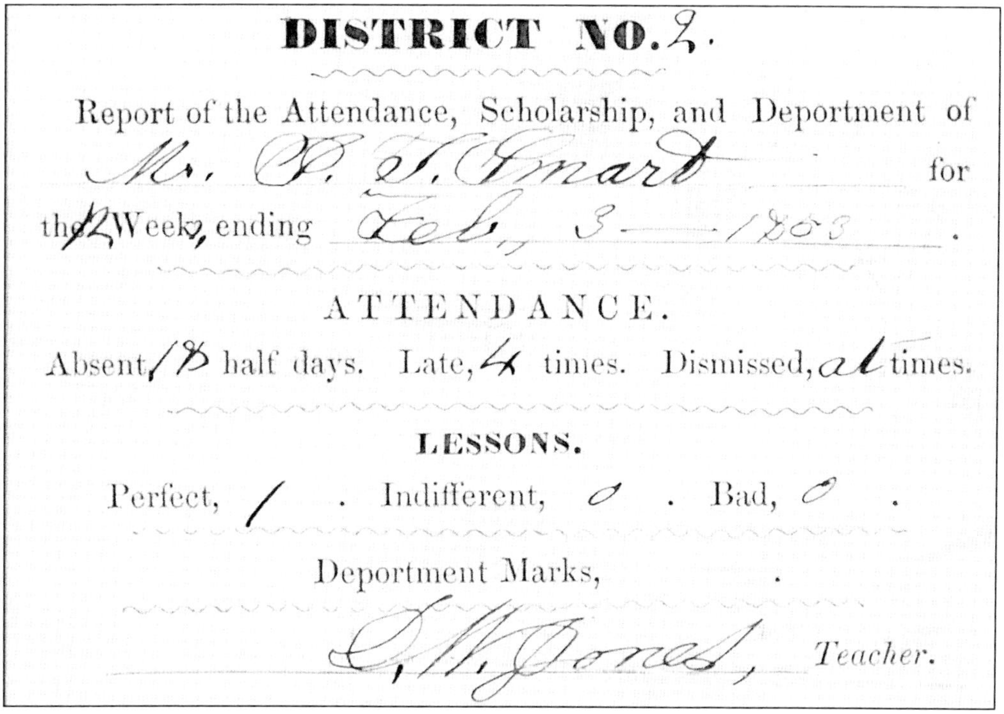

DISTRICT NO. 2.

Report of the Attendance, Scholarship, and Deportment of
Mr. P. T. Smart for
the 2 Weeks, ending Feb, 3 — 1853.

ATTENDANCE.

Absent, 18 half days. Late, 4 times. Dismissed, at times.

LESSONS.

Perfect, 1 . Indifferent, 0 . Bad, 0 .

Deportment Marks, .

D. M. Jones, *Teacher.*

A report card from the Division 2 school in 1853 for J.T. Smart. It looks like a quick step from perfect to indifferent. This was the Joseph T. Smart who became an enterprising butcher, furnishing fresh meat, hides, and tallow to Stratham, Exeter, South Newmarket (Newfields), North Hampton, Little Boars Head, Greenland, and the Rye Beaches. (LB.)

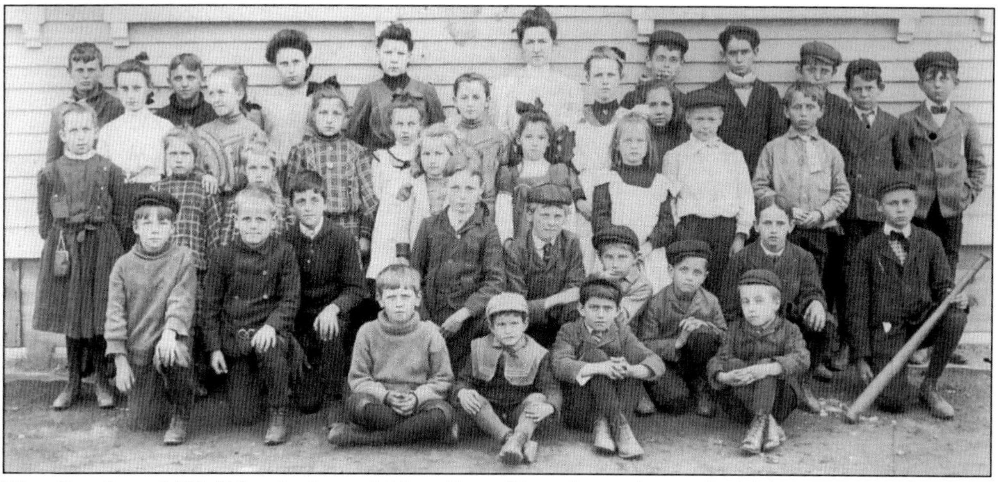

The Stratham Hill School class of Miss Susie French in the early 20th century. The one-room schoolhouses taught multiple grades together—hence siblings were educated together. Listed from left to right are as follows: (bottom row) Archie Chapman, Lauris Godfrey, Harold Odell, Harold Proctor, Norman Gregory, and John French; (second row) Eva Chadbourne, Vera Cottrill, Leah Cottrill, Nellie Chapman, Myrna Jewell, Mary Gregory, Flore Odell, Mary Chase, Ruth Godfrey, and Philip Gregory; (back row) Shirley Godfrey, Archie Chapman, Myrtle Beals, Susie French, teacher, Doris Littlefield, Archie Craig, Lawrence Chadbourn, Gertrude Beals, and Hugh Chase. (SHS.)

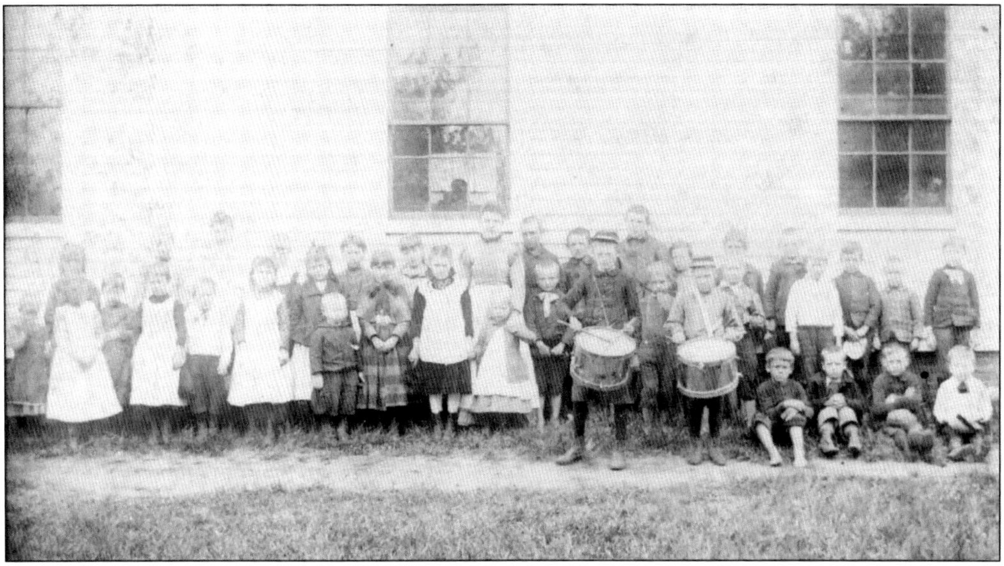

An early school picture, from the 19th century. In viewing the school pictures over time, notice how many generations of a family are apparent. (SHS.)

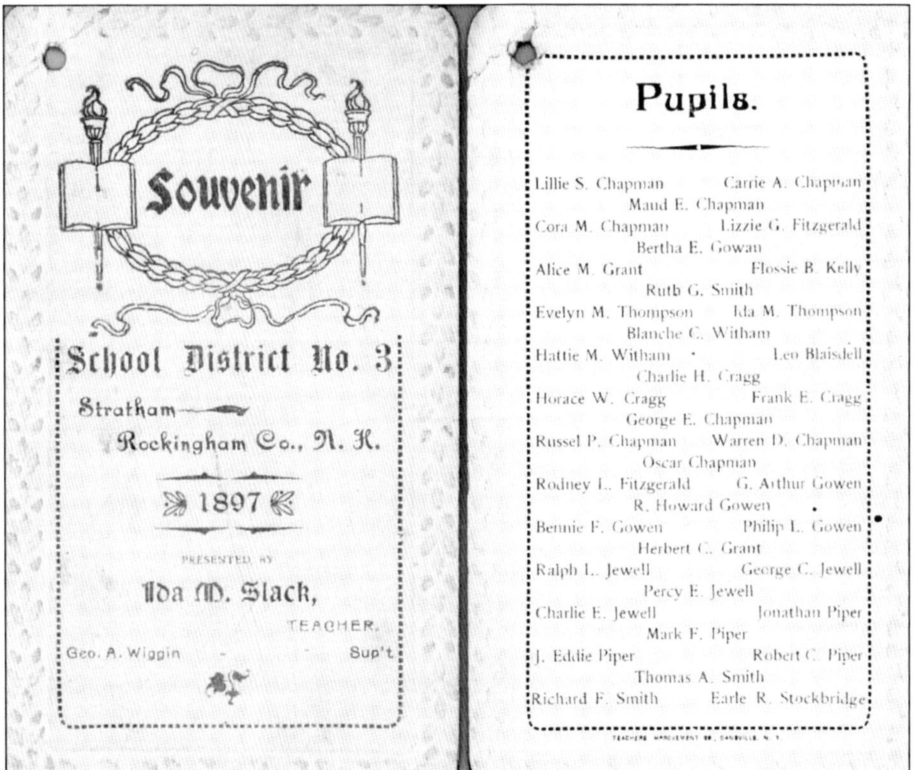

Souvenir

School District No. 3

Stratham

Rockingham Co., N. H.

1897

PRESENTED BY

Ida M. Slack,

TEACHER.

Geo. A. Wiggin - Sup't

Pupils.

Lillie S. Chapman Carrie A. Chapman
Maud E. Chapman
Cora M. Chapman Lizzie G. Fitzgerald
Bertha E. Gowan
Alice M. Grant Flossie B. Kelly
Ruth G. Smith
Evelyn M. Thompson Ida M. Thompson
Blanche C. Witham
Hattie M. Witham Leo Blaisdell
Charlie H. Cragg
Horace W. Cragg Frank E. Cragg
George E. Chapman
Russel P. Chapman Warren D. Chapman
Oscar Chapman
Rodney L. Fitzgerald G. Arthur Gowen
R. Howard Gowen
Bennie F. Gowen Philip L. Gowen
Herbert C. Grant
Ralph L. Jewell George C. Jewell
Percy E. Jewell
Charlie E. Jewell Jonathan Piper
Mark F. Piper
J. Eddie Piper Robert C. Piper
Thomas A. Smith
Richard F. Smith Earle R. Stockbridge

The program from the graduation ceremonies of 1897. Tied with a gold ribbon, the program included surnames long familiar in town, such as Chapman, Gowen, Jewell, Piper, Stockbridge, and Smith. Division 3 denotes the Winnicutt School at the corner of Barker Road and High Street. (LB.)

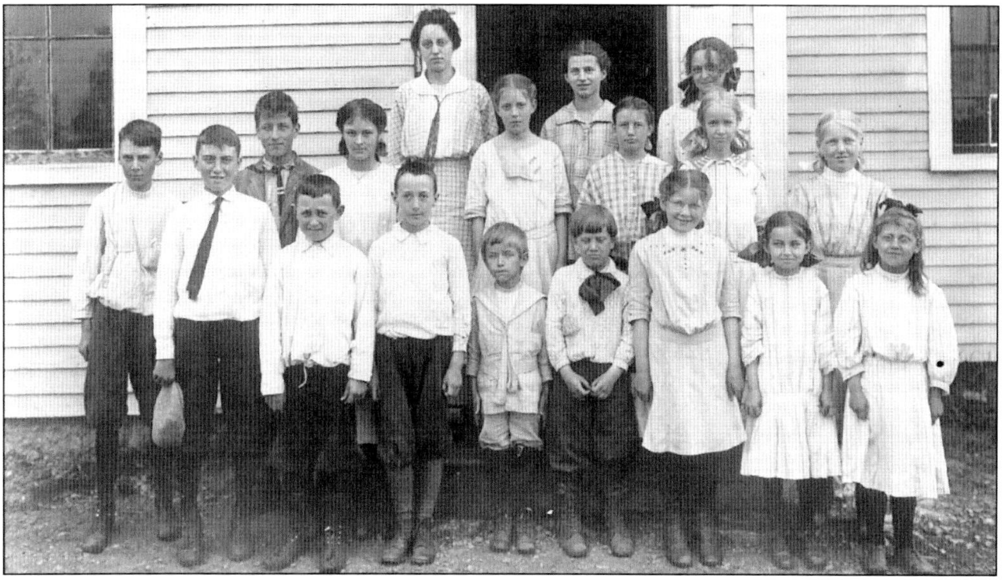

The Plains School, at 152 Heights Road, in 1910. Listed from left to right are as follows: (first row) Paul Chase, Warren ?, Howard Albert Wiggin, unidentified, ? Batchelder, Helen Batchelder, and two unidentified; (second row) Ralph Lane, Beatrice Barnard, Helen Batchelder, Ora Dining, Elsie Wiggin, and Francis Batchelder; (back row) Agnes Lane. (SHS.)

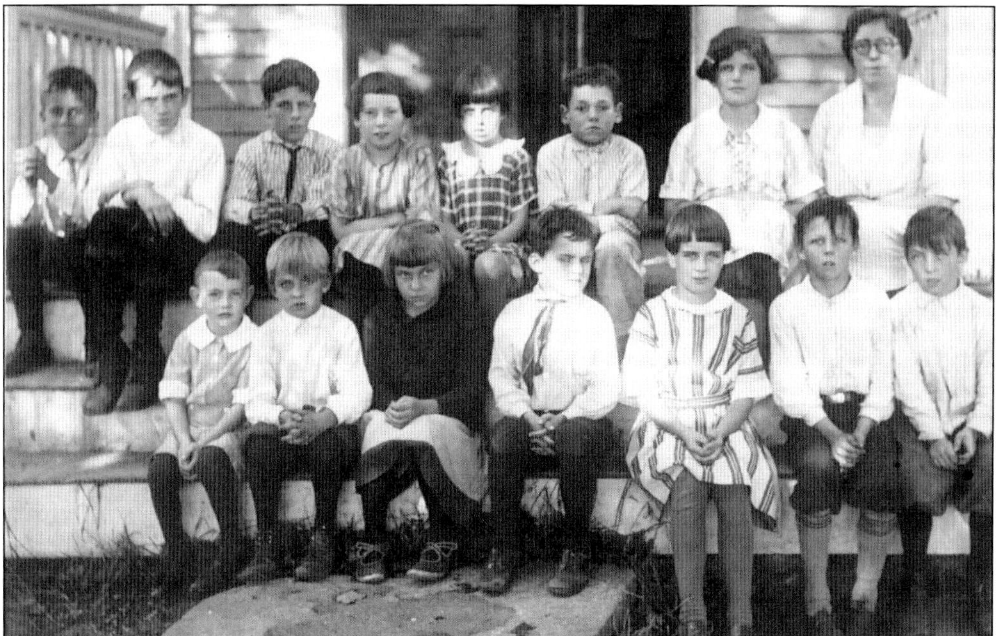

Miss Edna Crane's class at the Ridge School at 78 Portsmouth Avenue in October 1926. Included here are Wesley Varney, John Parkman, Robert Berry, Lucy Chapman, Dorothy Berry, Francis Wentworth, Marjorie Parkman, Miss Crane, Leslie Dining, Alfred Carbonneau,Hattie McIntyre, Thomas Berry, Barbara Berry, Octave Carbonneau, and Edgar Carbonneau. Miss Crane taught in the Ridge School and later in the Memorial School on Bunker Hill Avenue. (SHS.)

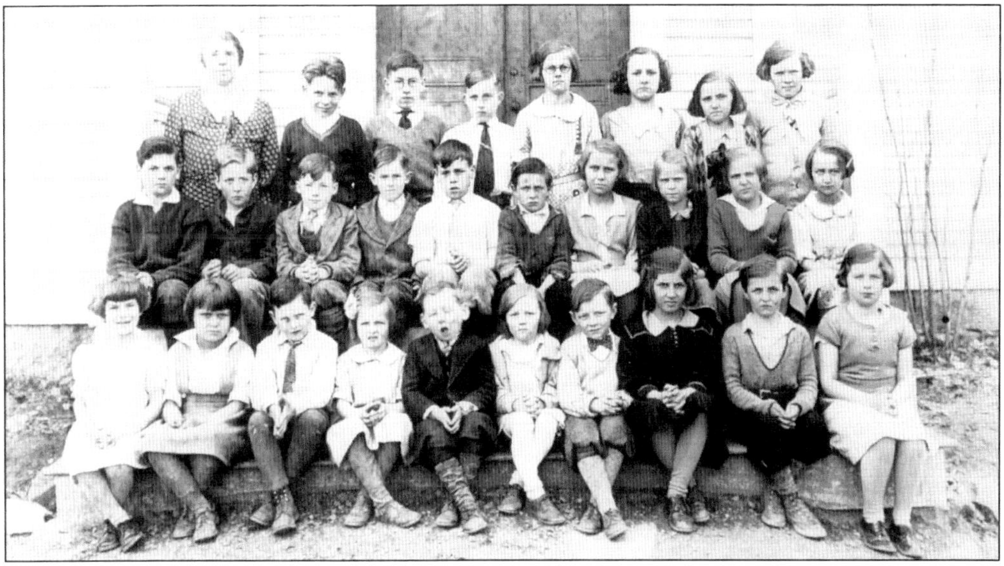

Ridge School, 1928–34. Among those listed here are Edna Crane, Herbert Boutwell, Richard Kinniburgh, Winfield Foote, Elizabeth Fisk, Frieda Wentworth, Barbara Wentworth, Dorothy Towle, unidentified, John Batchelder, Lester Carbonneau, Rudolph Towle, Joseph Boutwell, Alfred Carbonneau, unidentified, Mary Fisk, Betty Stockbridge, Eleanor Clarke, Miriam Fisk, Maude Boutwell, Mary Carbonneau, Herbert Rawson, Caroline Wentworth, another Rawson, Joan Batchelder, Calvin Carbonneau, Barbara Tuck, and two unidentified. (SHS.)

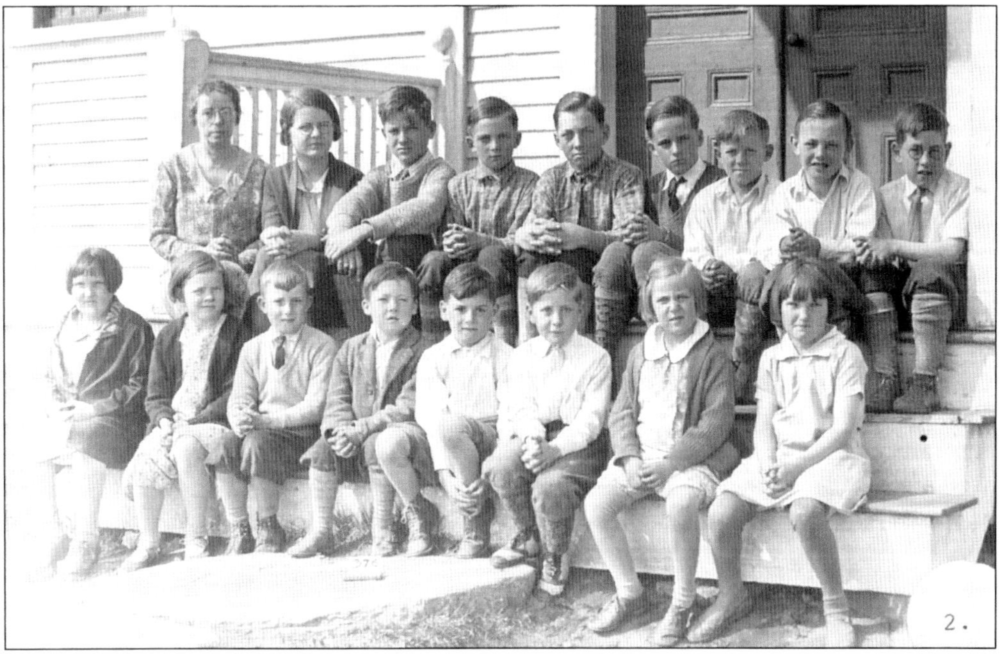

Miss Edna Crane's class at the Ridge School on Portsmouth Avenue in 1932. The students include Mildred Parker, William Parker, Edgar Carbonneau, Alfred Carbonneau, Leslie Dining, Thomas Berry, Allen Kelton, Richard Kinniburgh, Shirley Kent, Dorothy Towle, Winfield Foote, Rudolph Towle, John Batchelder, Lester Carbonneau, Eleanor Clarke, and Evelyn Kent. Edna Crane boarded with Annie W. Scammon for many years. (SHS.)

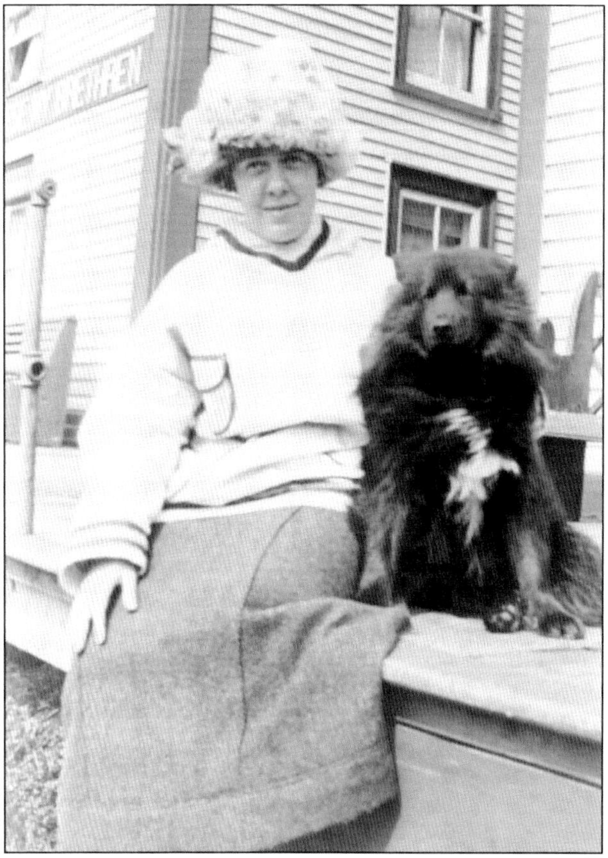

Schoolmistress Bessie Copping and her pet dog. Bessie sent this photograph as a holiday greeting to the Pearson family in 1912. She taught at the Ridge School and was the daughter of the Congregational minister. She later moved to Labrador. (SHS.)

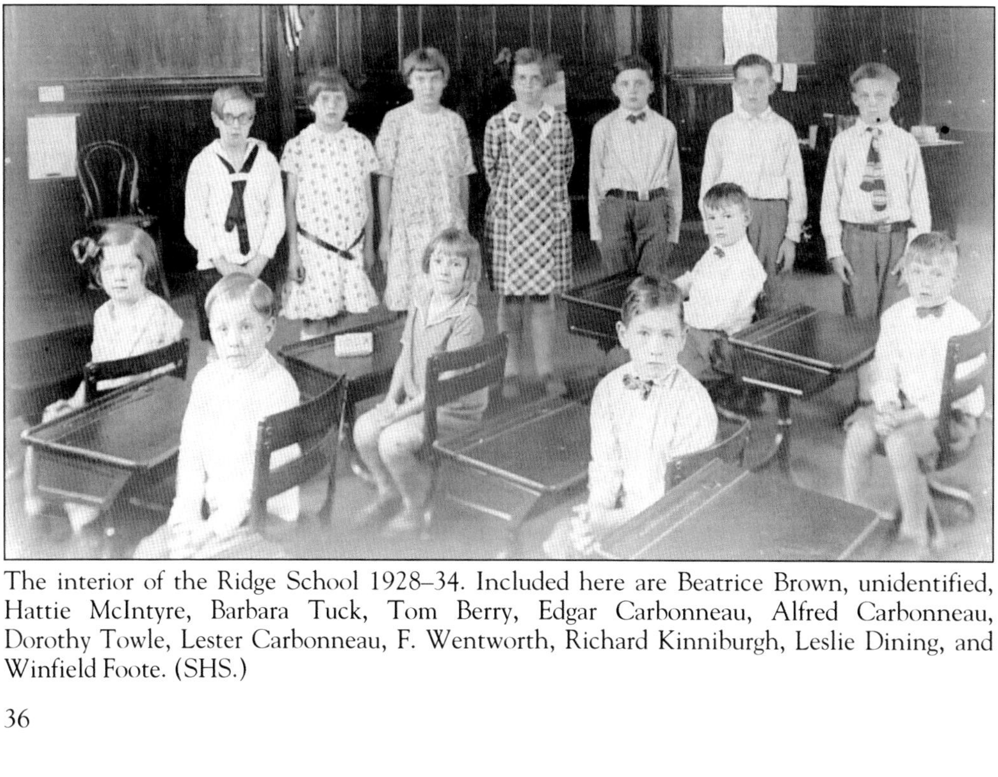

The interior of the Ridge School 1928–34. Included here are Beatrice Brown, unidentified, Hattie McIntyre, Barbara Tuck, Tom Berry, Edgar Carbonneau, Alfred Carbonneau, Dorothy Towle, Lester Carbonneau, F. Wentworth, Richard Kinniburgh, Leslie Dining, and Winfield Foote. (SHS.)

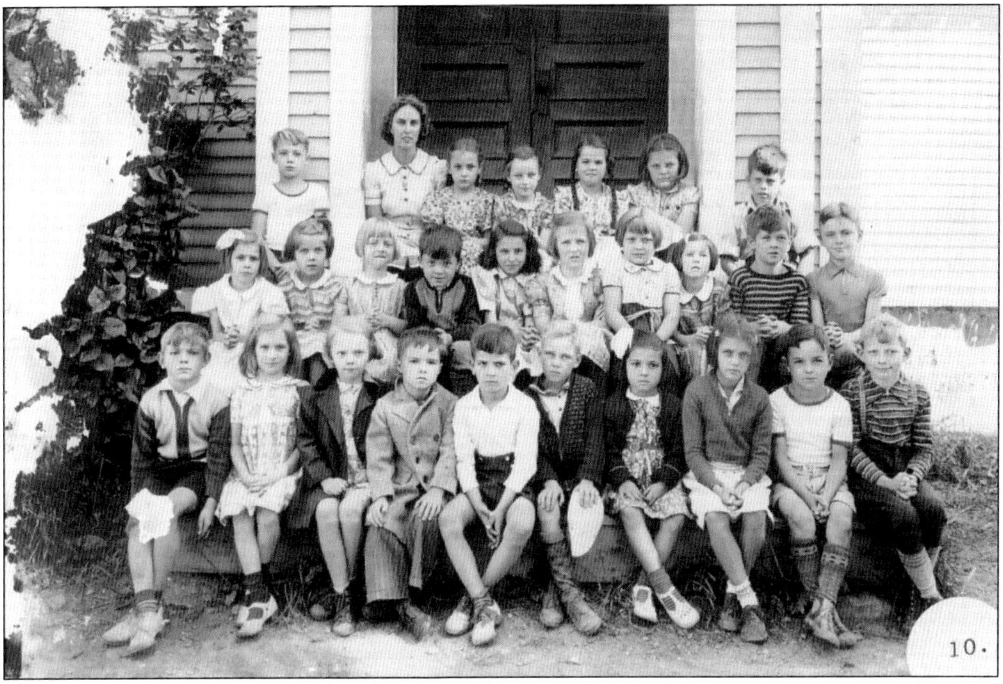

Marge Cleary's 1939–40 class at the Stratham Hill School at 240 Portsmouth Avenue. The students include Nelson Dolloff, Kenneth Stevens, Dick Wiggin, Charlie Picard, Anita Wentworth, Paul Wentworth, Cameron Sewell, Barbara Sewell, Charlie Pentaluscco, Marjorie Rawson, Billy Fisk, Rae Wiggin, Carl Winich, and Freddy Dougherty. (SHS.)

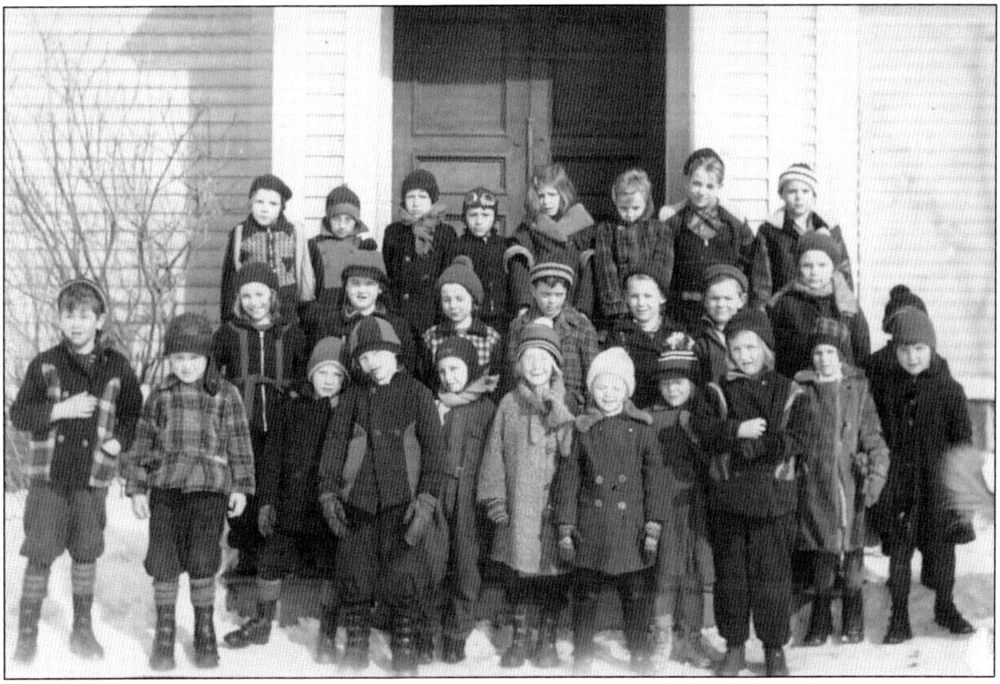

Stratham Hill School during the winter of 1939–40. Teacher Marge Cleary brought a camera to school and photographed the same first through third graders pictured above. (SHS.)

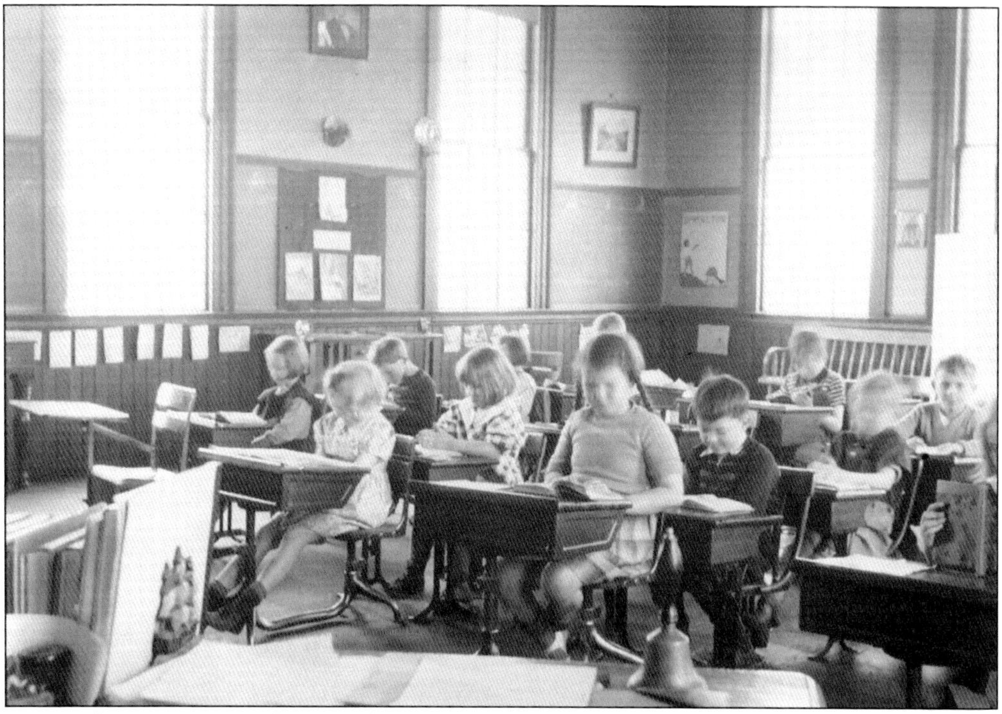

Marge Cleary's 1939–40 class, inside the Stratham Hill School. (SHS.)

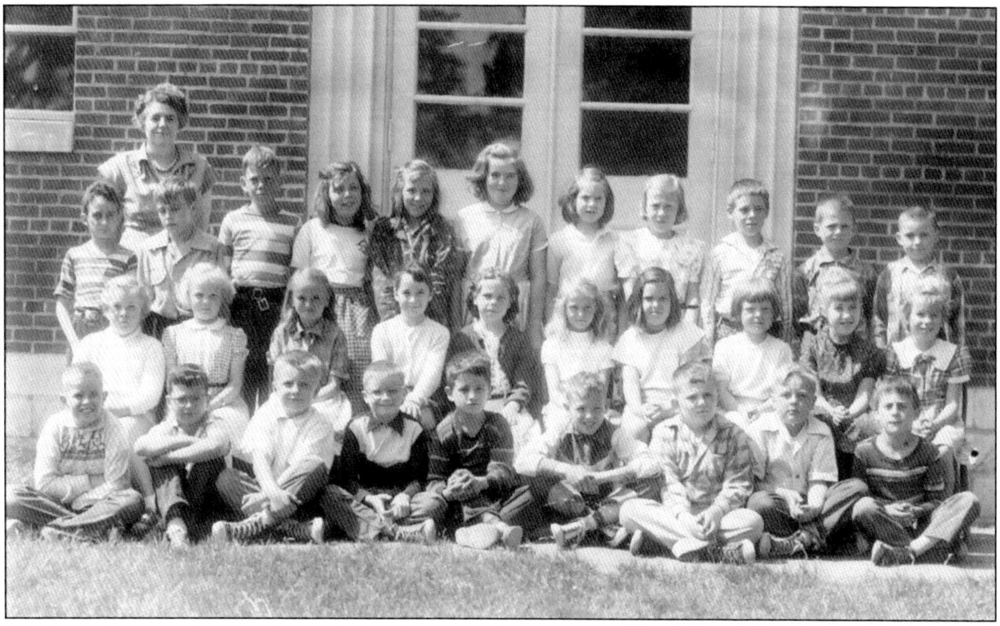

Gladys Clements' second- and third-grade class at the new Stratham Memorial School in the early 1950s. Students include Paul Walker, Martha Peabody, Dan Rawson, Nicky Schorch, Ron Houghton, Fred Hutton Jr., Dick Connant, Winston Hershey, Kathy Wiggin, Linda Scamman, Nancy McNally, Lauren Dixwell, Lucy Hutton, Beverly Batchelder, Tommy Weeks, Jeff Laviolette, Karen Meeks, Carlene Grant, Donna Goodrich, Maureen O'Leary, Kenny Gunther, and Les Barker. (LC.)

Four

WORKING THE LAND

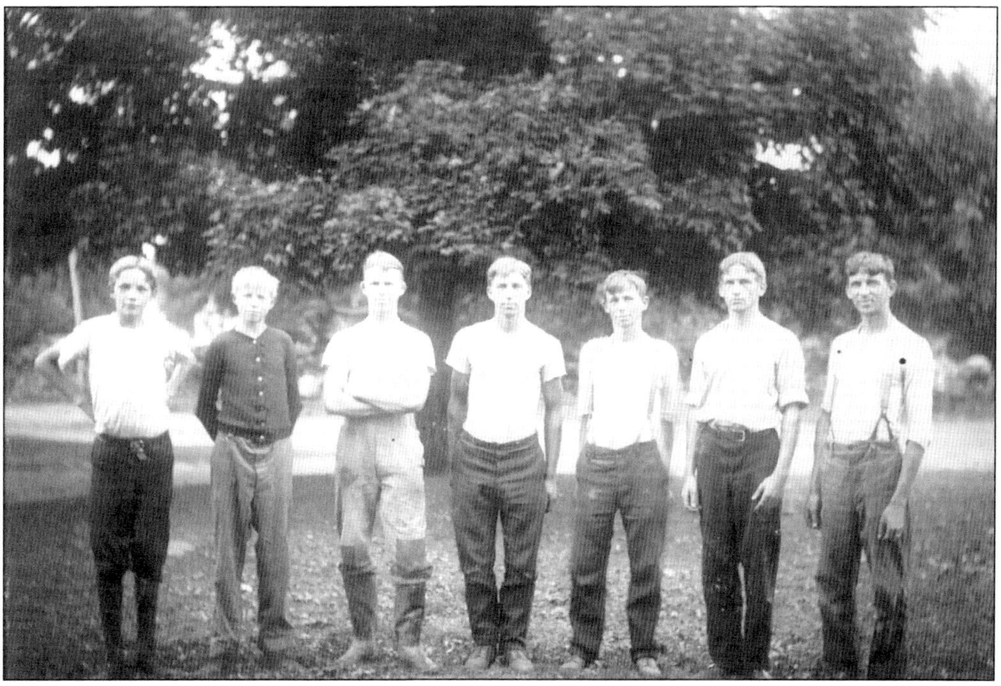

The original caption, "In order—right from work." The sons of George Gowen pose after a day working on the farm around the turn of the century. They are Shirley, Phillip, Ben, Howard, Arthur, Ralph, and Clarence. (HC.)

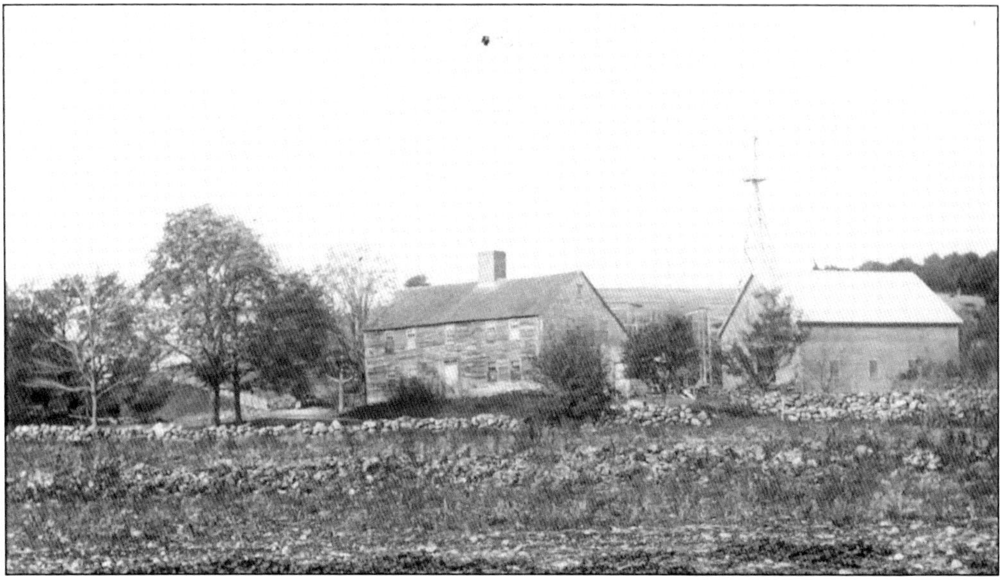

The Hillside Farm, the old Gowen family farm, pre-1900. This house was torn down after a new house was built. (HC.)

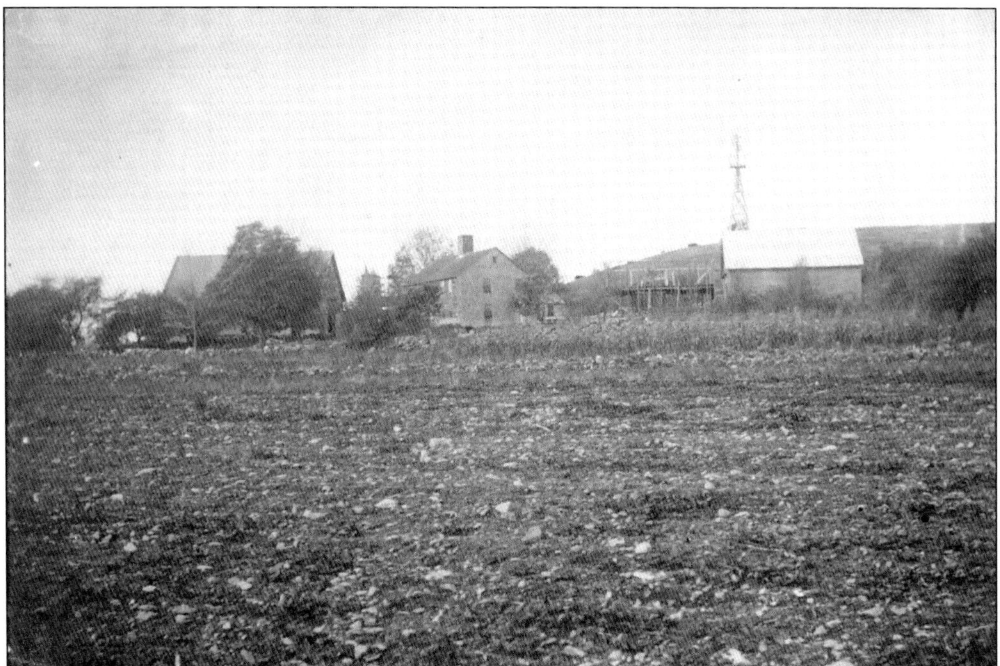

Another view of the Hillside Farm showing many of the barns and out buildings, pre-1900. (HC.)

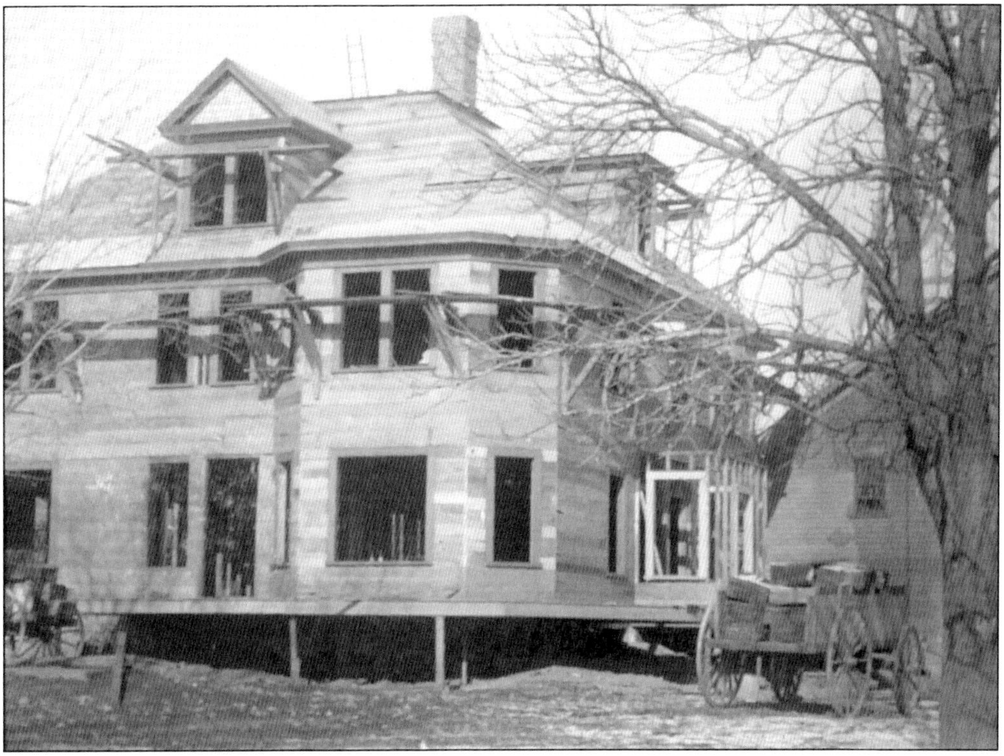

The "new" Gowen house at 83 High Street under construction, *c.* 1900. (HC.)

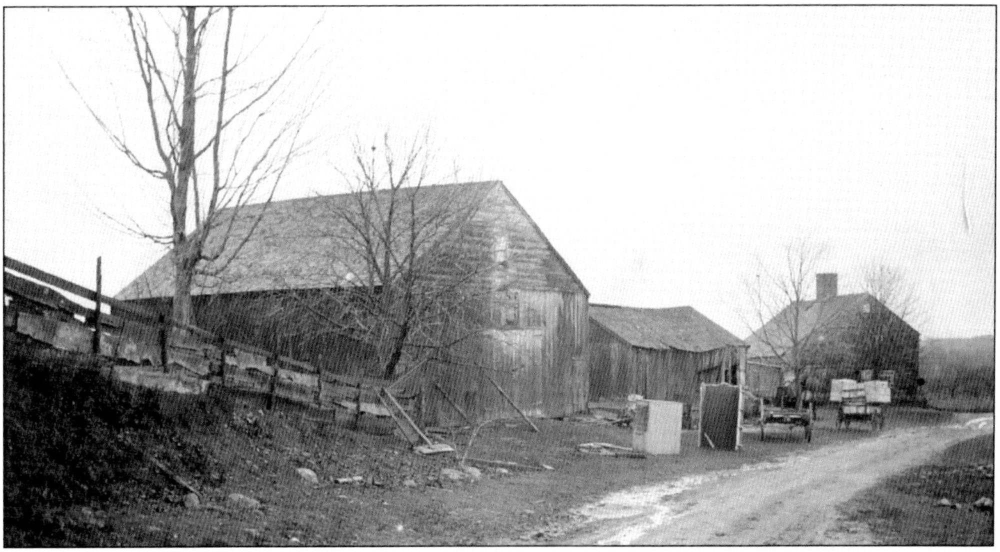

The old Gowen Farm, called Hillside, adjacent to 83 High Street. They are moving from the old house to the new house, which they built next door, *c.* 1900. (HC.)

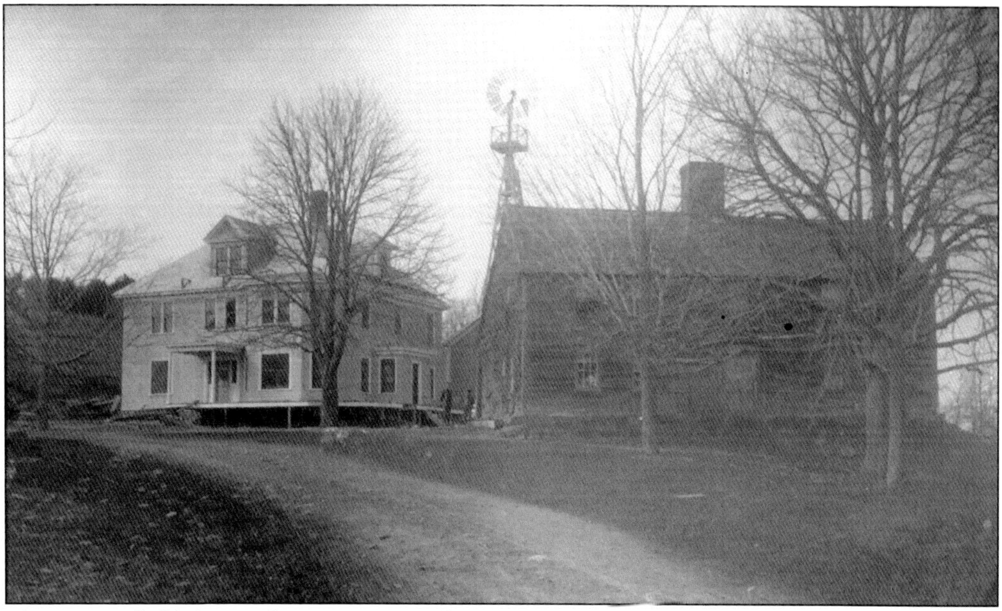

The new and old Gowen houses at 83 High Street near Barker Road, *c.* 1900. (HC.)

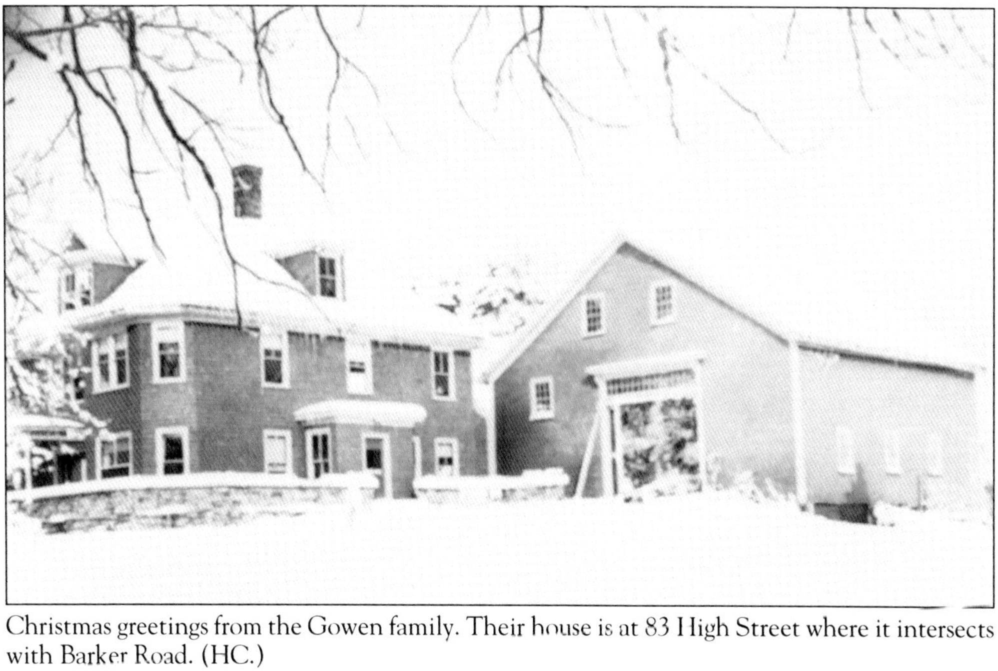

Christmas greetings from the Gowen family. Their house is at 83 High Street where it intersects with Barker Road. (HC.)

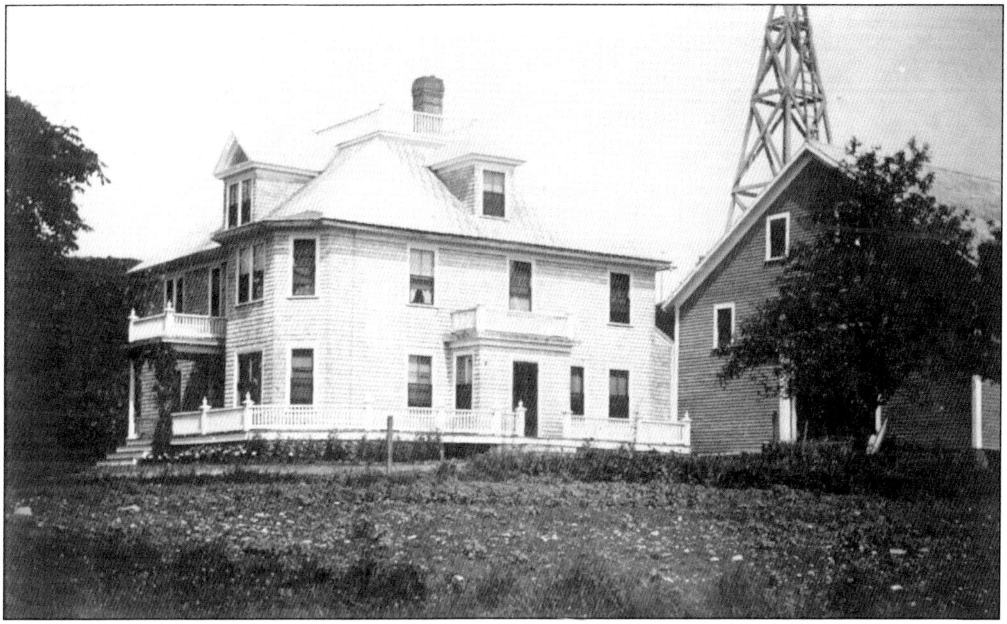

The new Gowen house at the Hillside Farm on High Street, *c.* 1900. (HC.)

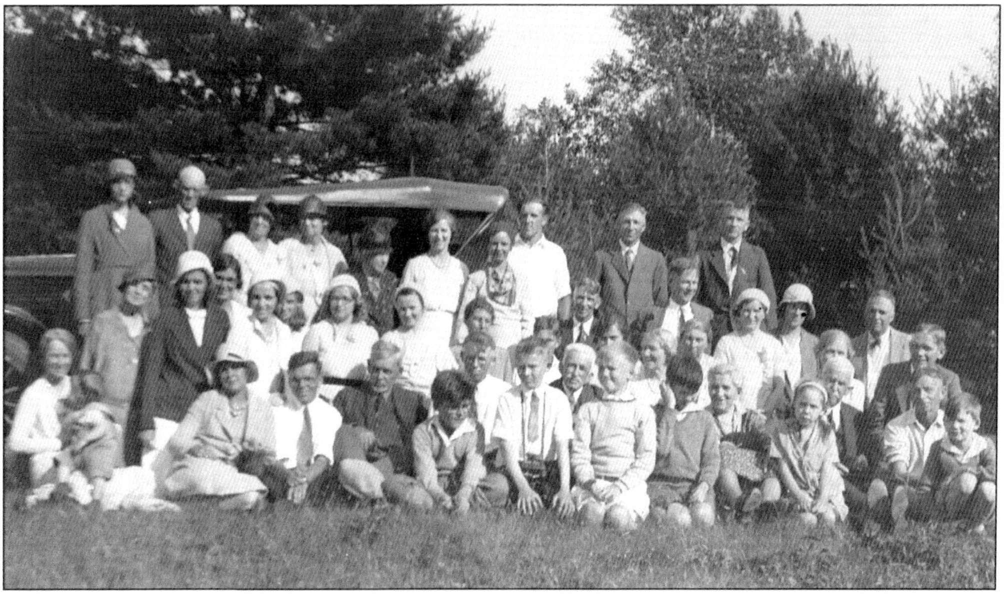

The Gowen family at the Stratham Hill Park for a reunion in 1932. These include the boys from p. 39 and their families. Listed from left to right are as follows: (front row) Edna Smith, Cameron Sewell, Helen and Oscar Pearson, Francis Gowen, Robert G. Gowen, Ralph Gowen, Robert H. Gowen, John Gowen, Agnes Smith, May Ellen, and Arthur and Frederick Gowen; (second row) Nan and Margaret Pearson, Janice Gowen, Helen Smiley, Lottie Gowen, Ben Gowen, George Gowen, Vera and Helen P. Gowen, Myra Gowen, Rachel Smiley, May and Shirley Gowen; (third row) Grace Pearson, Mary Sewell, Helen Chase, Fredericka Smith, Olive Smith, Dorothy Pearson, Clarence and Philip Gowen, Helen Linley Gowen, and Frank Pearson; (back row) Florence and Marshall Chase, Mary Gowen, Bertha Chase, Dougald Sewall, and Howard and Ralph Gowen. (SHS.)

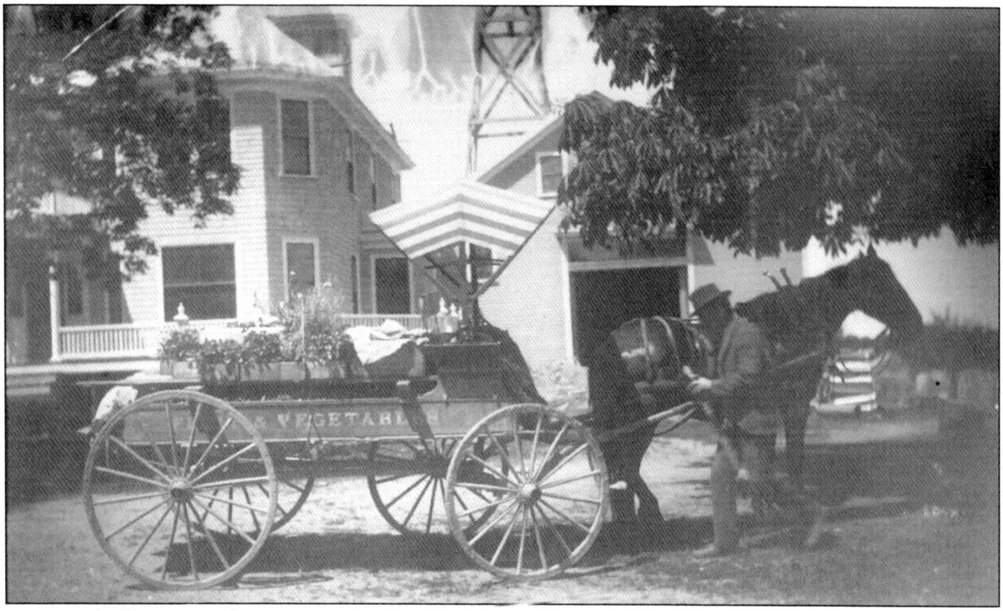

George E. Gowen and carriage on High Street, *c.* 1900. (HC.)

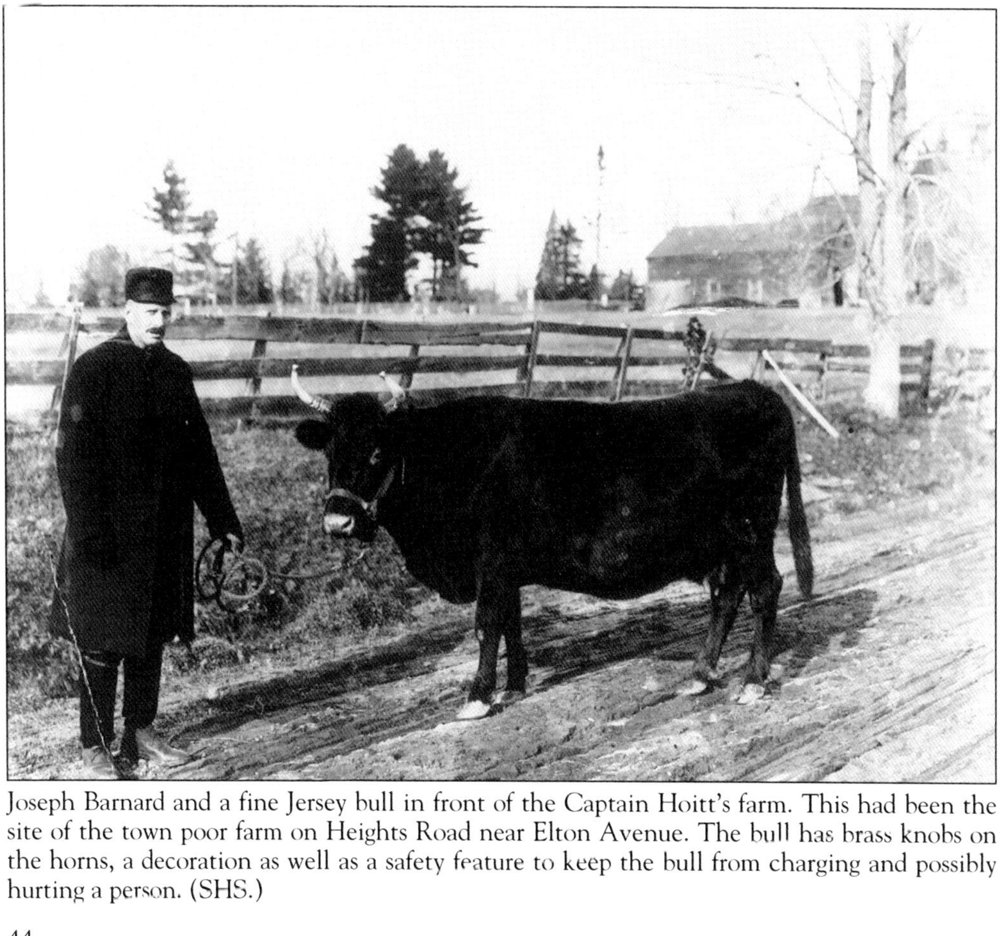

Joseph Barnard and a fine Jersey bull in front of the Captain Hoitt's farm. This had been the site of the town poor farm on Heights Road near Elton Avenue. The bull has brass knobs on the horns, a decoration as well as a safety feature to keep the bull from charging and possibly hurting a person. (SHS.)

Stratham, N.H.
1905

100 acre farm, 35 in mowing and tillage, balance in woodland and pasture, house of 13 rooms in A-1 condition; barn 90 ft. long, 2 hay lofts; 3 miles from Exeter; 8 miles from Rye Beach; 1/2 mile from electrics; 51 miles from Boston, Western Div. B. & M.

This property is situated on the brow of a hill with a fine view of the surrounding country; farm at present time leased, but if purchaser wished to occupy at once no doubt satisfactory arrangements could be made with the present tenant. This would make a fine place for summer home.

Price $5000. Mort. $2200. which can remain. Owner, E.F. Folsom, 16 Gorham Ave., Brookline, Mass. Tel. 1314-3 Brookline.

A 1905 sales advertisement for the farm at 61 Heights Road. (CR.)

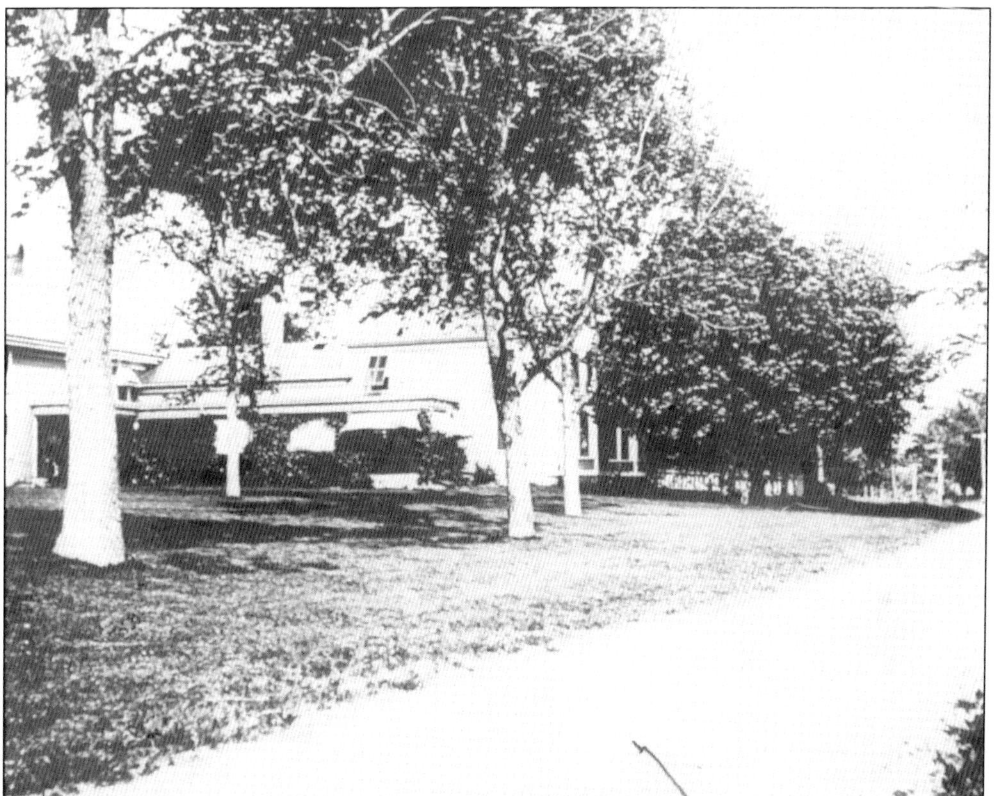

One of the grand houses built by the Folsom family in the 19th century at the crest of Heights road overlooking Exeter. It has been a country seat, summer residence, and a working farm, and is now a certified organic farm and protected conservation land. (CR.)

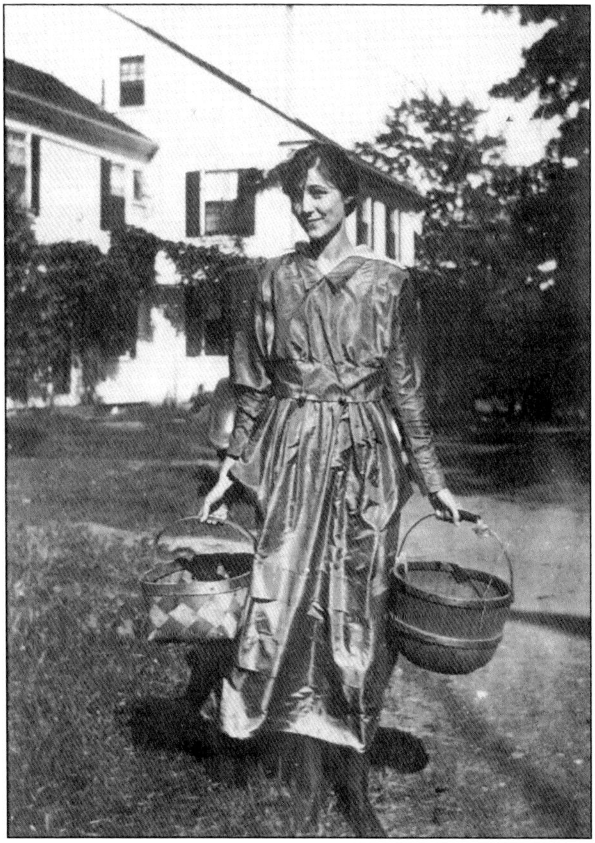

Jessamy Fountain, a student at Smith College, visiting her parents' farm at 69 Portsmouth Avenue. Her parents, George Morton Fountain and Ellen Ellison Fountain, ran the farm from 1915 to 1927 and raised horses, sheep, cattle, and goats. After graduating from Smith in 1916, Jessamy was a social worker in New York City and a frequent visitor to Stratham until she married Arthur Benjamin Haley, a dean, coach, and teacher at Phillips Exeter Academy. They met at a dance at the academy on one of her visits home. (D and SS.)

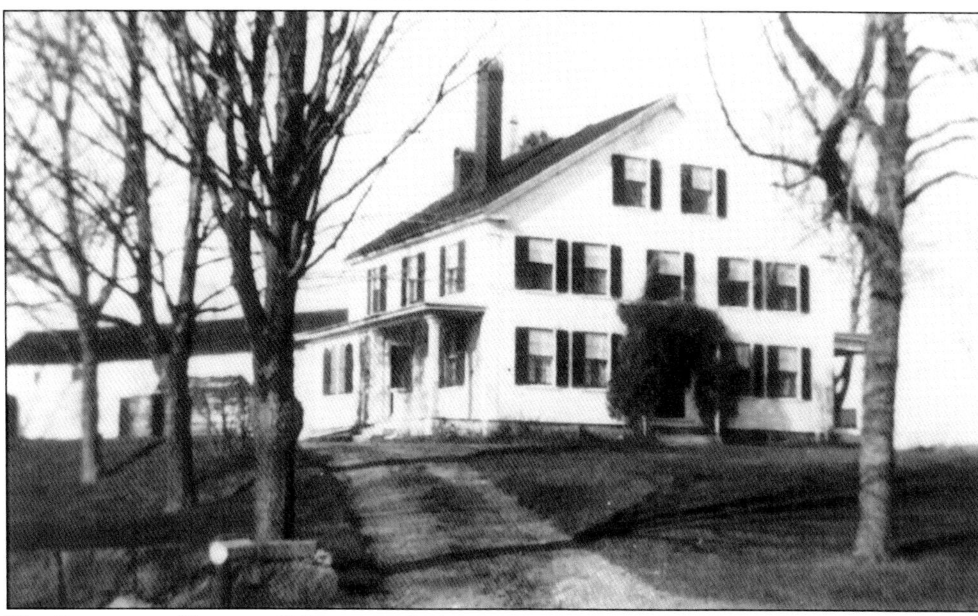

The Bittersweet Farm at 69 Portsmouth Avenue, *c.* 1915–1927, pictured while owned by the Fountain family. Arthur Benjamin Haley, dean at Phillips Exeter Academy, proposed to Jessamy Fountain, the farmers' daughter, beneath the elms. (D and SS.)

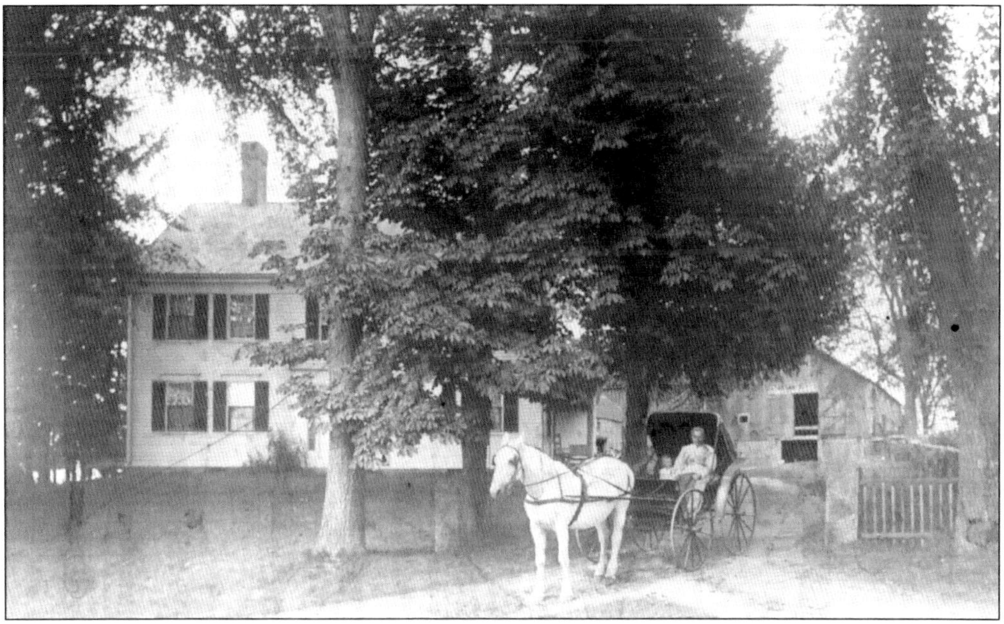

An 1890s view of the Berry family farm at 25 Heights Road. George Wesley Berry and his mother, Emma, sit in the carriage drawn by either Molly or Dolly. (B and MB.)

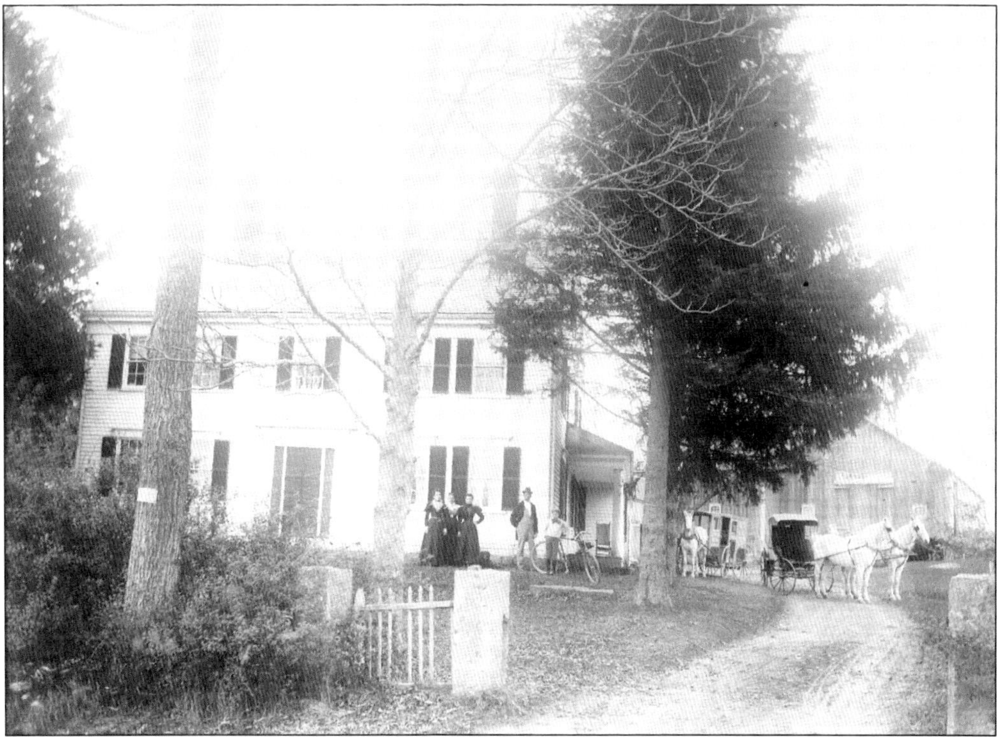

The Berry family farm at 25 Heights Road in the 1890s. The people are identified as proprietor James Wesley Berry, one of the women is his daughter Amanda, and the other two women are unknown. The boy is, most likely, George Wesley Berry. The horses are Molly and Dolly. (B and MB.)

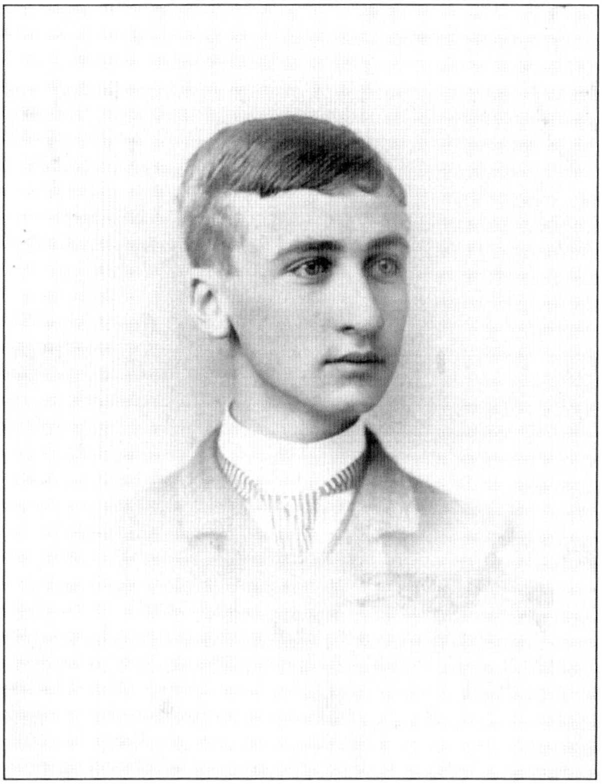

John Fred Emery c. 1885, known as J. Fred. Mr. Emery was a pioneer market gardener in town supplying produce to Exeter, Dover, and Portsmouth, as well as to a farmstand on Emery Lane. A noted Democrat, he was a state representative in 1903 and a state senator in 1909. He was prominent for many years in town affairs and was noted for making oral presentations in verse. (SHS.)

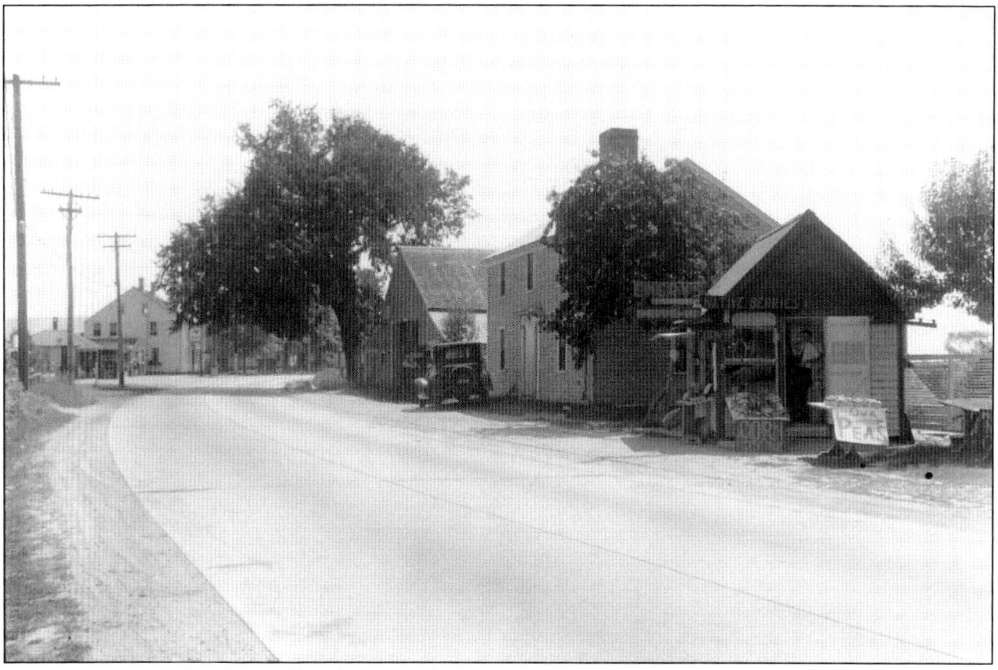

J. Fred Emery in the door of his farmstand at 12 Emery Lane. Before the road was moved in the 1950s, Emery Lane was part of Portsmouth Avenue, the main road through town that was laid out as Kings Great Hyway in 1671 as the primary ground-route inland. (SHS.)

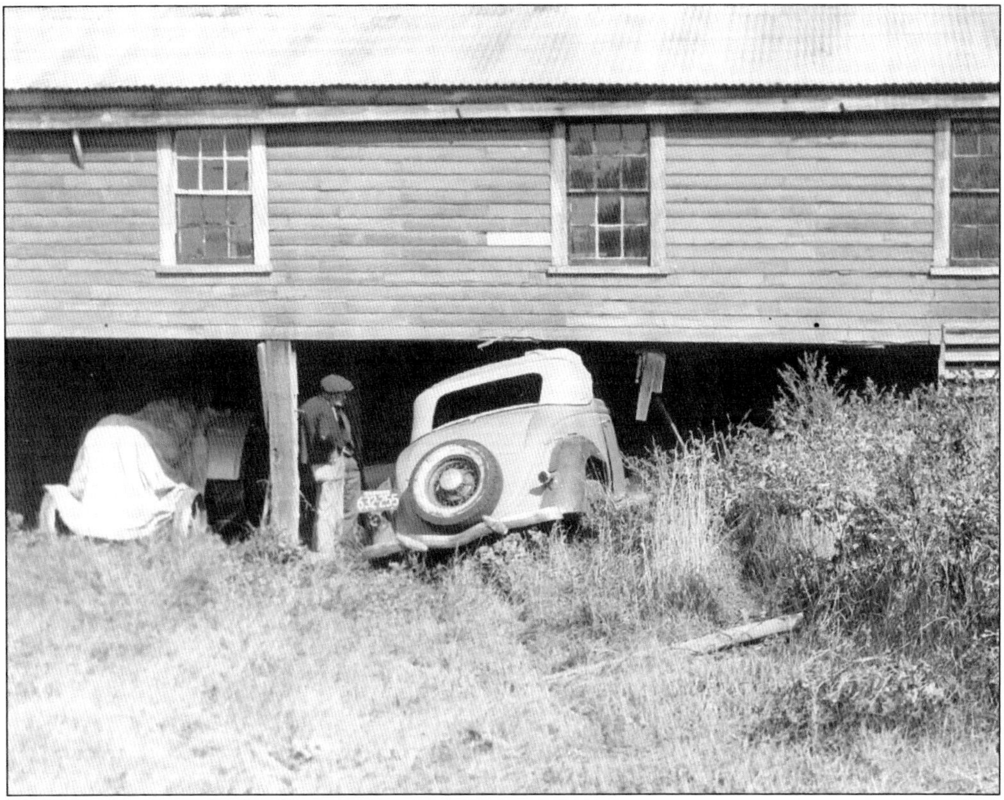

J. Fred Emery on his farm. He is looking at a car that ran off the road and finally stopped beneath his barn. (SHS.)

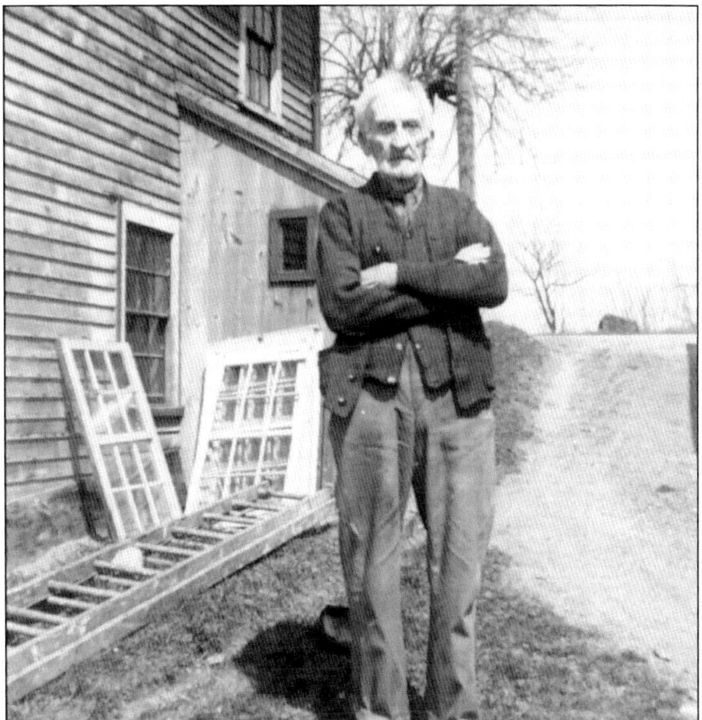

J. Fred Emery at age 85 in 1954. Emery was a member of the fraternal organization the Order of Red Men. In 1893 he served as Great Sachem of New Hampshire and later was a representative on the Great Council of the United States. (SHS.)

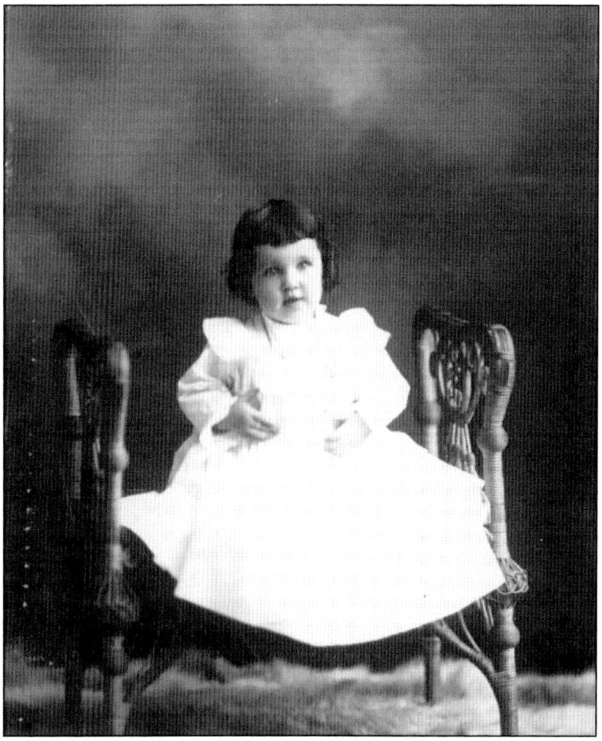

Mary Emery at 18 months in July 1902. The daughter of J. Fred and Frances Emery, Mary trained as a schoolteacher and taught at the Franklin, New Hampshire, junior high school for over 25 years. (SHS.)

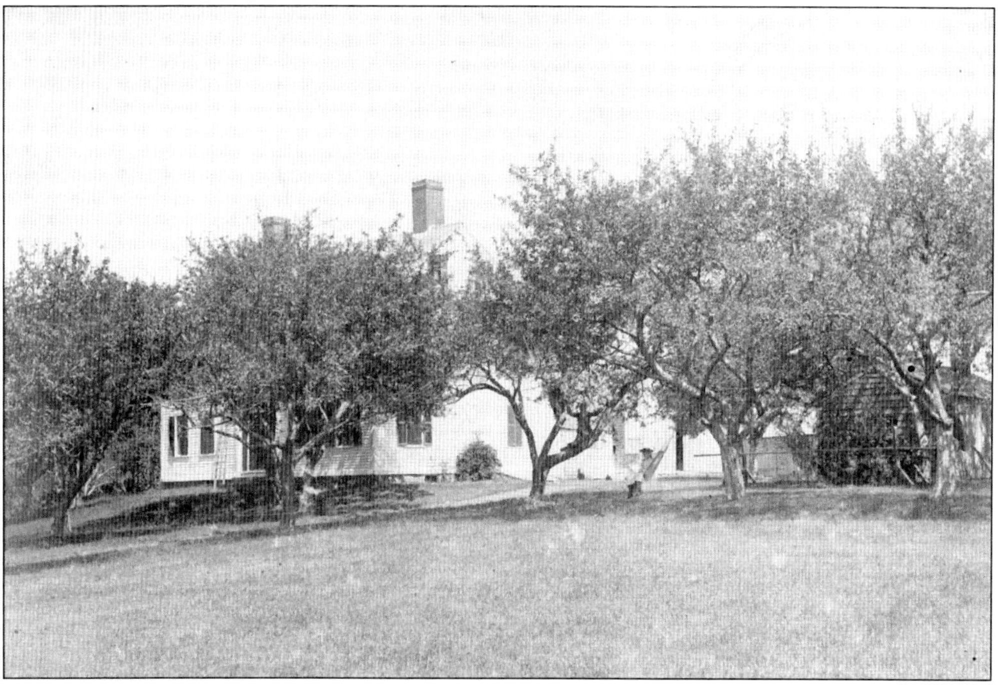

A girl, possibly Mary, enjoying a summer's day in the orchard on the Emery Farm. Stratham has been prime agricultural land since settlement by European immigrants. Dairy, poultry, and truck farms have provided ample provisions to natives as well as to New England city dwellers. (SHS.)

House on top, 15 Jackrabbit Lane; house on bottom, 17 Jackrabbit Lane. At the turn of the century these were Brown family homes at what is now Stratham Hill Park. (HC.)

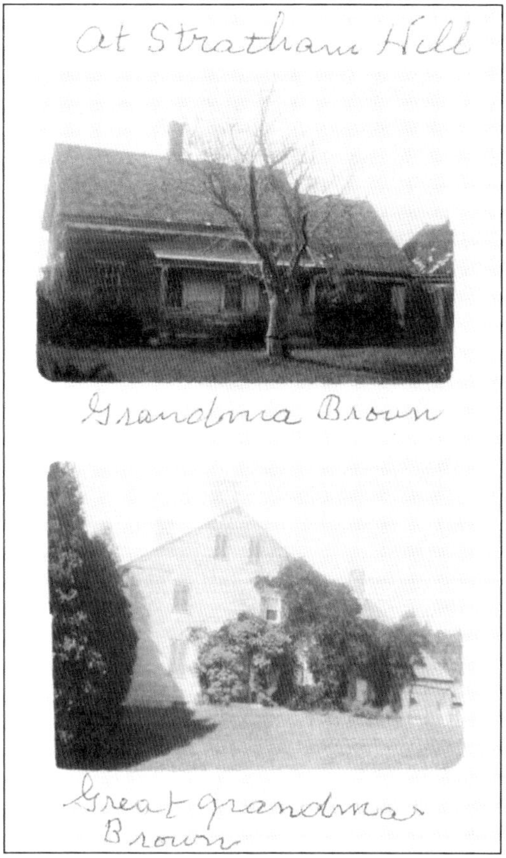

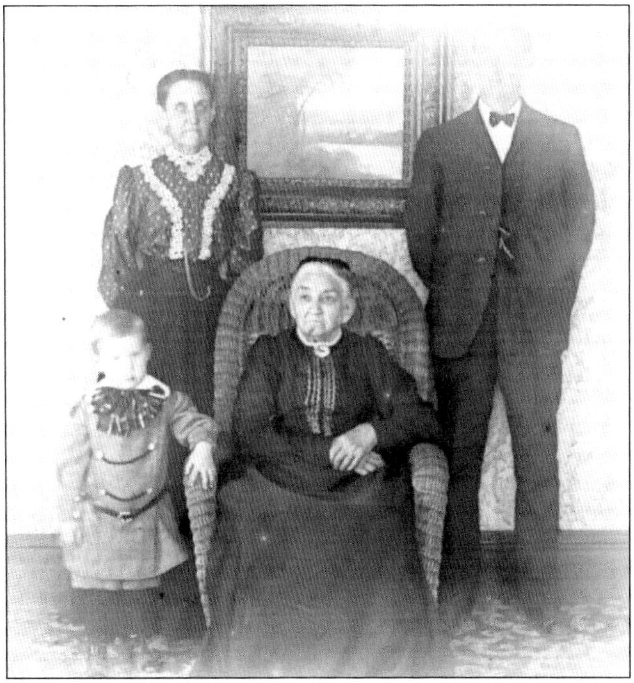

Four generations of Browns and Chases in the 19th century. They are Oliver Brown Chase, Great-grandma Brown, Grandma Chase, and John Emmon Chase. (HC.)

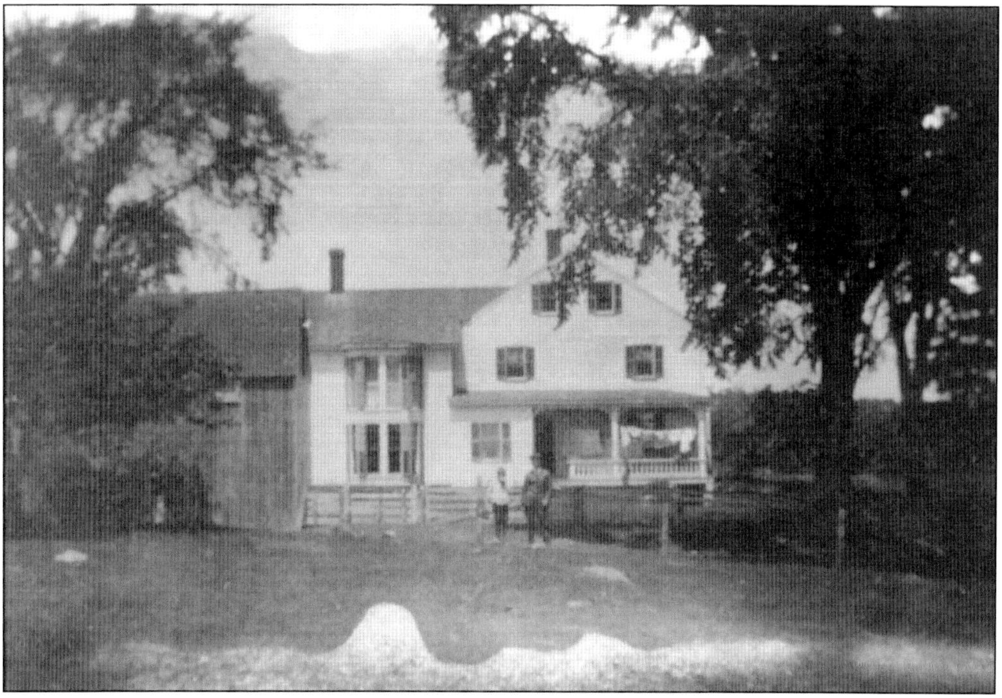

The Chase Farm at 114 Bunker Hill Avenue. (HC.)

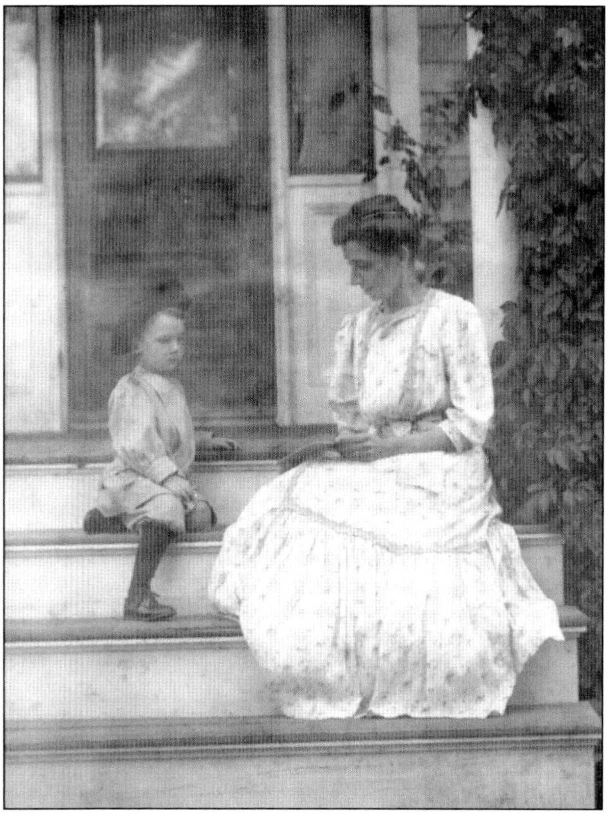

Paul Gowen Chase and his mother, Bertha Gowen Chase. They are pictured here reading on the porch of the Gowen Farm at 83 High Street, c. 1908. (HC.)

Paul Gowen Chase and his mother, Bertha Gowen Chase. Mother and son are feeding the piglets at the Chase Farm on Bunker Hill Avenue, *c*. 1912. (HC.)

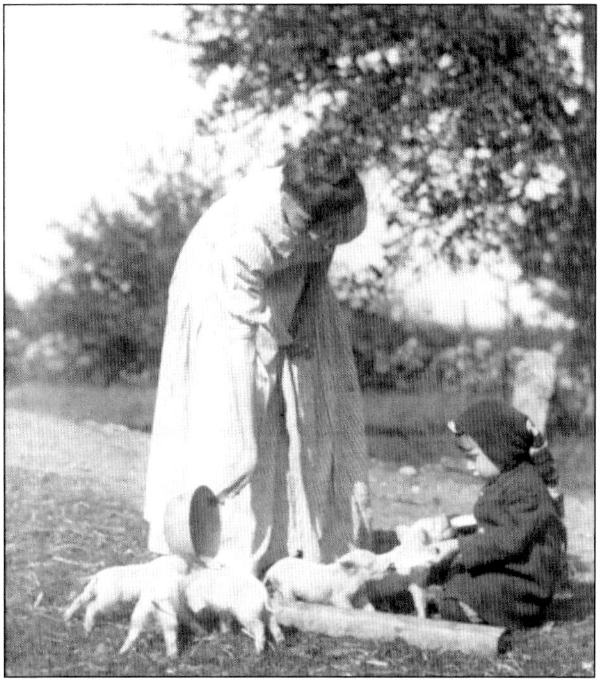

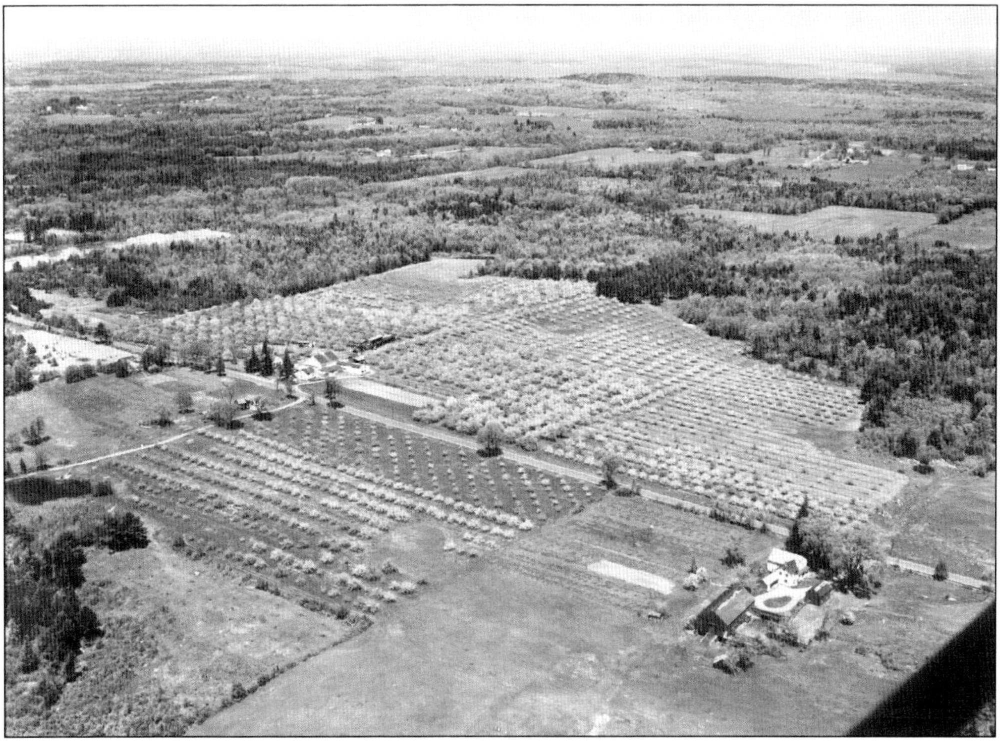

A 1960 aerial view of the Sewell home and orchard at 97 Bunker Hill Avenue (the building complex is on the left). Great Bay is visible in the distance. The Cushman home, which is now a cellar hole, is visible across the street slightly to the left. The house and barn on the right are the Chase's, at 114 Bunker Hill Avenue. (C and JS.)

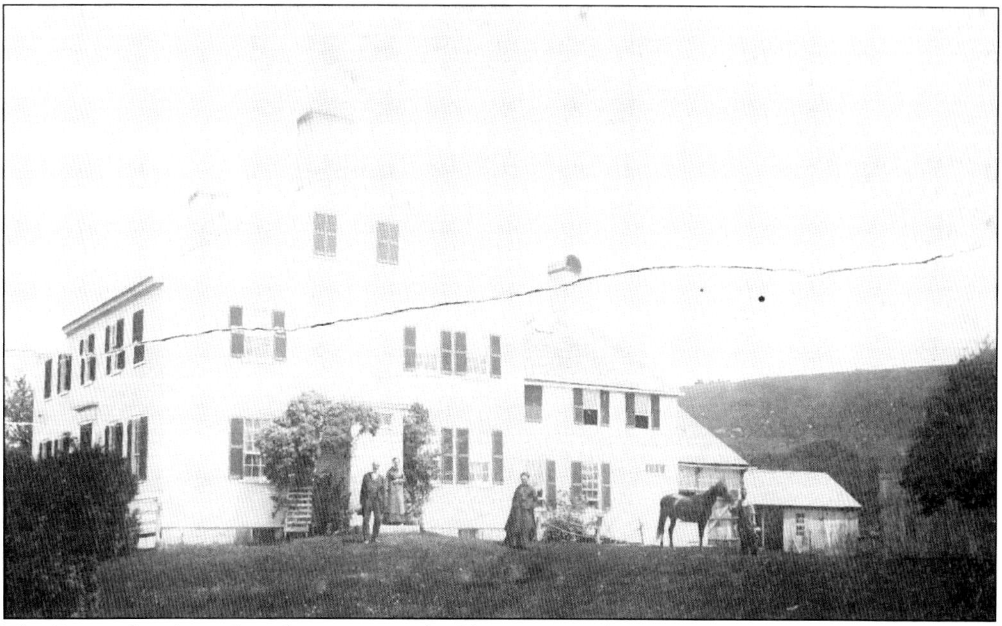

The Brown family at their farm at 17 Jackrabbit Lane in the 19th century. This house and land are part of Stratham Hill Park. (HC.)

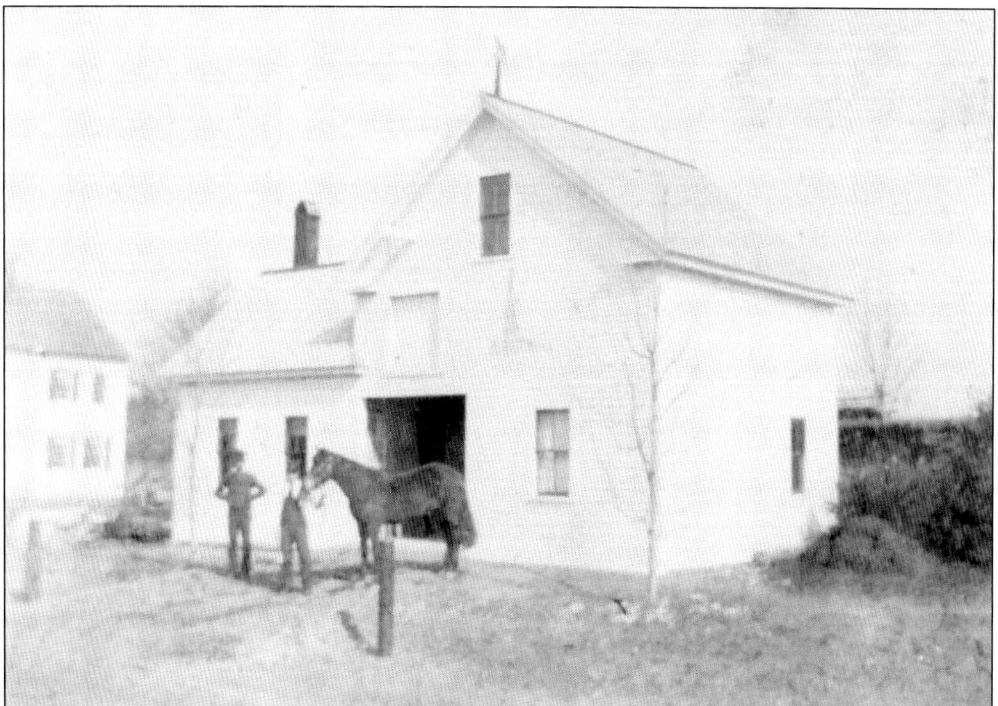

Ridgely Marsh and Charlie Gear. Marsh's house in the background is at 104 Union Road where Barker Road intersects. Gear ran a store out of the adjacent carriage house and wrote the accounts on the wall. Gear also worked as a teamster driving between Portsmouth and Exeter. (BB.)

Eugene Carbonneau, Paul Gowen Chase, and Rex on the porch of the Chase Farm, 114 Bunker Hill Avenue, c. 1915. (HC.)

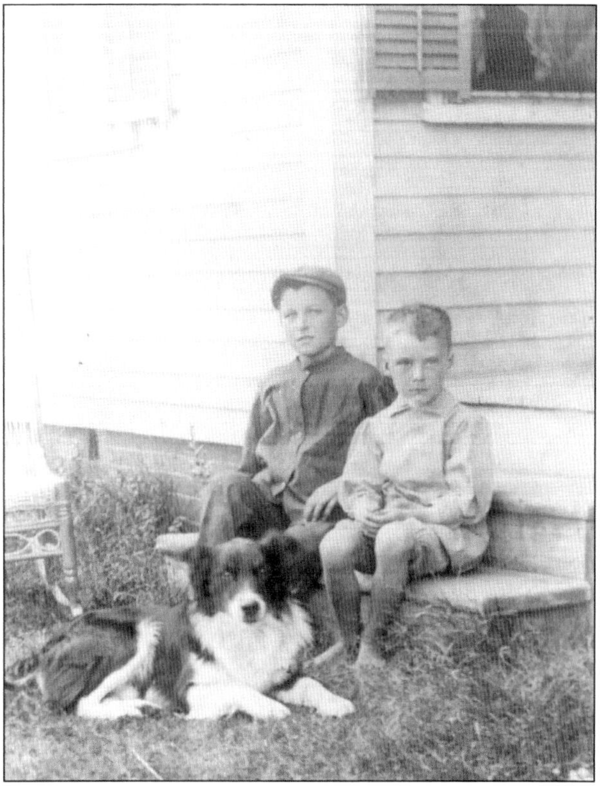

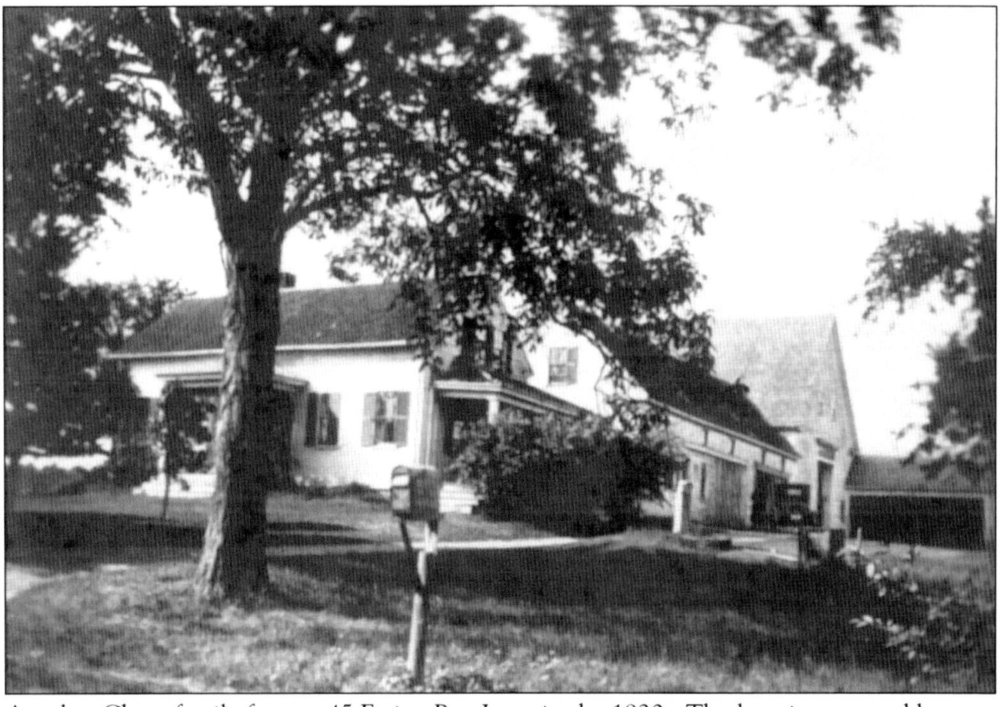

Another Chase family farm at 45 Frying Pan Lane in the 1920s. The lane is so named because in earlier days one frying pan was shared among neighbors. (HC.)

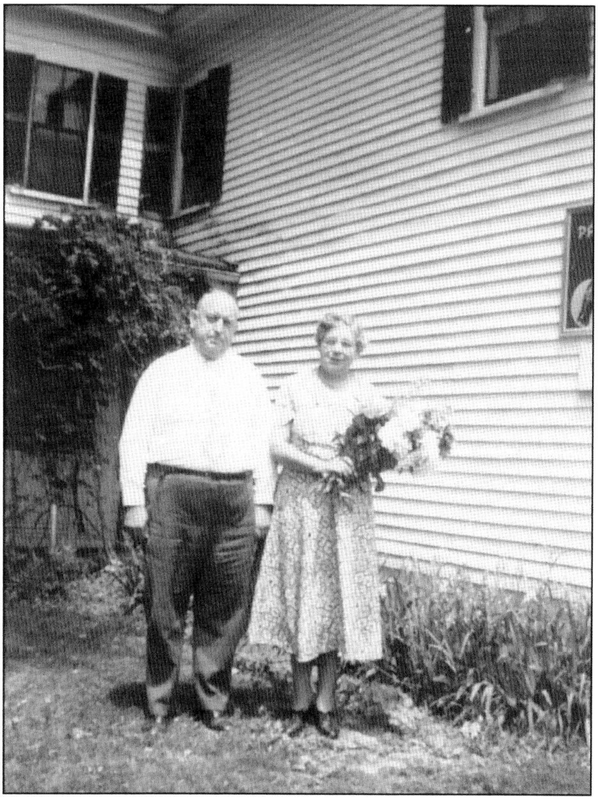

Joseph and Bertha Stickney Parks. Longtime residents and very active in the Grange, they are shown near the Stratham Village Market on Portsmouth Avenue. At that time the market was owned by the Edmund's family and Joseph and Bertha lived above the store. Bertha grew up on the Stickney Farm, now the site of the NHSPCA. Joseph was a World War I veteran. (SHS.)

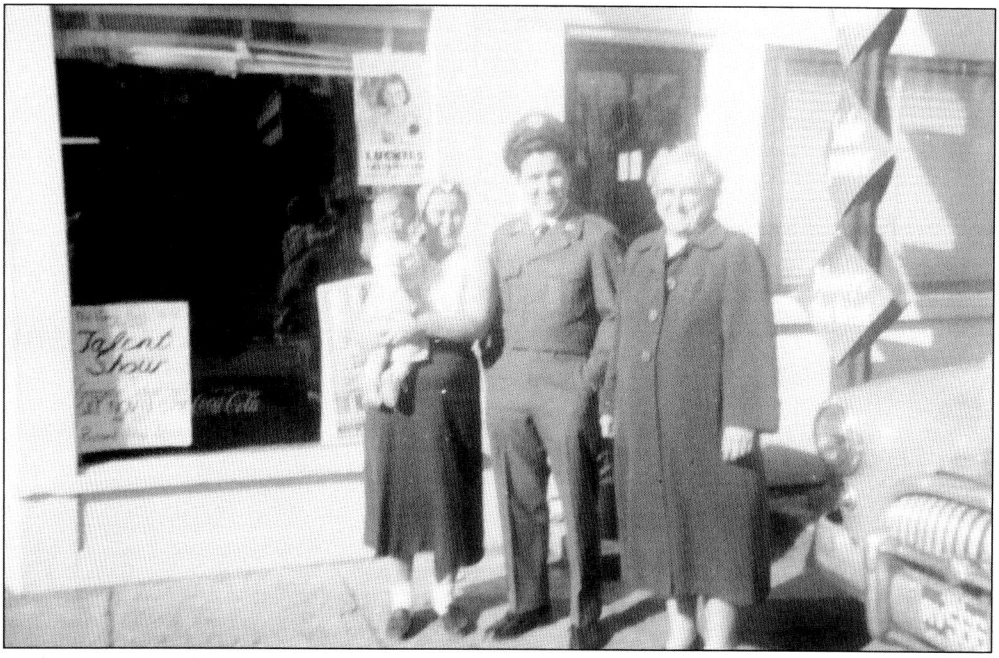

Dick Wiggin in his Air Force uniform with his mother, Eleanor Wiggin, and sister-in-law, Jean Cottrell Wiggin (holding Bruce Wiggin) in front of the Wiggin Variety Store on Portsmouth Avenue in the 1950s. (E and EW.)

The Jonathon Leavitt House. In 1875 it was owned by Andrew Chase. His daughters, Alice Marie Chase and Priscilla Sally Chase, are in the foreground. The house was later moved by Mr. Stickney to the corner of Bunker Hill and Portsmouth Avenue, where burned down in the 1960s. (SHS.)

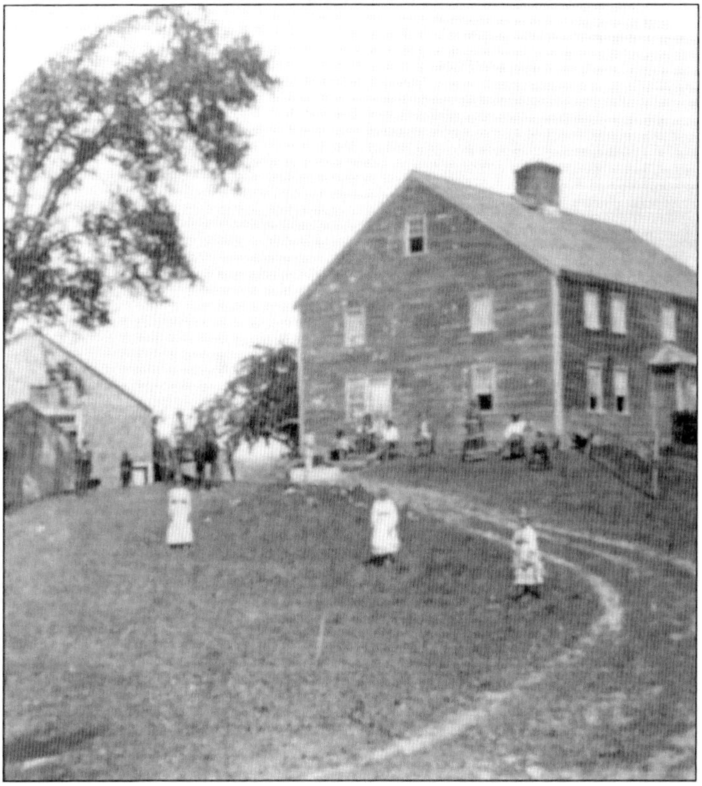

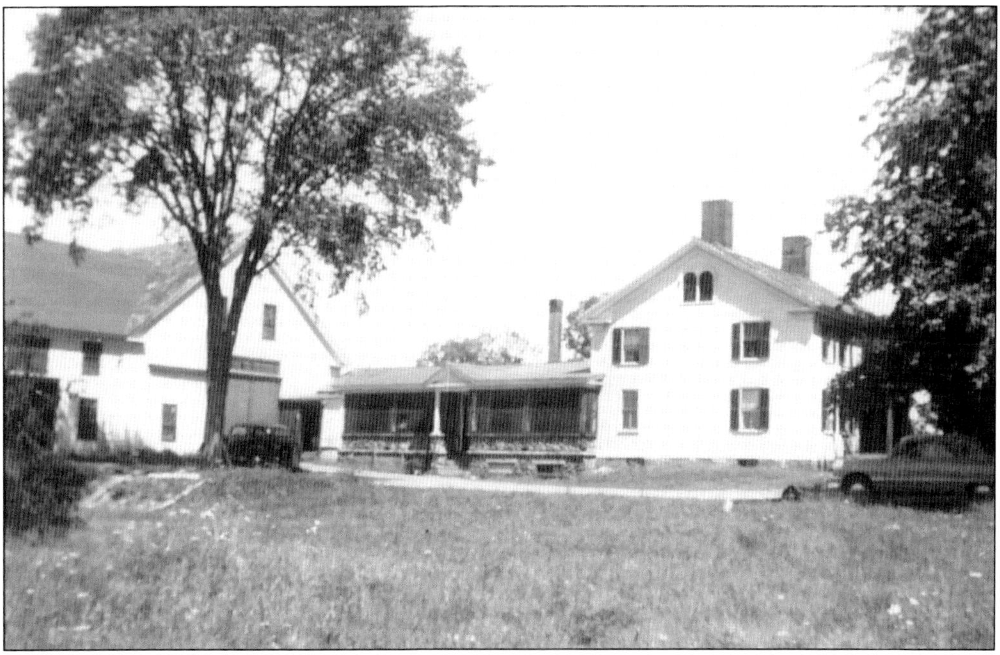

The Wiggin Farm at 271 Portsmouth Avenue. Note the stone piazza linking the house and the barn. As with most farms keeping dairy cows, there was a milk room between the house and the barn. (E and EW.)

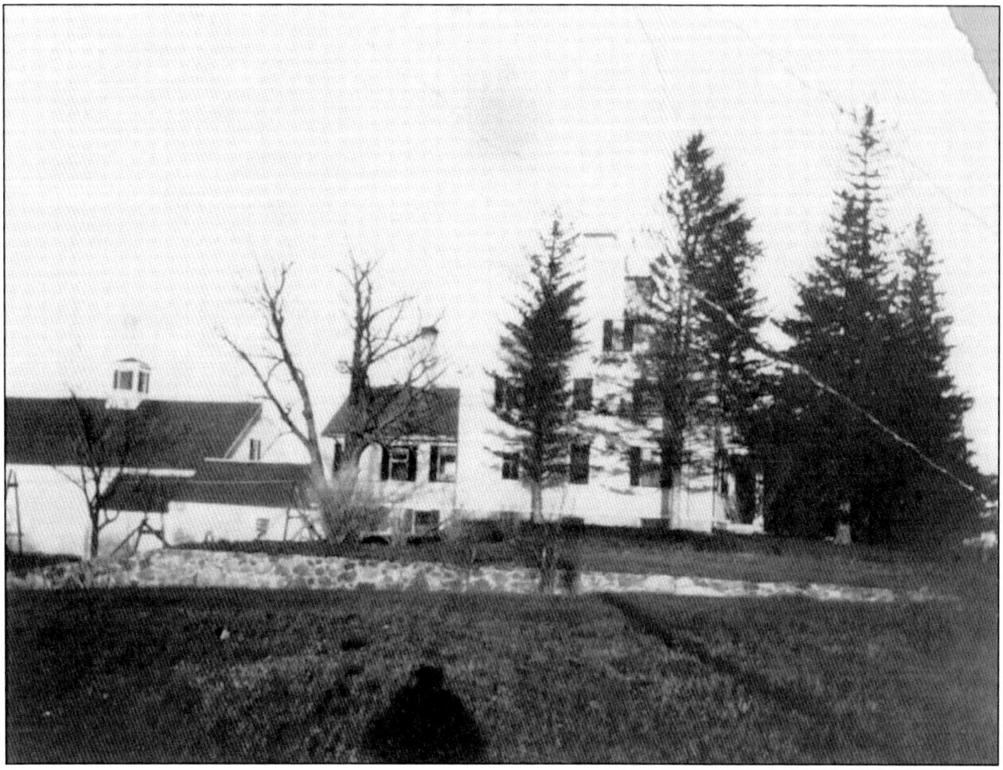

A side view of the Sewell Farm at 97 Bunker Hill Avenue. The stone retaining wall is no longer visible. This farm has been owned by the Odell, Sinclair, Brooks, and Rowes families. (C and JS.)

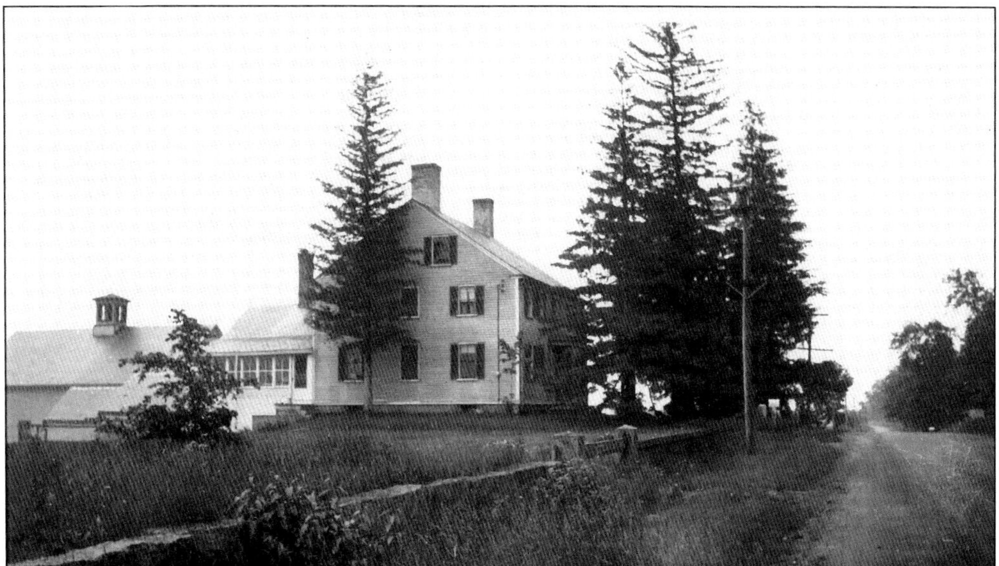

Another *c.* 1942 side view of the Sewell Farm on Bunker Hill Avenue. The road was much farther from the house. (C and JS.)

The twins, Elmer and Earl Wiggin, in 1908. They were lifelong residents and both became farmers on Portsmouth Avenue and Squamscott Road, respectively. In later years they were known, along with their friends Stan French, Irving Scamman, and Bob Clements, as the Jolly Boys. It seems they regularly spent time in the "chapel" by the shore of the Squamscott; the chapel looked more like a shack and was a fine place for a regular game of cards. (E and EW.)

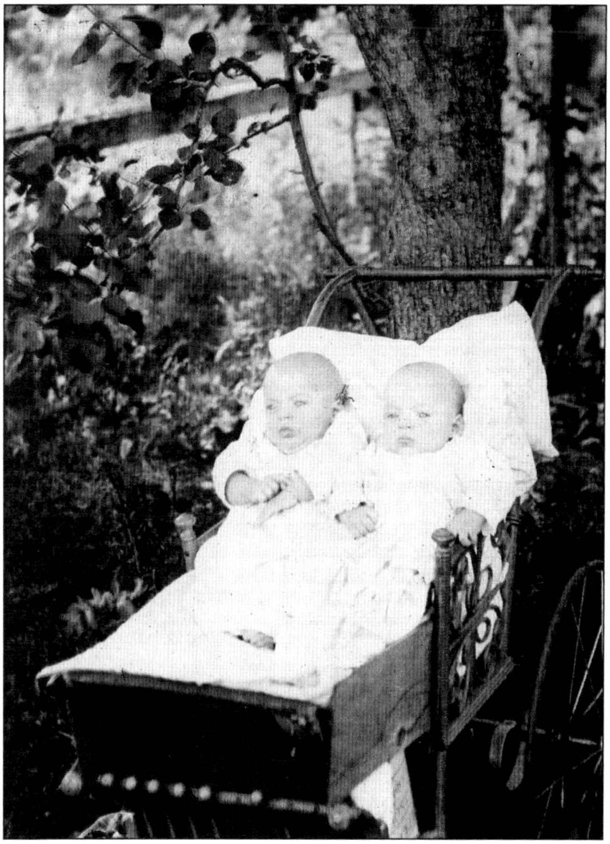

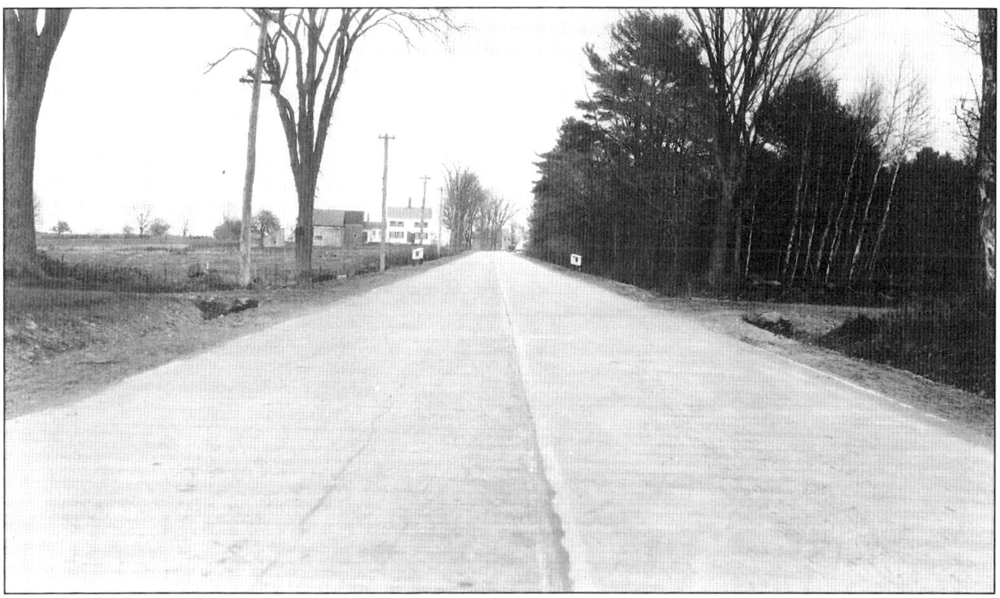

A 1930 view of Portsmouth Avenue with Jackrabbit Road on the right and Elmer Wiggin's old farm at 261 Portsmouth Avenue on the left. (D and SS.)

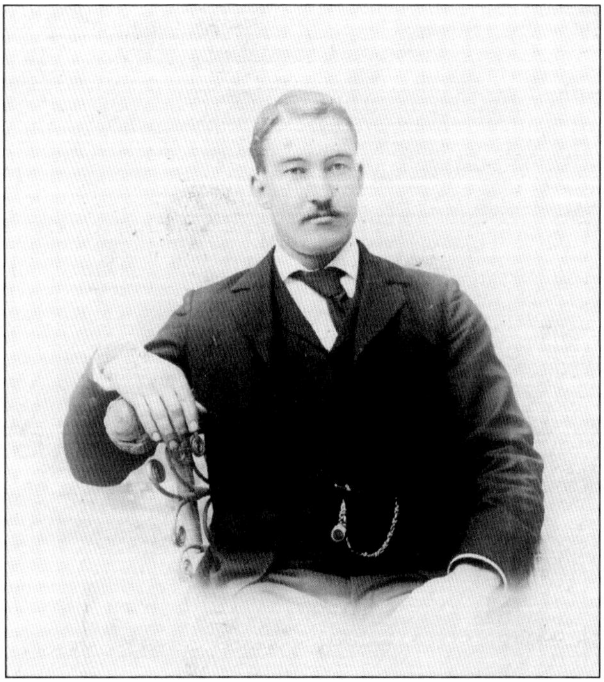

True Roby as a young man at the turn of the century. Roby married Neva Marsh, lived on Portsmouth Avenue, and was the proprietor of Roby's Cabins. (E and EW.)

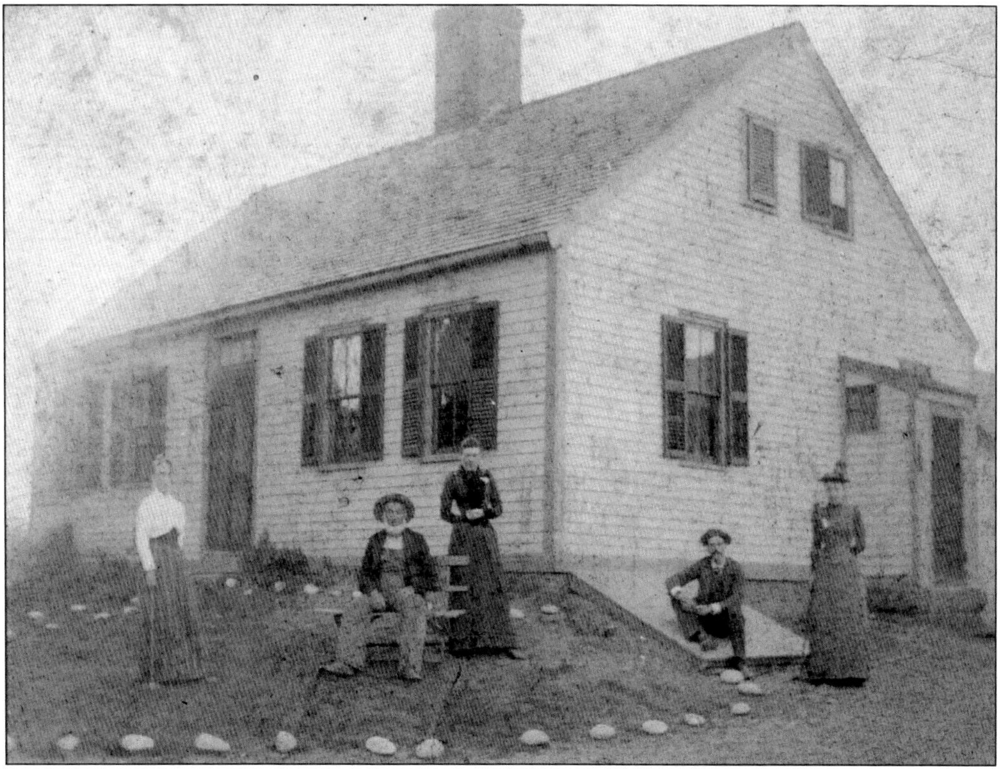

When coming out of Lovell Lane onto Portsmouth Avenue, look opposite slightly to the right. This house, with an additional story, still stands at 309 Portsmouth Avenue. It was once the home of William Roby; his son, James True Roby, added the additional story. (SHS.)

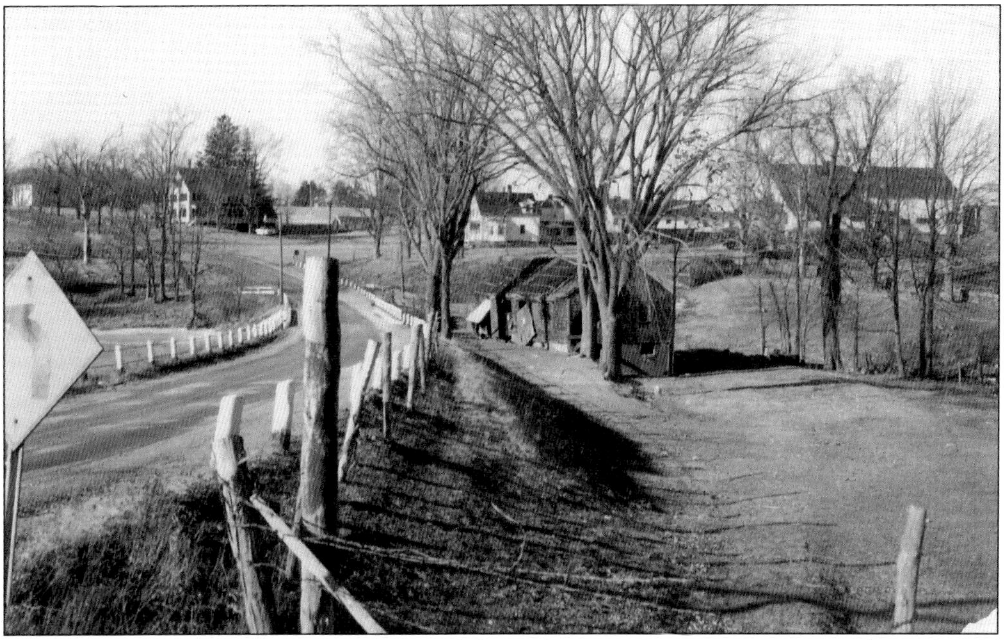

The old Winnicutt Road near the river and dam. This view from 173 Winnicutt shows the old Sanderson/Jewell Place and some of the extensive barns. Roby Jewell had a huge horse dealing and auction center including stalls, stockyard, and goals. Farmers came from all over to purchase draft teams from Roby Jewell. The house in the upper left is 163 Winnicutt Road. (C and KP.)

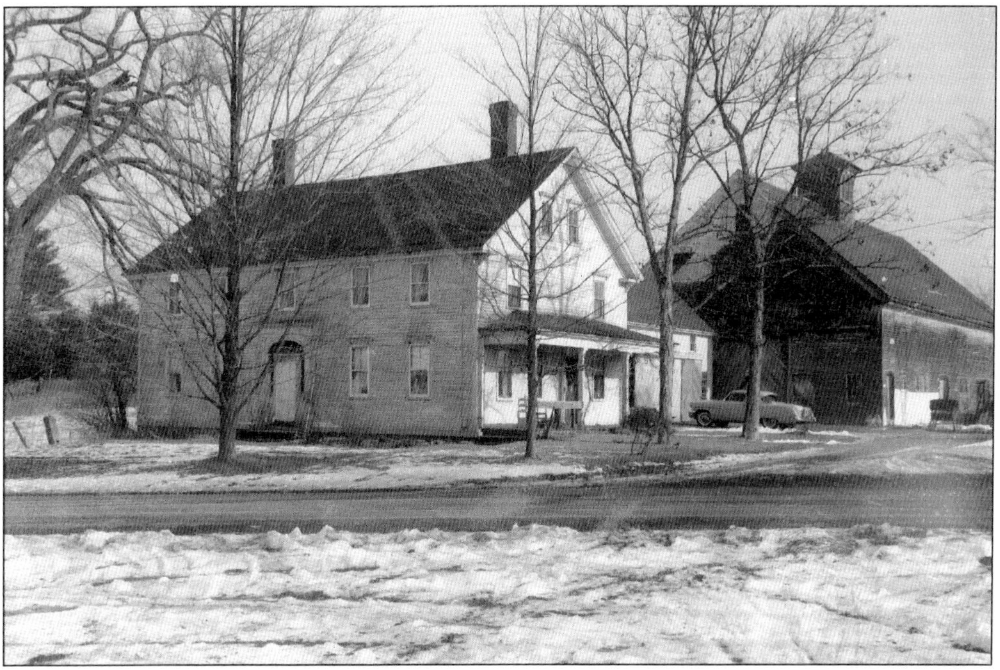

The Jewell/Peabody Farm at 173 Winnicutt Road near the bridge. This was before the road was moved. The home was formerly a tavern; notice that the front door faces the road. The house next-door, at 175 Winnicutt, was where ladies visiting the tavern stayed. (C and KP.)

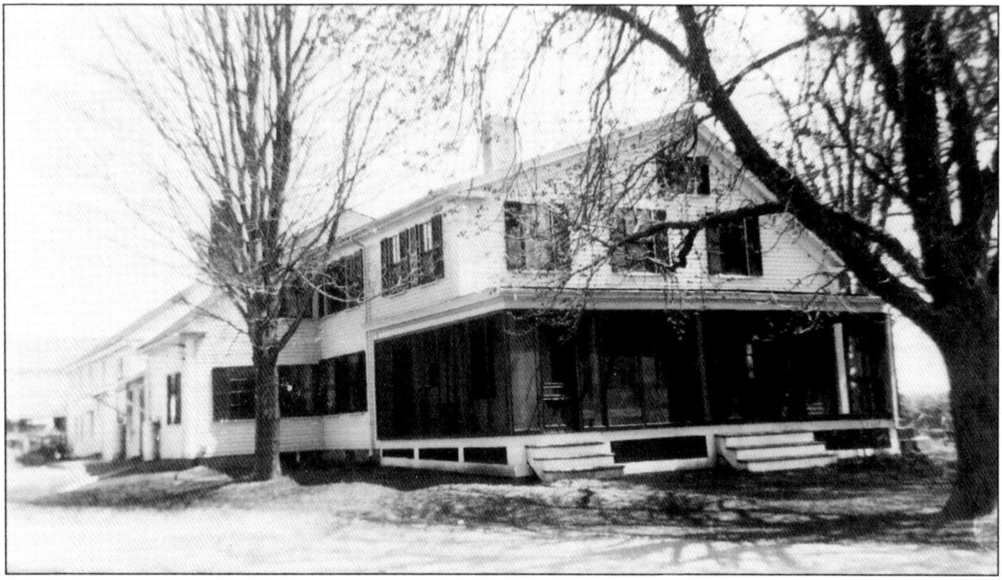

The old Sanderson/Jewell Place near 163 Winnicutt Road. This was where there were extensive horse auctions. (SHS.)

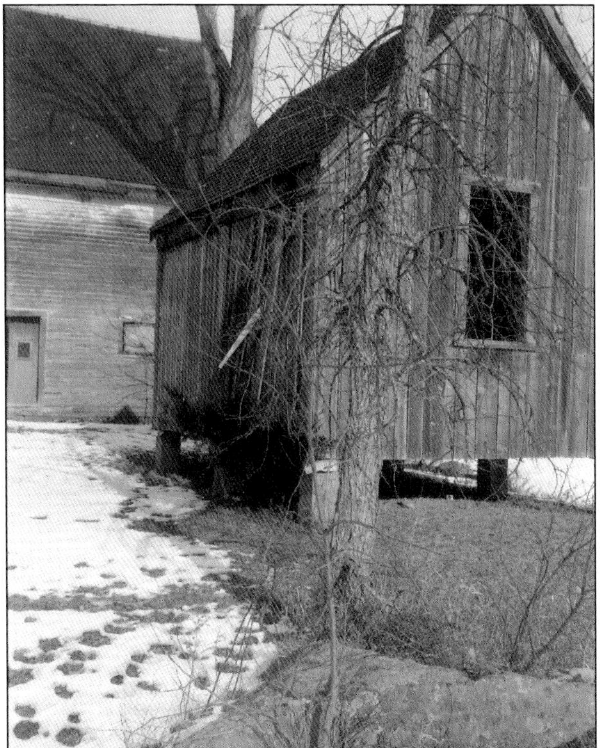

A corn crib, now long gone, on George Jewell's farm at 173 Winnicutt Road. (C and KP.)

Marion and Roby Jewell in the late 19th century. They grew up on their grandfather's farm at 163 Winnicutt Road. (E and EW.)

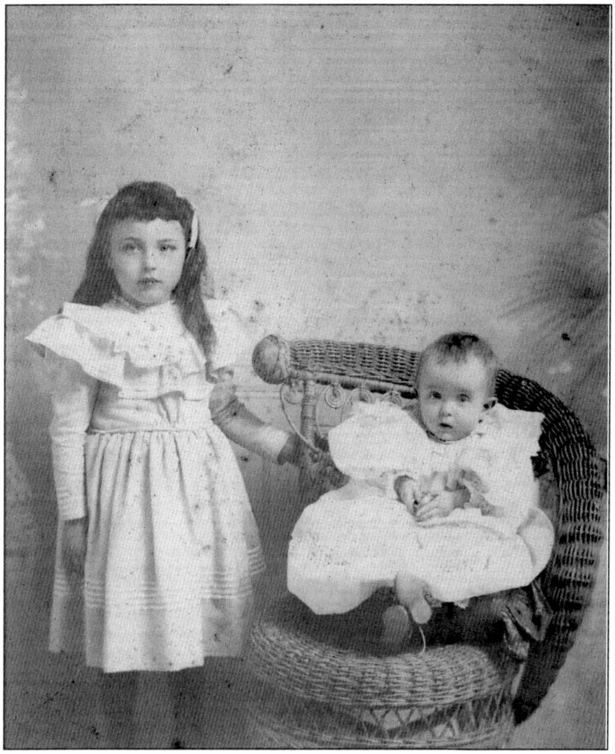

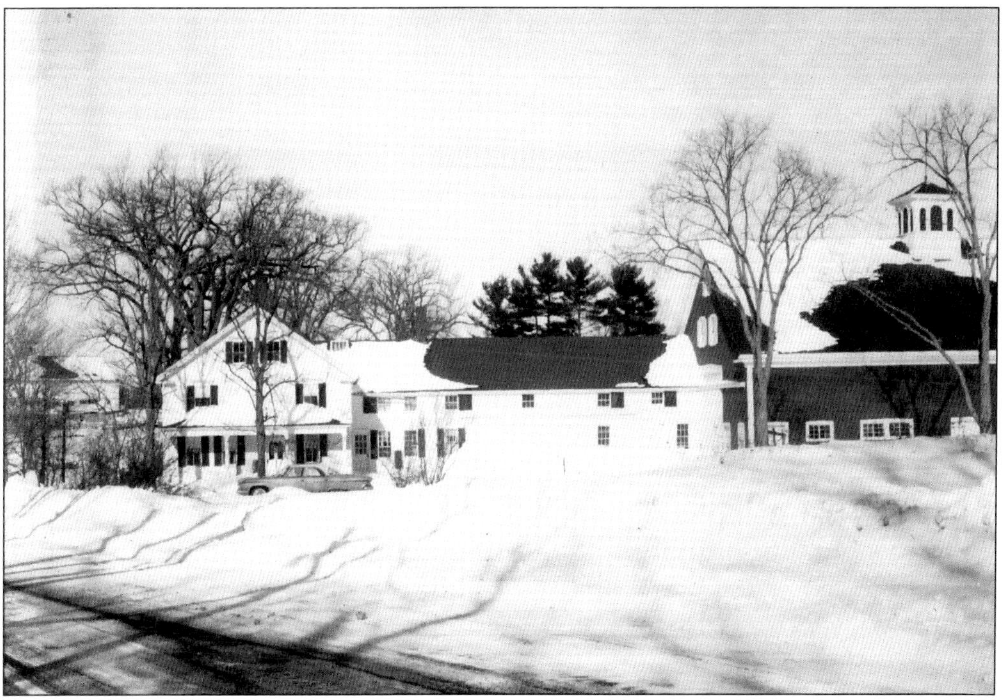

The side, long view of the Jewell/Peabody Farm at 173 Winnicutt Road during a winter in the late 1940s. This was the house where Dewitt Clinton Jewell, and later George and Alice Jewell, lived. (C and KP.)

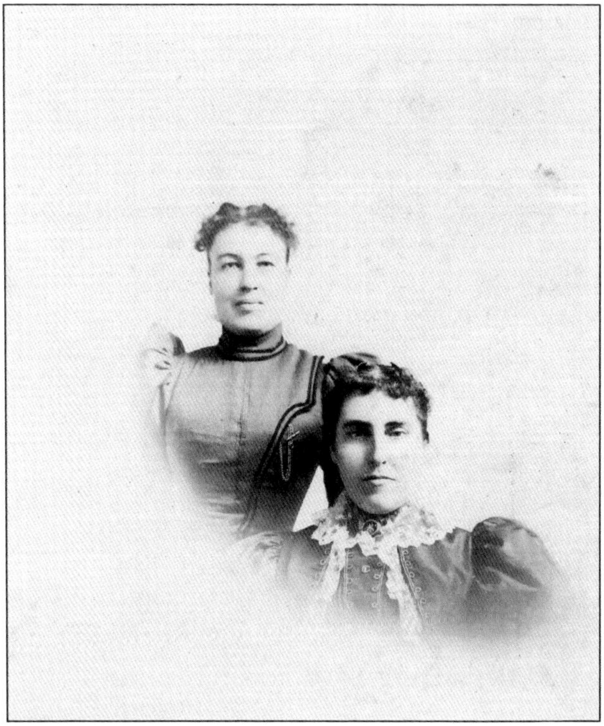

Josephine Roby Jewell and Mary Roby Jewell. These Roby sisters married Jewell brothers. Mary was the mother of Roby Jewell. Another sister, Alice Louise, married Fred Benjamin Wiggin; when they both died, Josephine and her husband, Henry, raised the five Wiggin children on their farm at 273 Portsmouth Avenue. (E and EW.)

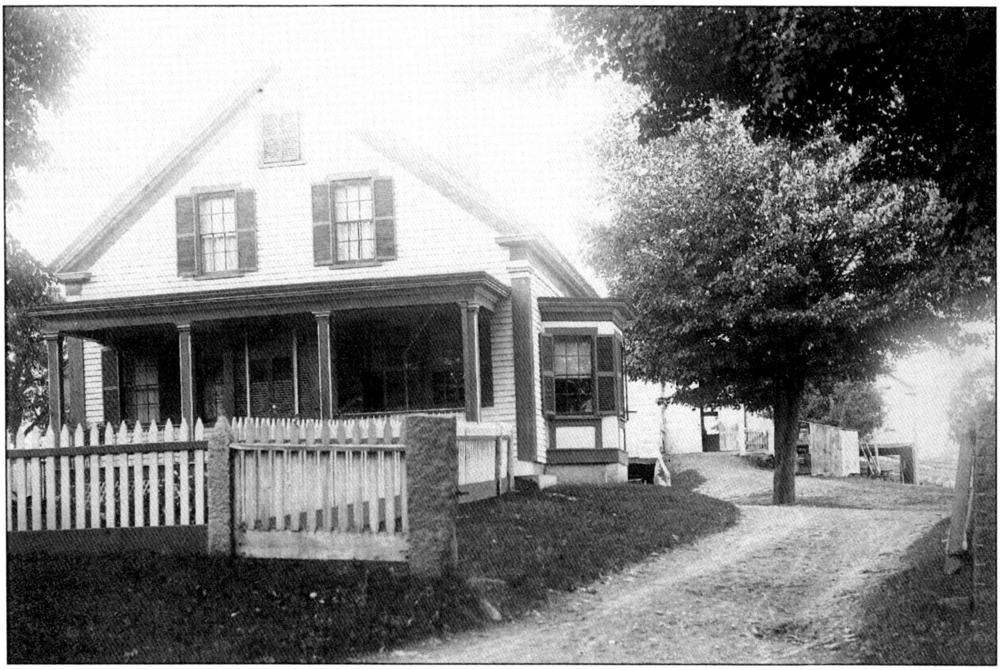

The old Jewell residence. This home, near 163 Winnicutt Avenue, was burned down as training for the fire department in the 1970s. Known as the old Jewell Homestead and as the old Sanderson place, it was the home of John Langdon Jewell (1813–1899) and Sophie Elizabeth Jewell until he built the new home farther up the hill. Notice the steep rise at the barn to load the hay. (LC.)

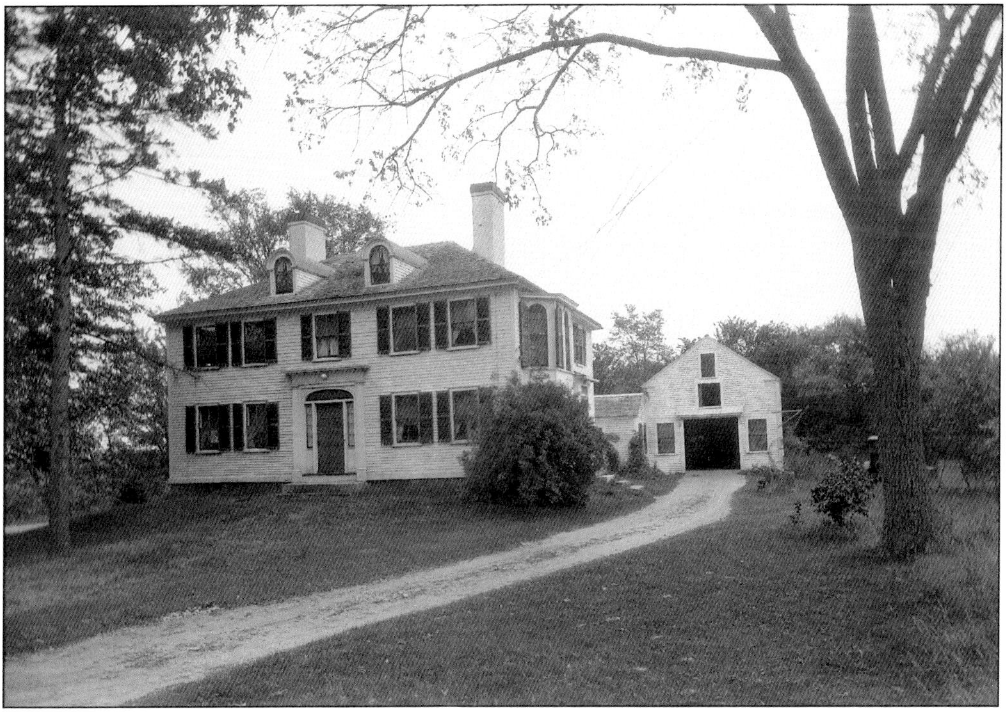

A 1934 view of the Bartlett House on the south corner of Bunker Hill and Portsmouth Avenues. This house was built in the early 19th century and was called the Bartlett House after Josiah Bartlett Jr. (who moved from Kingston to Stratham to marry Sarah Wingate, the daughter of Paine Wingate) and Josiah Bartlett III (1803–1853), his nephew, a prominent physician. (SHS.)

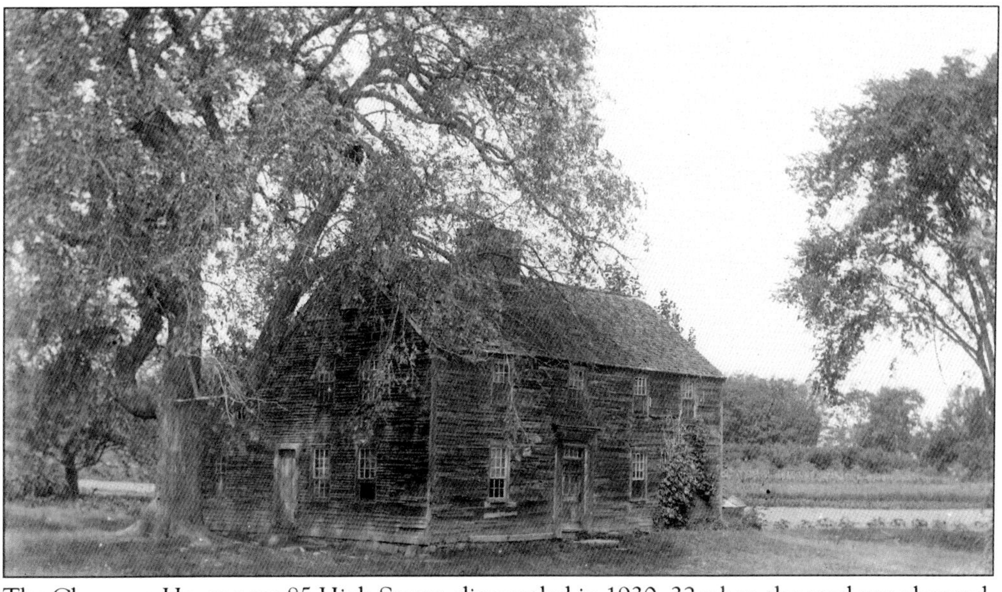

The Chapman House near 85 High Street, dismantled in 1930–32 when the road was changed. There was also a gas motor-powered box mill nearby that made small boxes. (SHS.)

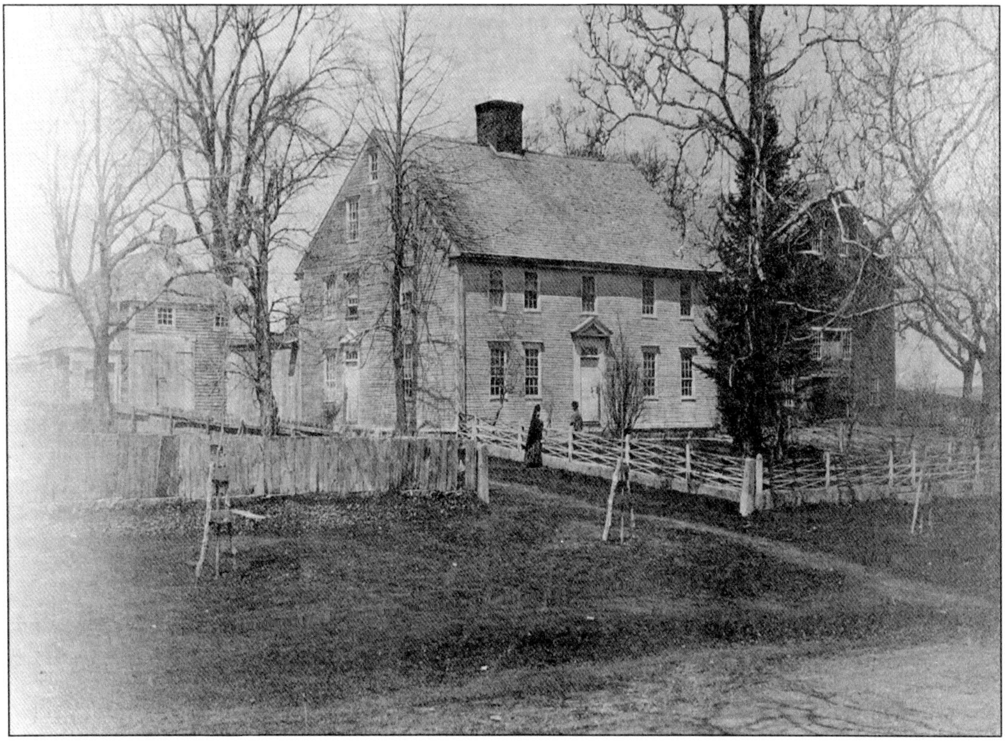

The Wingate House, at the circle, c. 1875. This was the home of Joseph C.A. Wingate, appointed consul to China in 1880. The fence and the outbuildings are long gone and the interior has been totally changed. (SHS.)

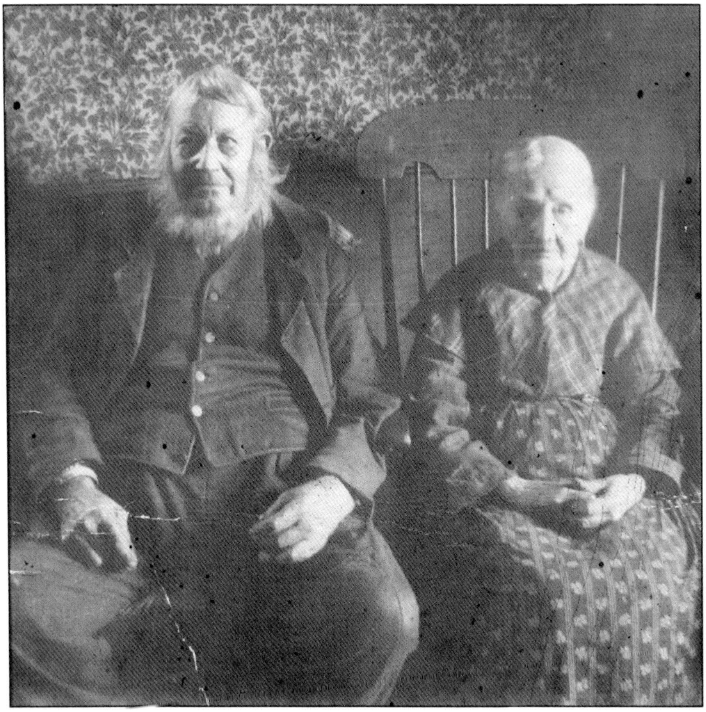

Major Thomas and Mrs. Mary Stockbridge Tuttle when they were a hundred years old in 1898. His title comes from service in the state militia. He first voted for James Monroe and was a staunch democrat throughout his life. They lived, and the picture was taken, in the home she grew up in on Rocky Hill Road, now Bunker Hill Avenue. (SHS.)

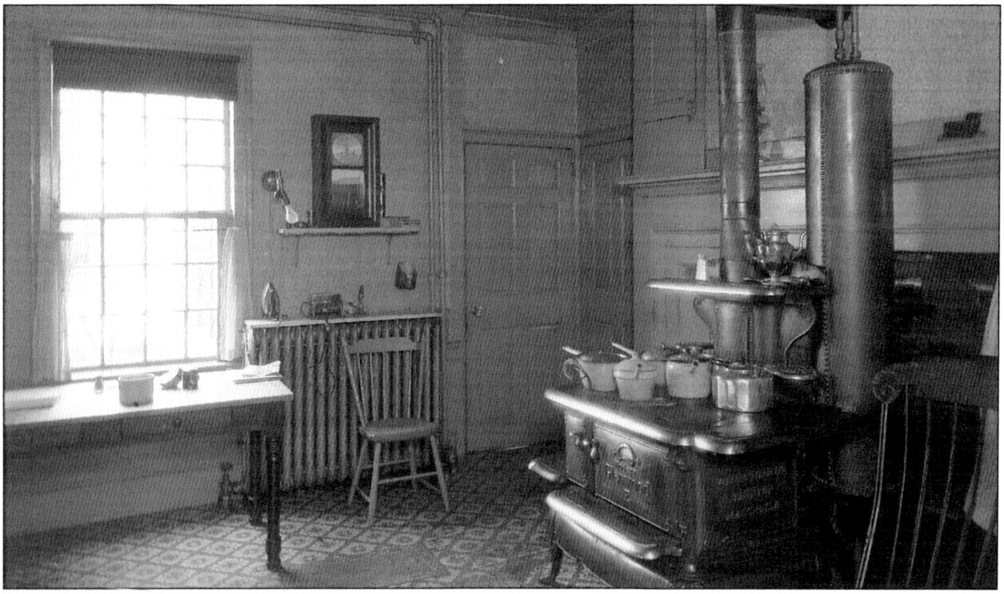

An interior view of the home of John Wingate at the circle on Portsmouth Avenue. The house was built for him at the time of his marriage in 1808. The original window and the high mantle over the huge fireplace are shown in this image. The first door to the left of the fireplace leads to the cellar and the woodwork to the cellar way was paneled. The second door to the left of the fireplace originally led to a hallway and an outside door. Beneath the window, on the outside, was an entrance to the stone dairy. (SHS.)

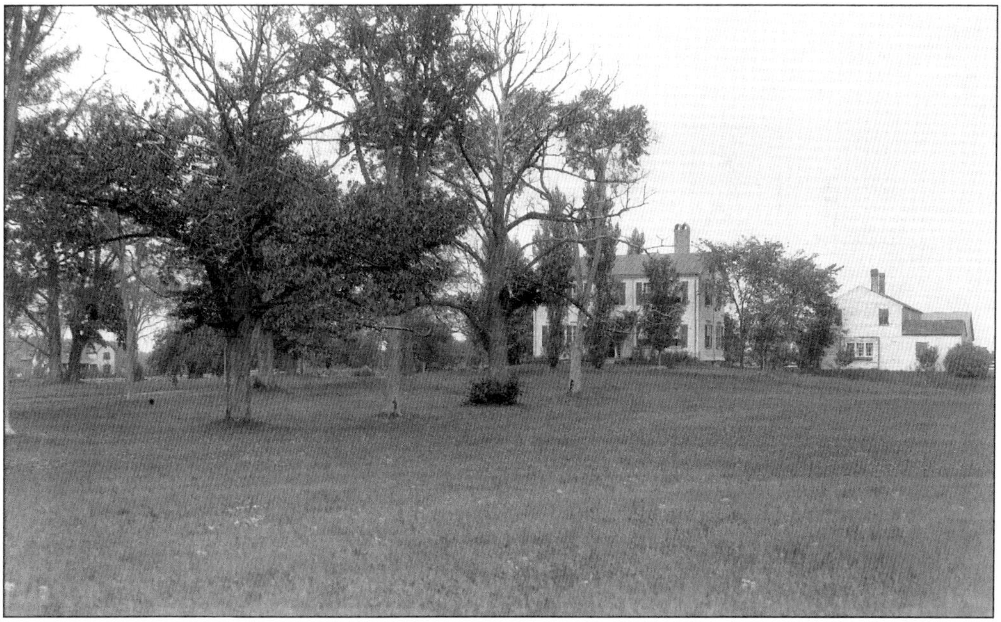

The home of John Wingate, son of Paine Wingate (who signed the Declaration of Independence). George Washington visited this home on November 3, 1789. The view is from Portsmouth Avenue and shows the smaller garrison-style house that was for the farm keeper. This was a private home until the early 1970s, when it became a restaurant and later professional offices and a spa. (SHS.)

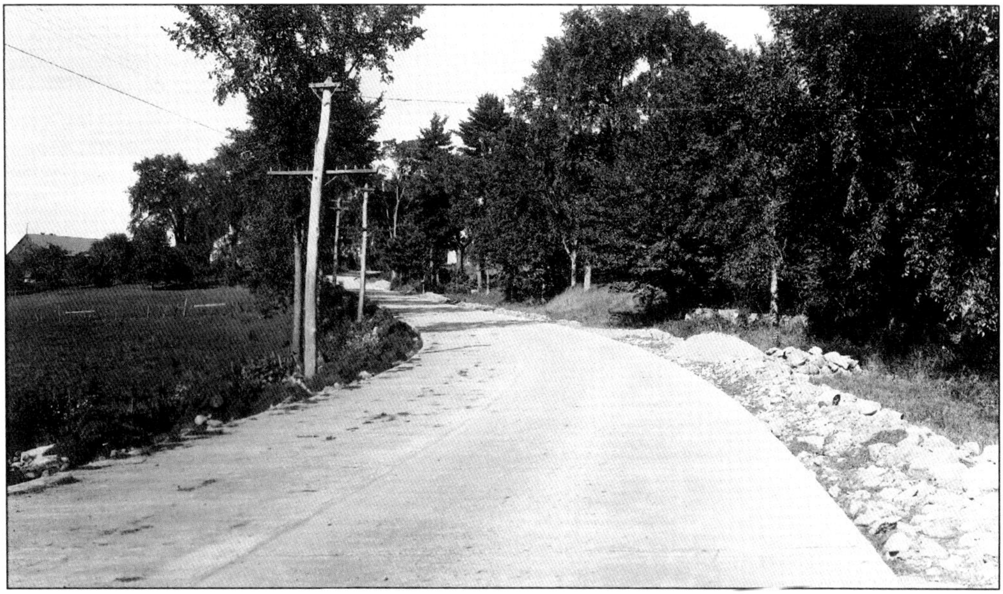

A view of cement-paved Portsmouth Avenue. The state of New Hampshire paved the road in 1929. A young W. Douglas Scamman would milk his cow on Willowbrook and Lovell Road and walk to Portsmouth Avenue to sell the fresh milk to the work crews. This scene is likely near 217 Portsmouth Avenue. (D and SS.)

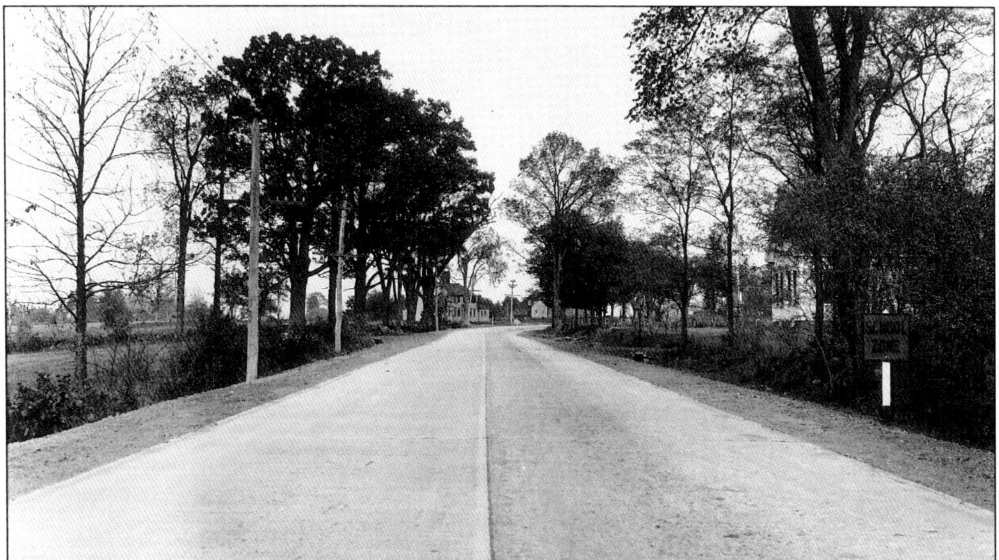

Newly paved Portsmouth Avenue with the Stratham Hill School on the right and the Kenniston Tavern and Depot Road on the left. (D and SS.)

Working on paving Portsmouth Avenue in 1929. (D and SS.)

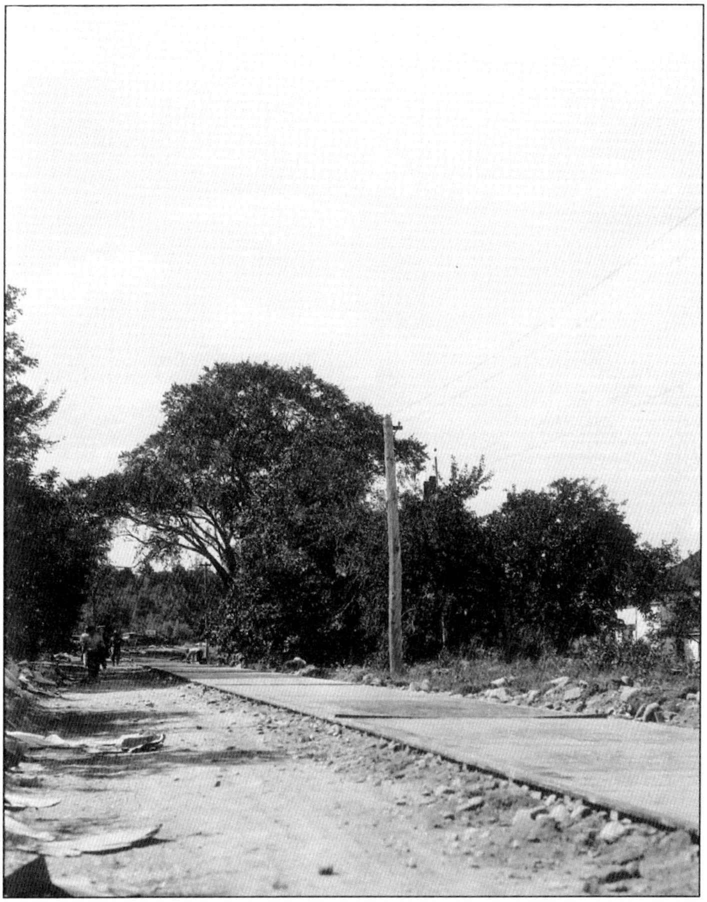

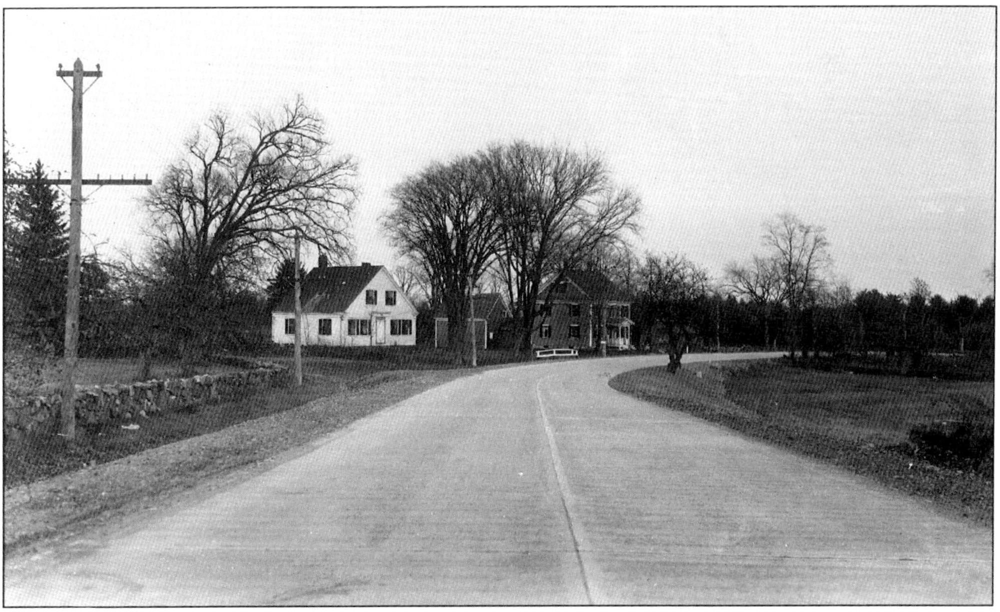

Portsmouth Avenue in 1929 near Stratham Lane. (D and SS.)

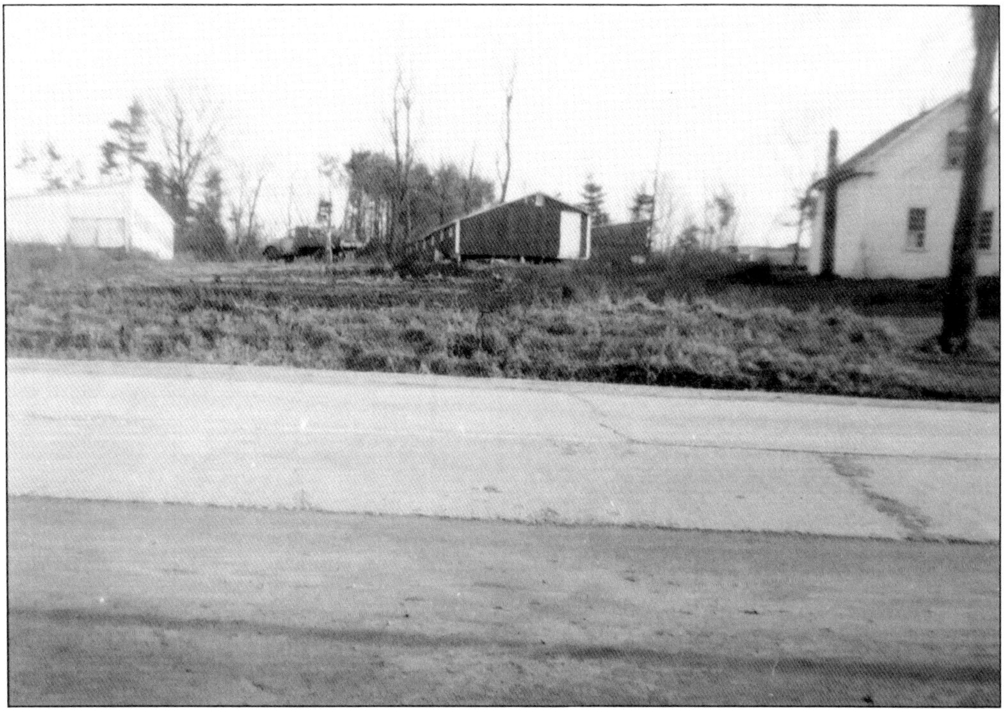

A view of some of the hen houses at the Cole Farm, 156 Portsmouth Avenue, opposite the Stratham Village Market in the 1940s. Stratham was a noted chicken farming area with chicken farms along Portsmouth Avenue, two large barns on Barker Road, and, at that time, the Stuart Farm on College Road was a poultry operation. (E and EW.)

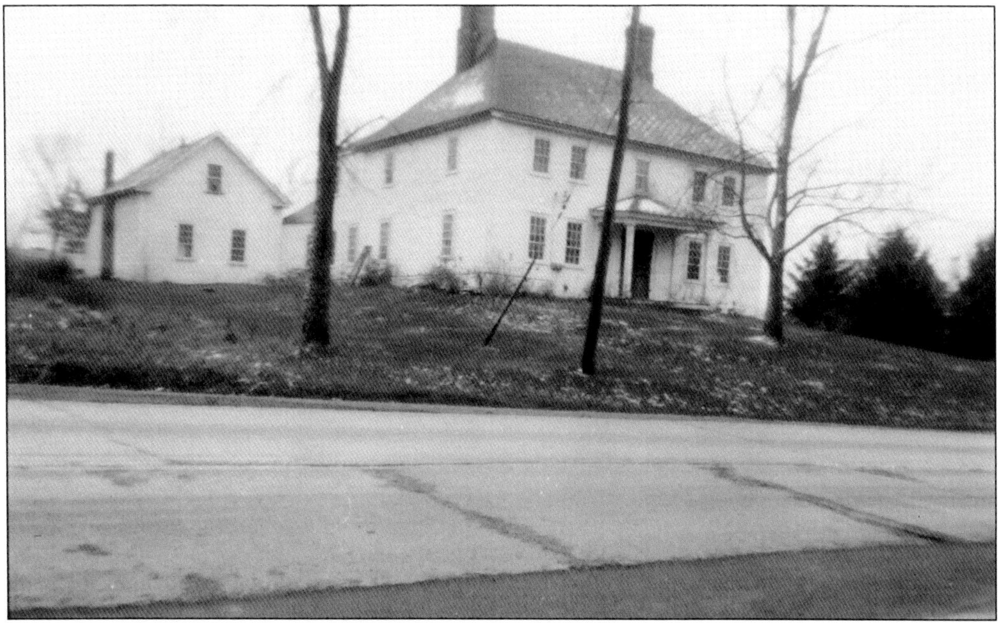

The Cole hen farm at 156 Portsmouth Avenue across from the store. Portsmouth Avenue was then a concrete road; it was widened in 1955. Many of the concrete slabs are beneath the ballfield in Stratham Hill Park. (E and EW.)

Five

NON-FARM WORK

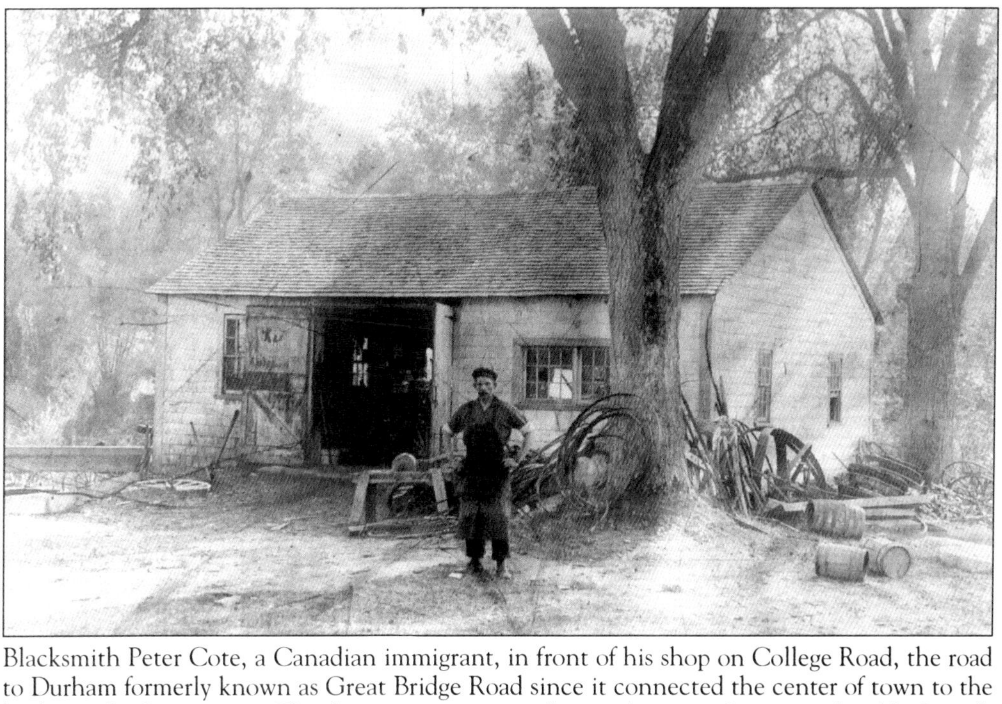

Blacksmith Peter Cote, a Canadian immigrant, in front of his shop on College Road, the road to Durham formerly known as Great Bridge Road since it connected the center of town to the bridge at the Squamscott. The shop is now a private home. At times there were four blacksmith shops in Stratham including one at 148 Portsmouth Avenue, one in the old trolley barn, one at the Gifford place, and one on Stratham Lane. (SHS.)

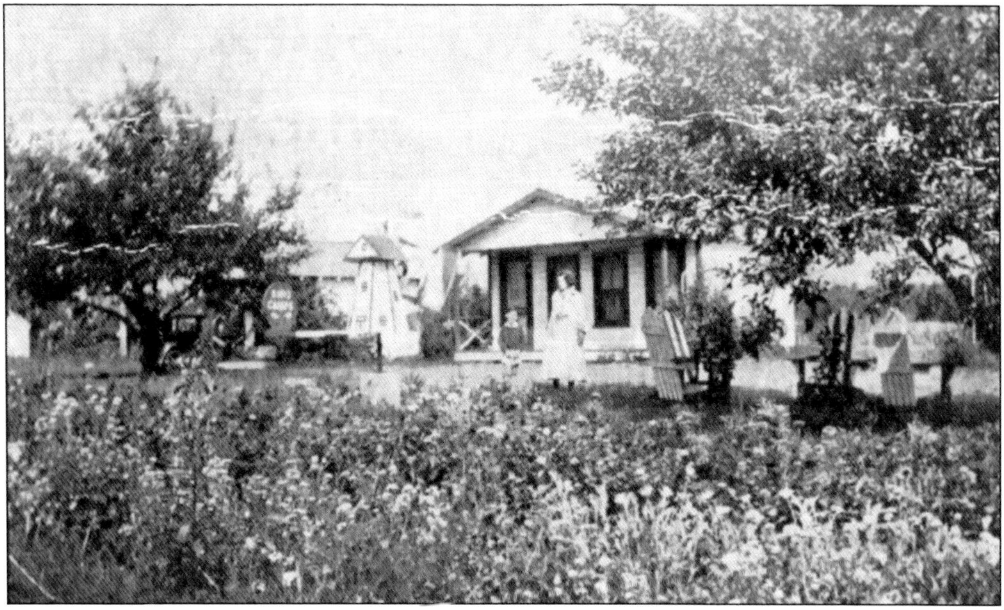

An advertisement for Roby's Cabins located at 313 Portsmouth Avenue and owned by True Roby. Vacationers could enjoy bucolic Stratham and easily catch the trolley to Portsmouth, Exeter, or Hampton. (SHS.)

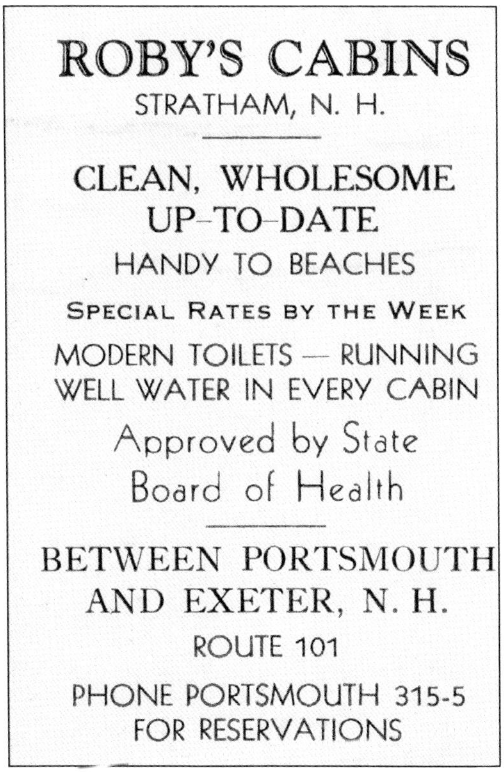

Advertising for Roby's Cabins. (SHS.)

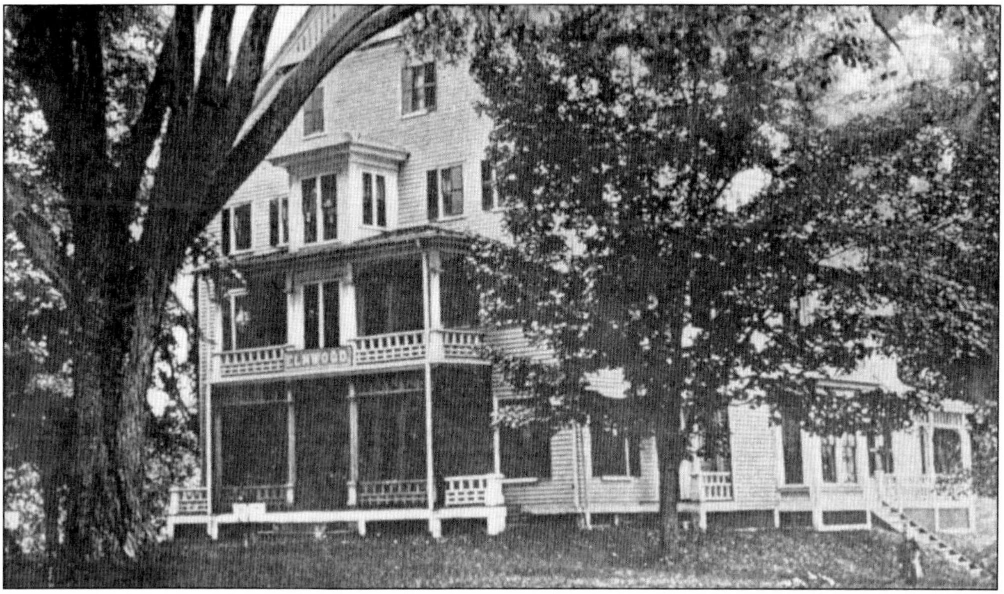

A postcard of the Elmwood, also known as the Elms, Stratham's resort hotel on Portsmouth Avenue across from the entrance to Winnicutt Road. This intersection was formerly known as Essex Corner. (SHS.)

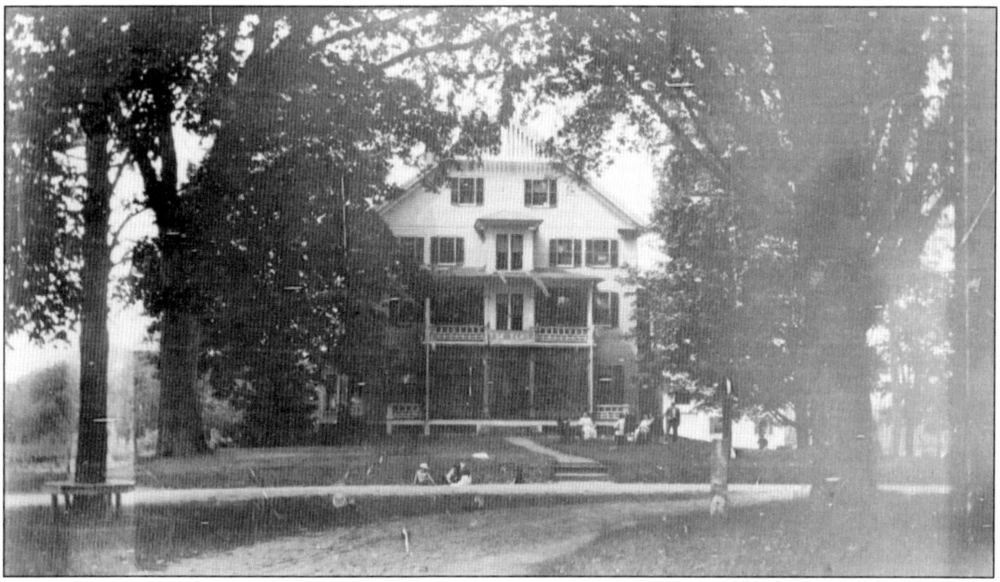

The Elms, Stratham's resort hotel. In the 1880s visitors came from all over to sample the waters supposedly good for "scrofula, all scrofulous diseases and swellings, kidney complaints, liver affection, rheumatism, gout, St. Anthony's fire, lassitude, lack of appetite, tumors, all eruptions of the skin, dyspepsia, indigestion, general debility, piles and dropsy." The water was also available by the jug at the well and in local pharmacies. The building, stripped of its finery, still exists as apartments at 159 Portsmouth Avenue across from Winnicutt Road. At one point there was a bowling alley behind the building near the horse shed. (SHS.)

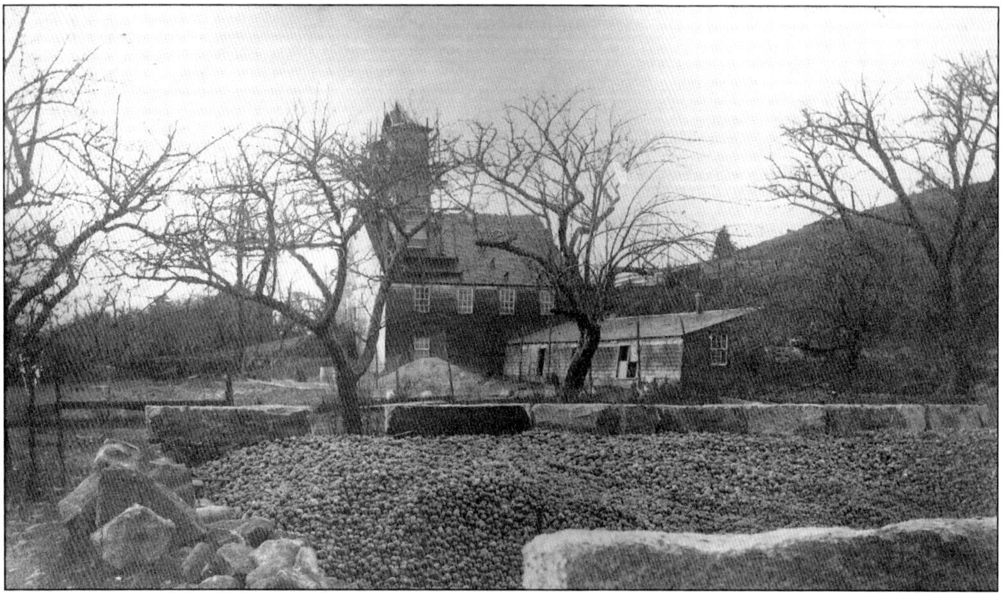

Apples in a barn cellar on the Gowen property on High Street near Barker Road. The Gowens pioneered use of an apple evaporator, which allowed them to ship nationally and internationally. Evaporated apples could be used out of season for cooking. (HC.)

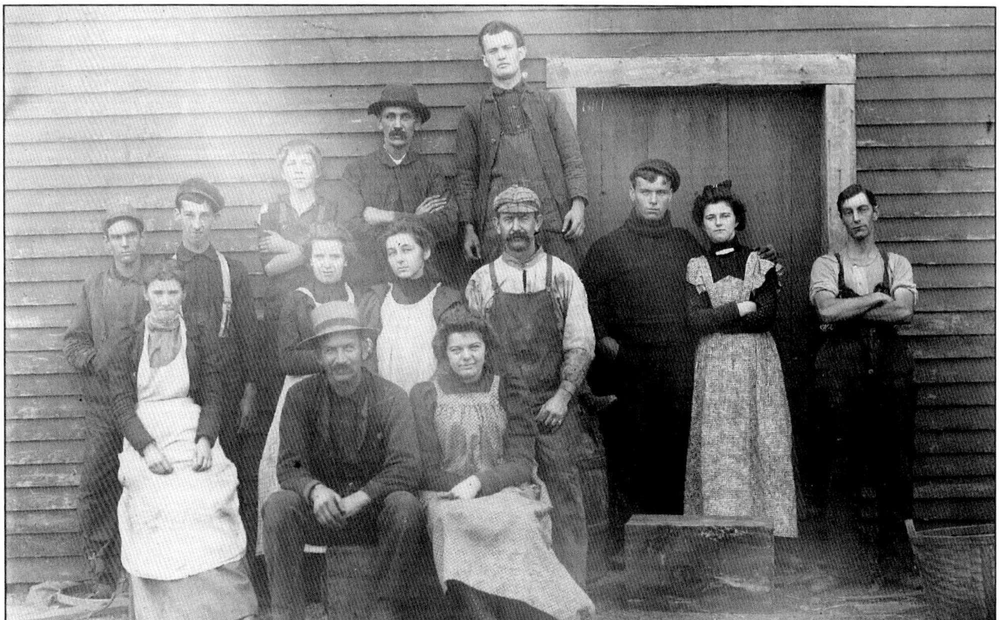

October 1900 farm workers on the Gowen Farm on Swamp Road or Heathey Swamp Road, now known as High Street. The Gowens were noted truck farmers and had an apple evaporator that enabled them to ship millions of pounds of apples to as far as England. Up to 20 people were hired as farm hands. Listed from left to right they are as follows: (first row) Lottie Cooper, George E. Gowen, Caine Chapman, and Asa Mason; (second row) Harry Hooper, Hugh Snell, Blanche Cooper, Bertha Gowen, Charles Grant, Eliot Cooper, and Maude Chapman; (back row) Howard Gowen, Jim Snell, and Frank Sewell. (SHS.)

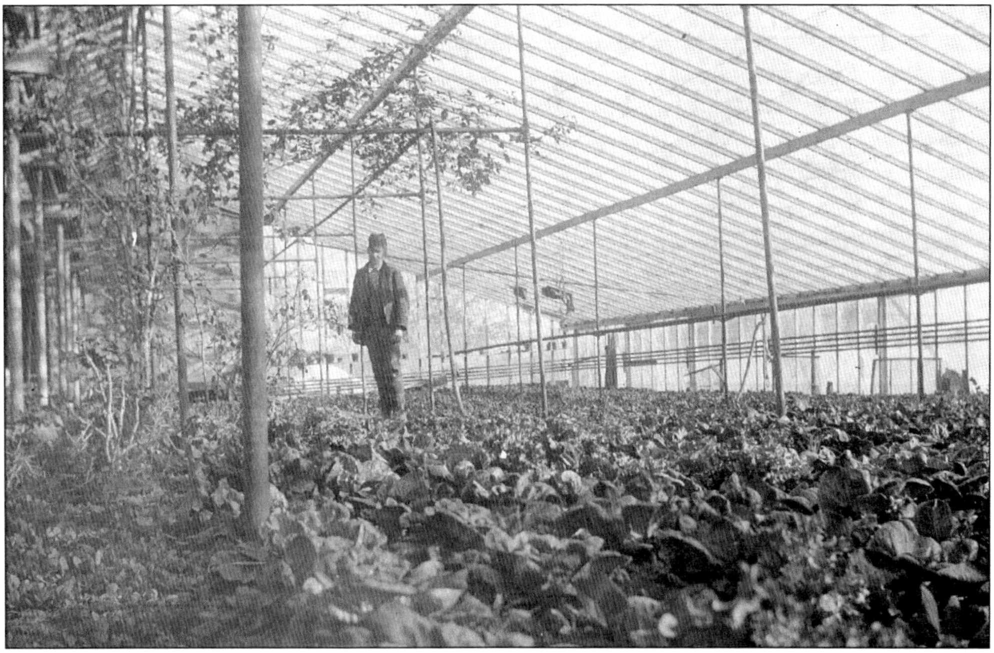
George Gowen with roses and lettuce in his greenhouse on the corner of High Street and Barker Road. In the early 20th century Gowen was among the leading truck farmers and orchardists in town. He worked fields, greenhouses, and hotbeds and shipped throughout the country and to Europe. (SHS.)

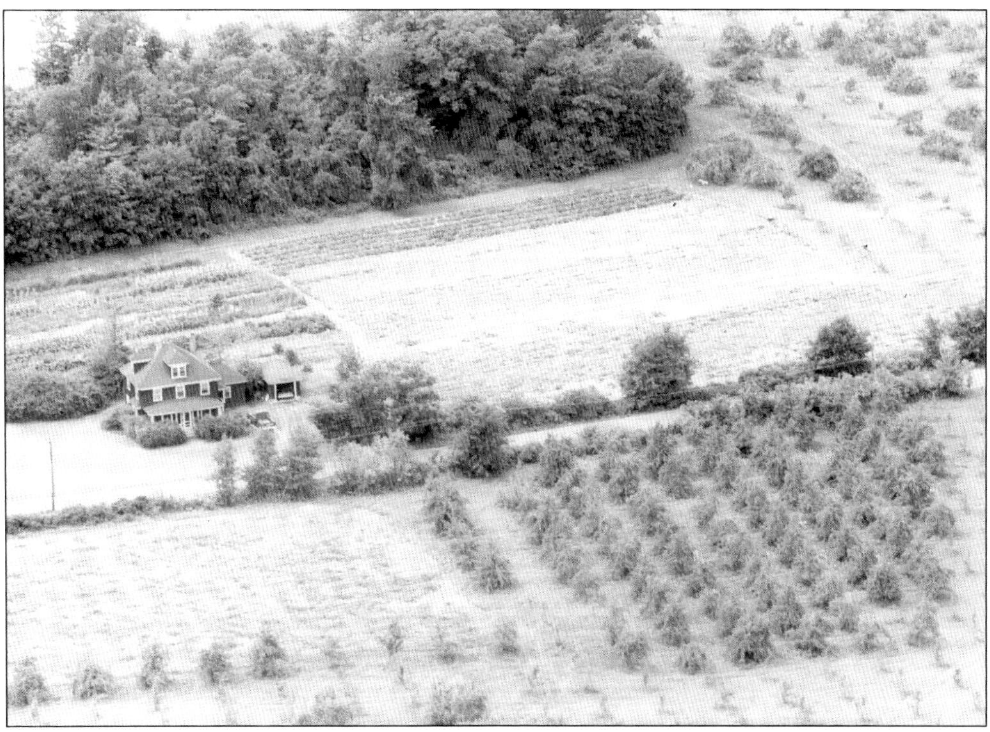
Ben Gowen's house and fields at 85 High Street. (SHS.)

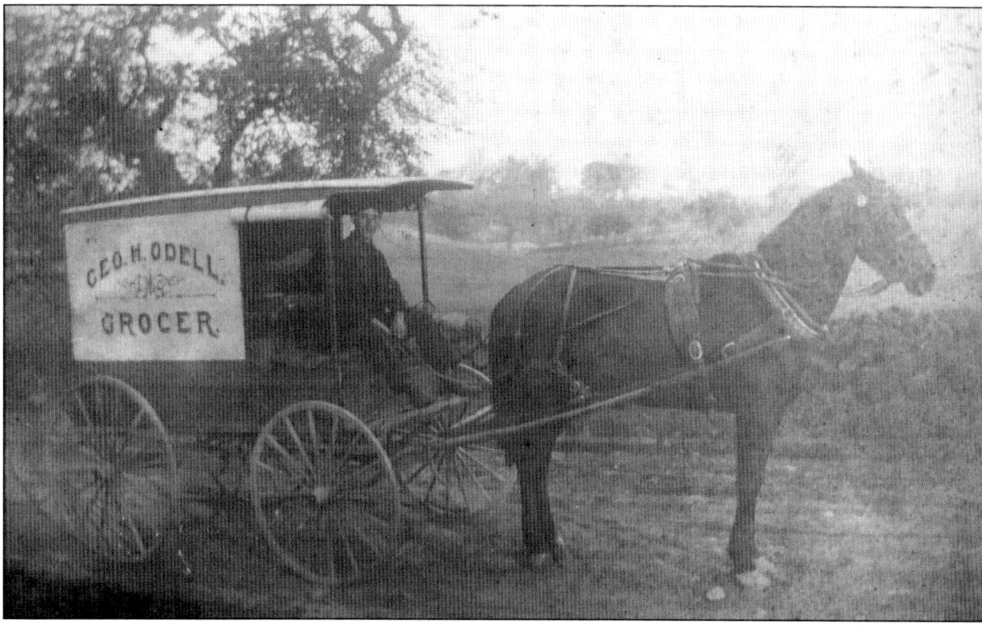

George Horace Odell, grocer, in his carriage. Odell's store, carrying hardware, groceries, and a large variety of miscellaneous goods, was at the intersection of Winnicutt Road and Portsmouth Avenue. People would bring their grocery list to the market and the grocer would deliver to their homes. (SHS.)

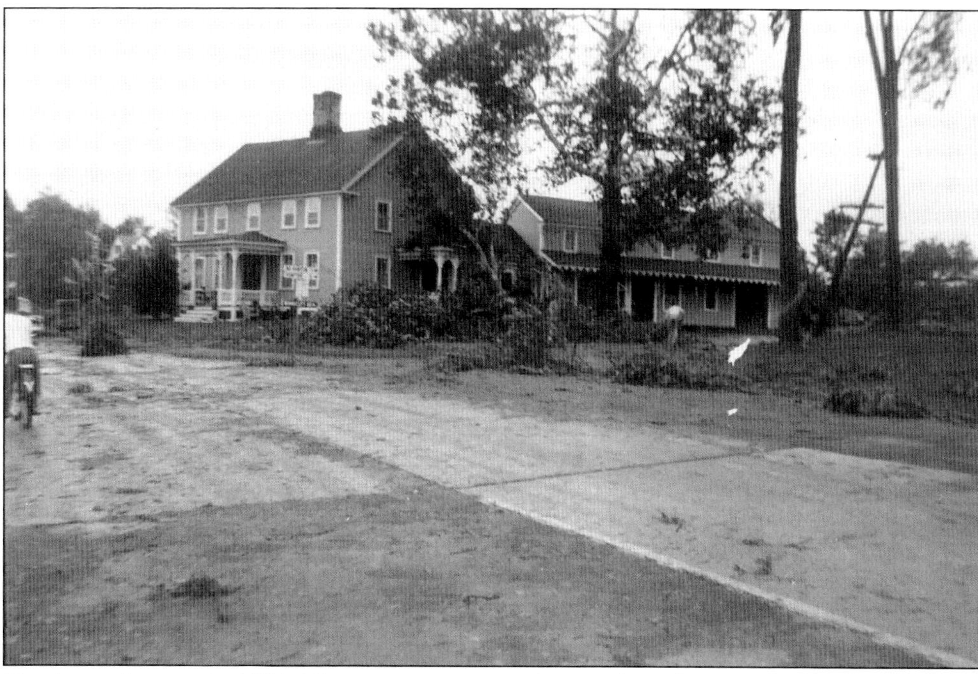

Hurricane damage in 1954. There was extensive damage from hurricanes Carol, Diane, and Edna. Formerly Horace Odell's and then Albert C. Lane's store, this boarding house was at the intersection of Portsmouth Avenue and Winnicutt Road. (SHS.)

The old gas pumps at the store at the intersection of Portsmouth Avenue and Winnicutt Road. Horace Odell's and then Albert C. Lane's store, which later became an apartment house, is on the left; the Wiggin Memorial Library is on the right. (E and EW.)

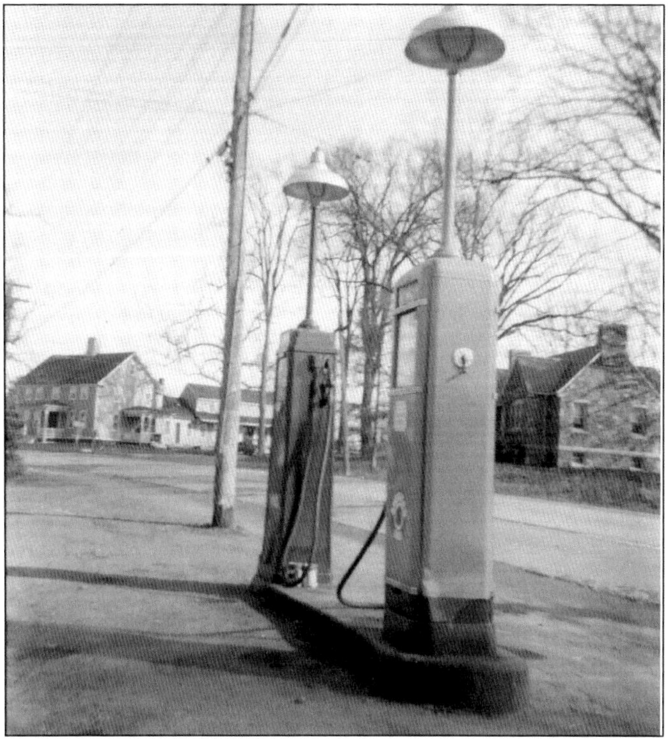

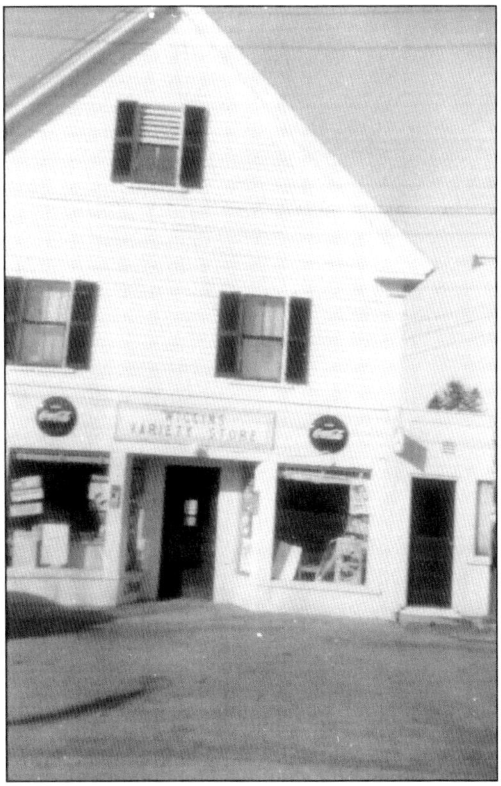

An exterior view of Wiggin's Variety Store on Portsmouth Avenue, c. 1950. This building was torn down and rebuilt in the 1980s. (E and EW.)

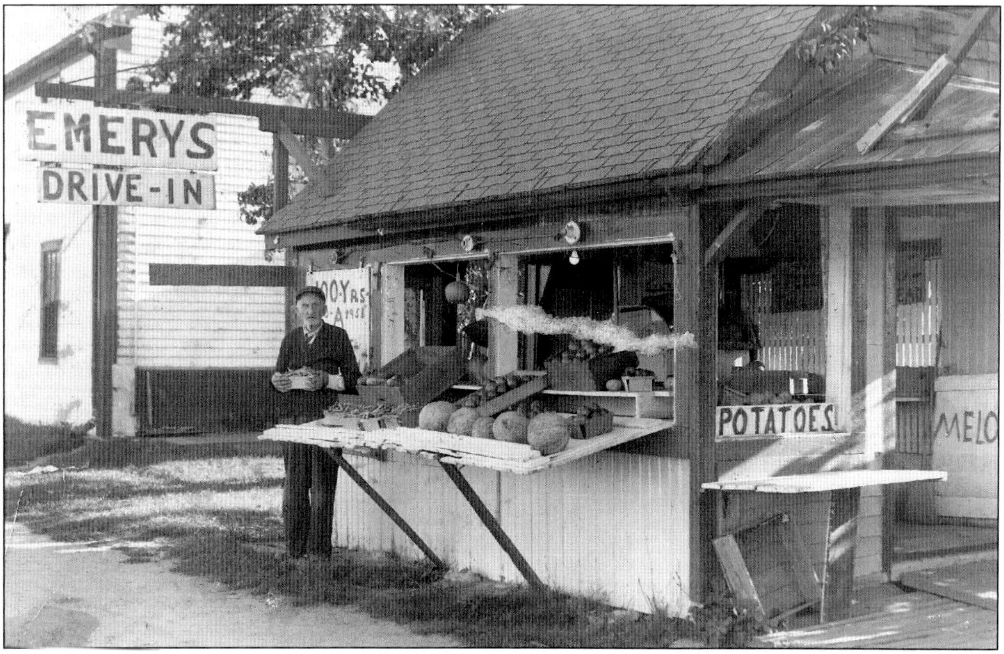

Fred Emery at his farmstand opposite Mark Pipers farmstand on Emery Lane. Evidently, Emerys had run farmstands for a century by 1953. There was a sign inside which read "God helps those who help themselves but God pity those found here helping themselves." (SHS.)

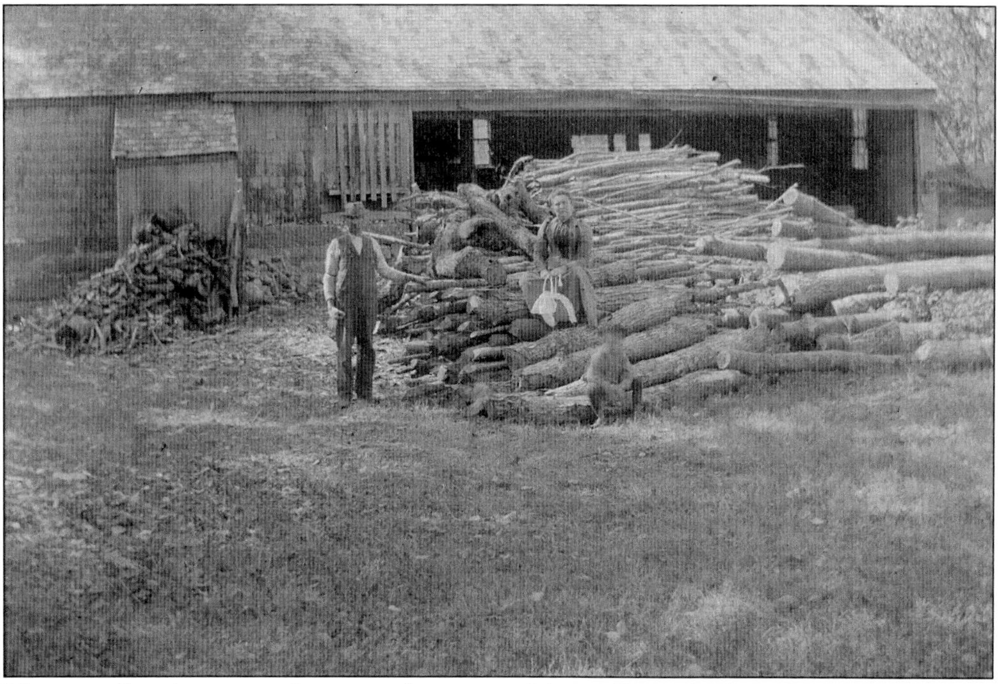

The sawmill in the center of town, in the center of the traffic circle. (SHS.)

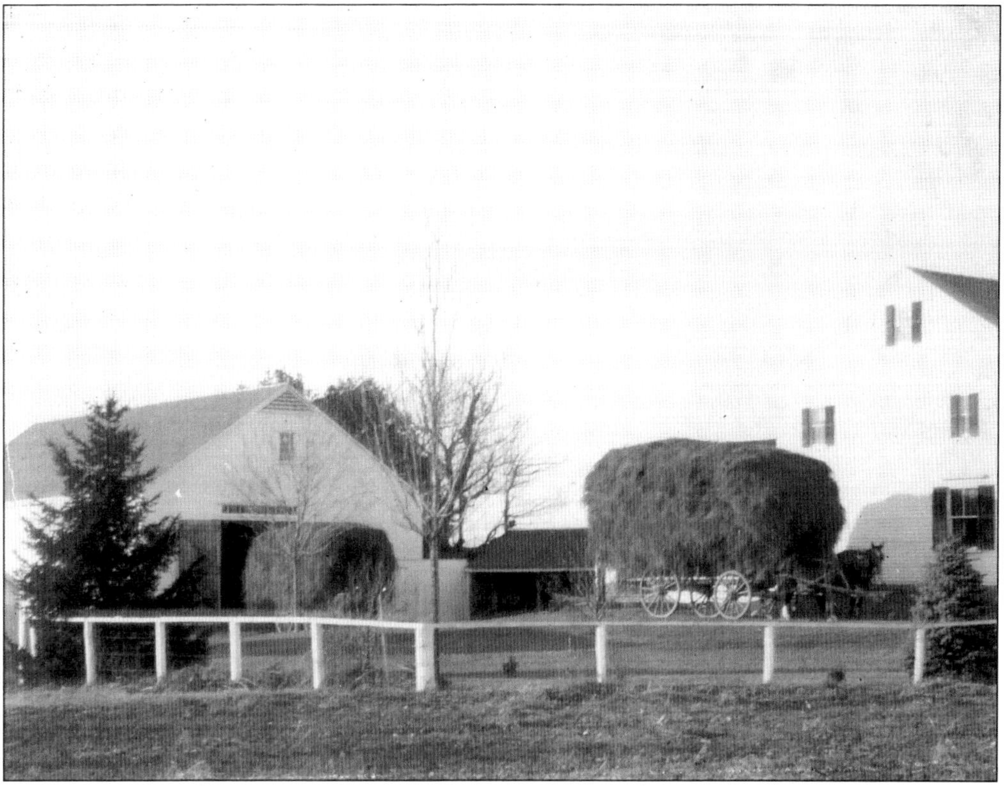

Two wagons full of hay at the Scammon Farm on River Road. (SHS.)

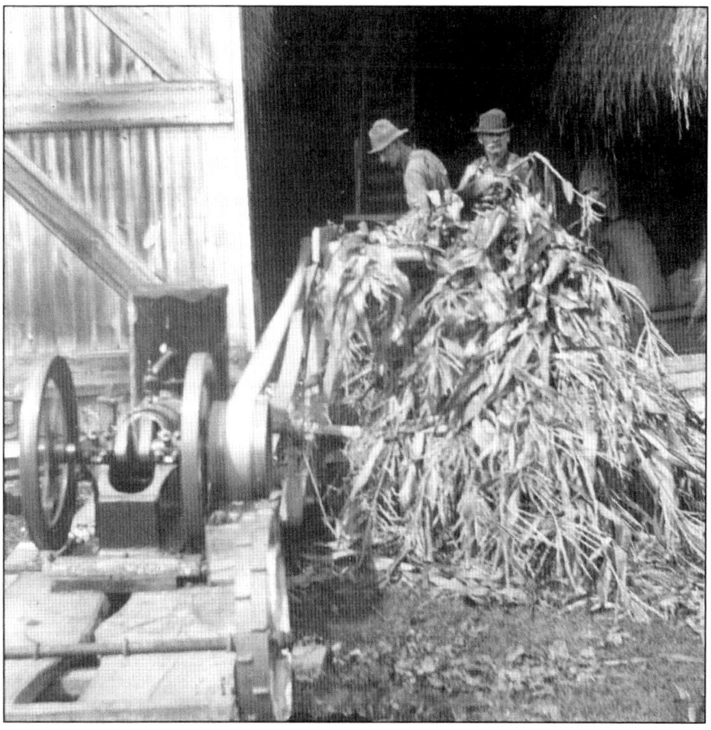

Fritz Olsen, a native Swede, worked the farm on River Road for Annie W. Scammon. He's shown here with a stationary corn chopper and blower. It will blow the chopped corn into the silo. River Road was formerly known as Quabaag Lane. (SHS.)

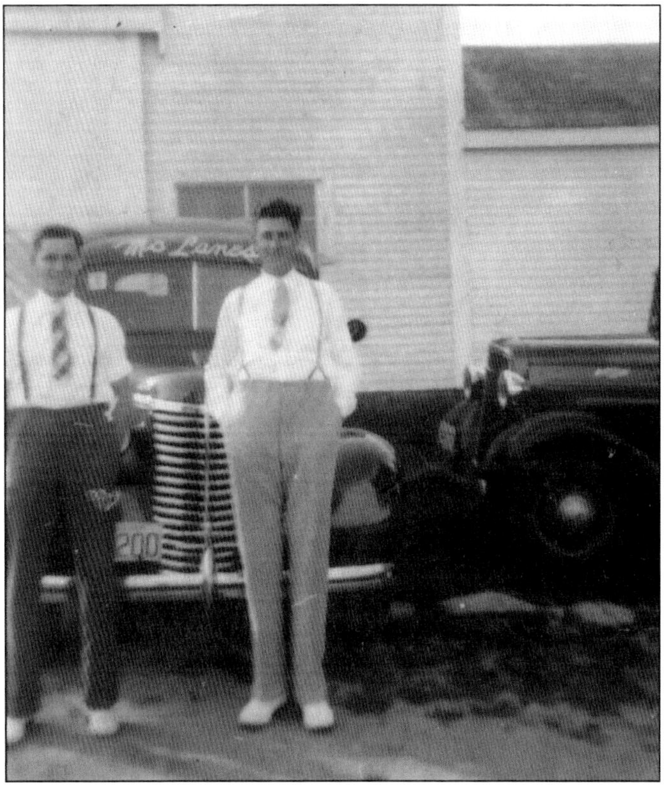

Bill and Howard McLane, 2 of the 11 McLane children, in front of a McLane Bakery truck in 1938. The McLane Bakery, at 21 Depot Road, had five delivery trucks and delivered fresh baked goods throughout the Seacoast in the 1930s. (VW.)

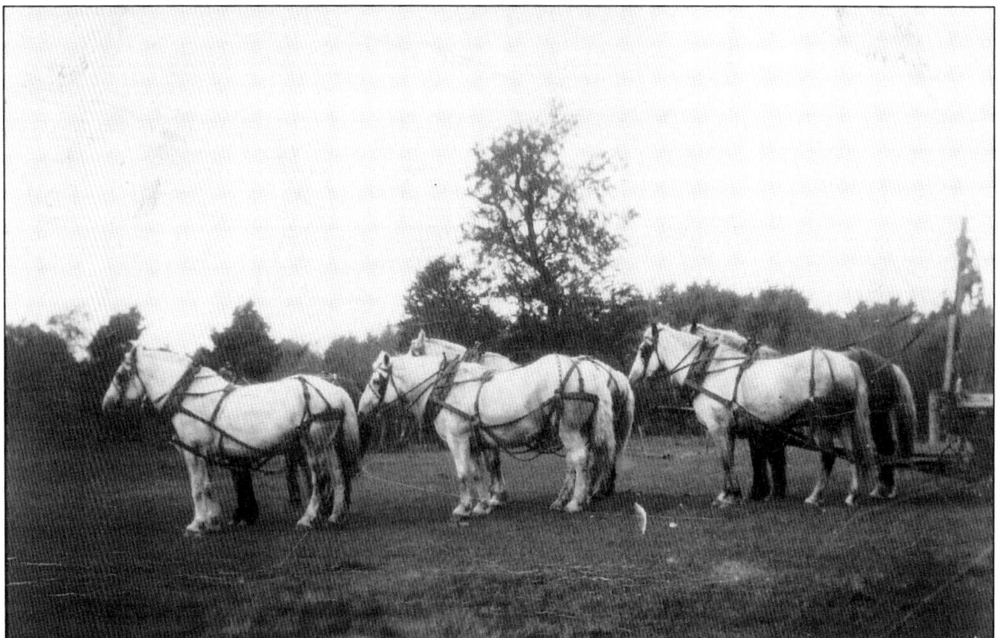

Ernest Wiggin's horses. Wiggin was a farmer, storekeeper, and on occasion, horse dealer with Roby Jewell. Jewell bought horses in Canada and brought them to Stratham, where Wiggin would prep them for sale at Jewell's auction. (E and EW.)

Clearing snow in Stratham in 1921. (SHS.)

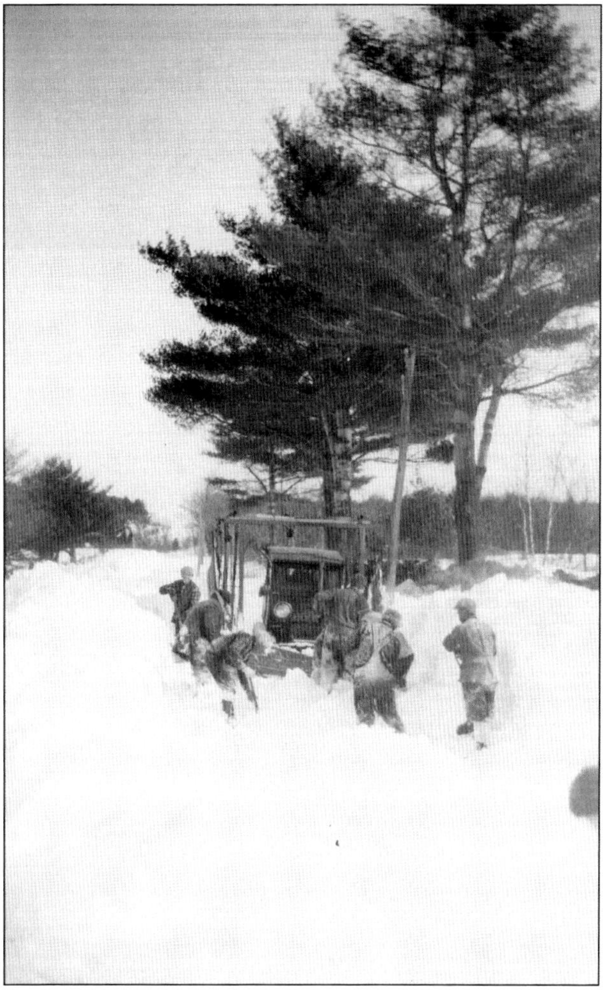

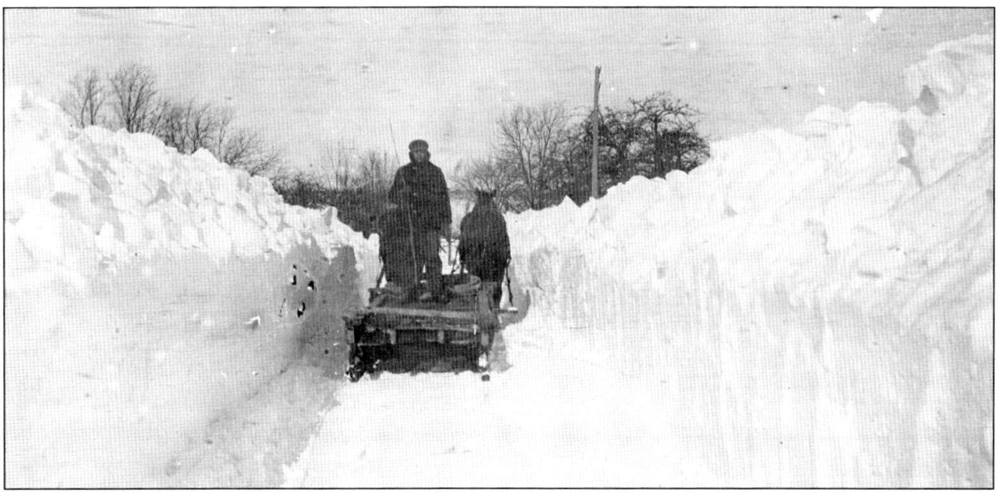

Howard Gowen on Depot Road in 1921 with the snow roller. Depot Road was formerly known as Bay View Road. (SHS.)

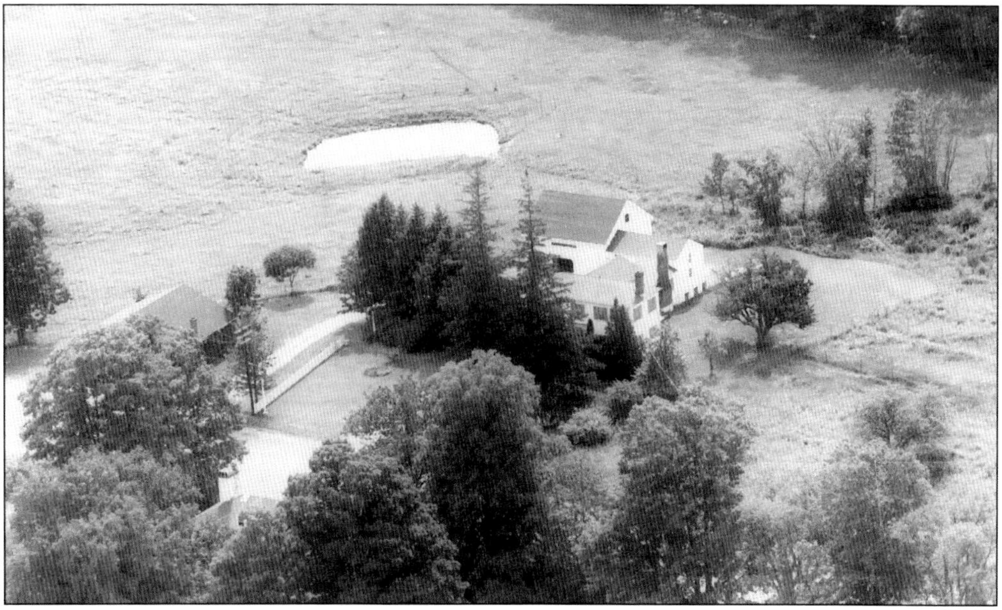

A 1966 aerial view of the Stockbridge House at 129 Portsmouth Avenue. The roof visible in the lower left is of the old gas station. (SHS.)

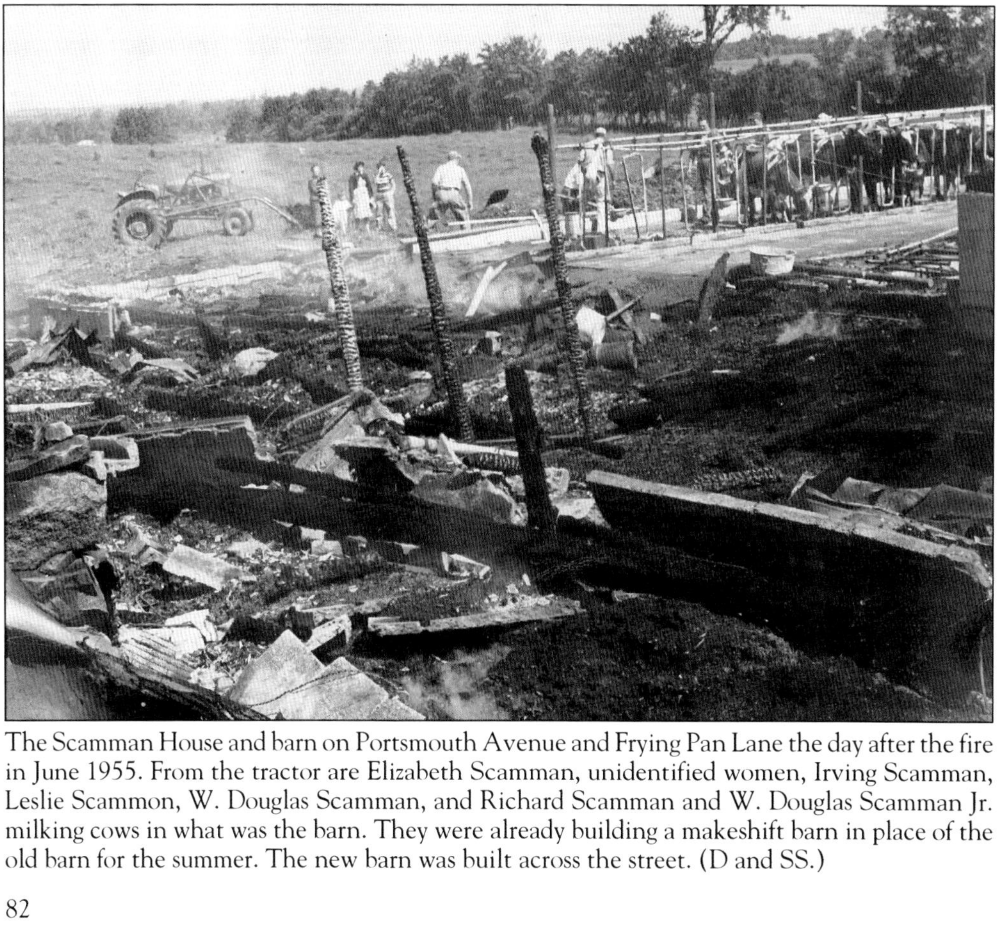

The Scamman House and barn on Portsmouth Avenue and Frying Pan Lane the day after the fire in June 1955. From the tractor are Elizabeth Scamman, unidentified women, Irving Scamman, Leslie Scammon, W. Douglas Scamman, and Richard Scamman and W. Douglas Scamman Jr. milking cows in what was the barn. They were already building a makeshift barn in place of the old barn for the summer. The new barn was built across the street. (D and SS.)

Six

The Bridge

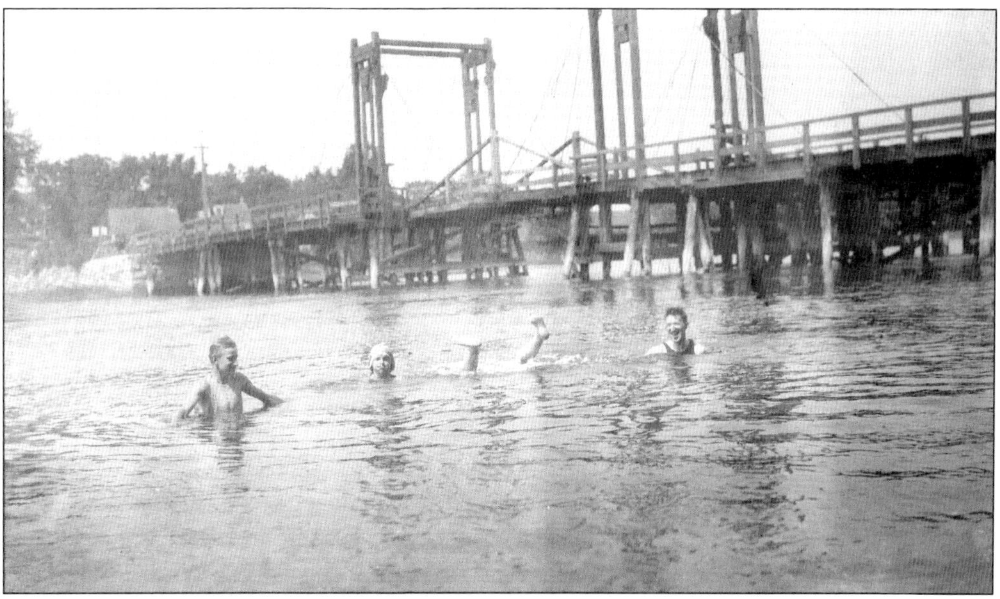

A favorite swimming spot on the Squamscott near the town landing and the old Newfields bridge. These 1920 swimmers are Stanley French, Dorothy Pearson, some unknown legs, and Charles Hall. (SHS.)

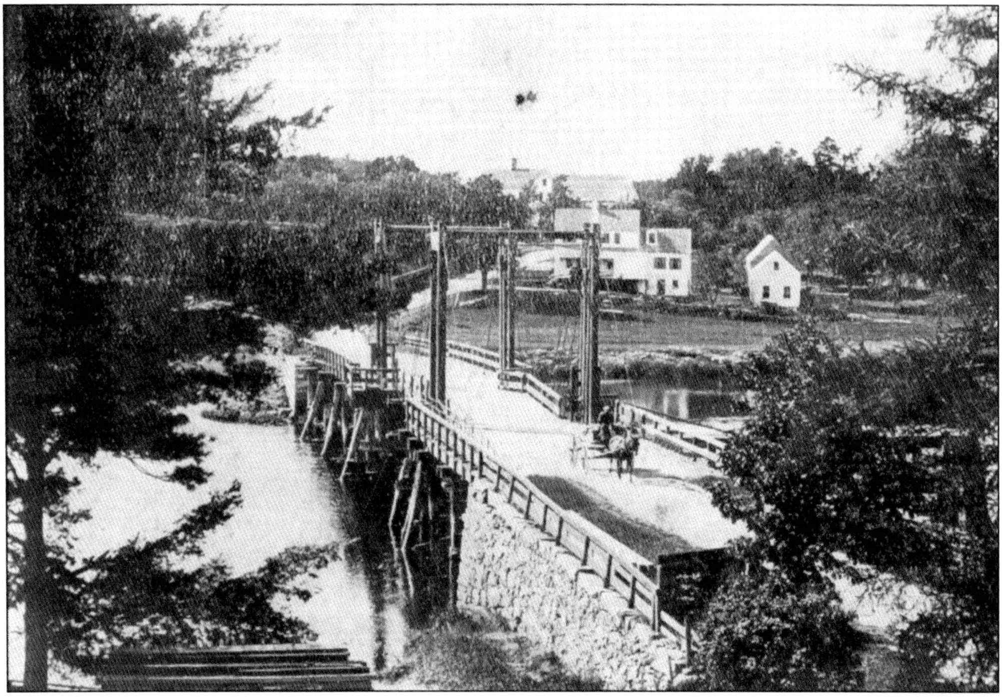

A horse and carriage on the old toll bridge on the Squamscott. The original toll bridge was opened December 1807 and was rebuilt in 1838 and again in 1889. This is the 1889 bridge in a view looking toward Newfields. (D and SS.)

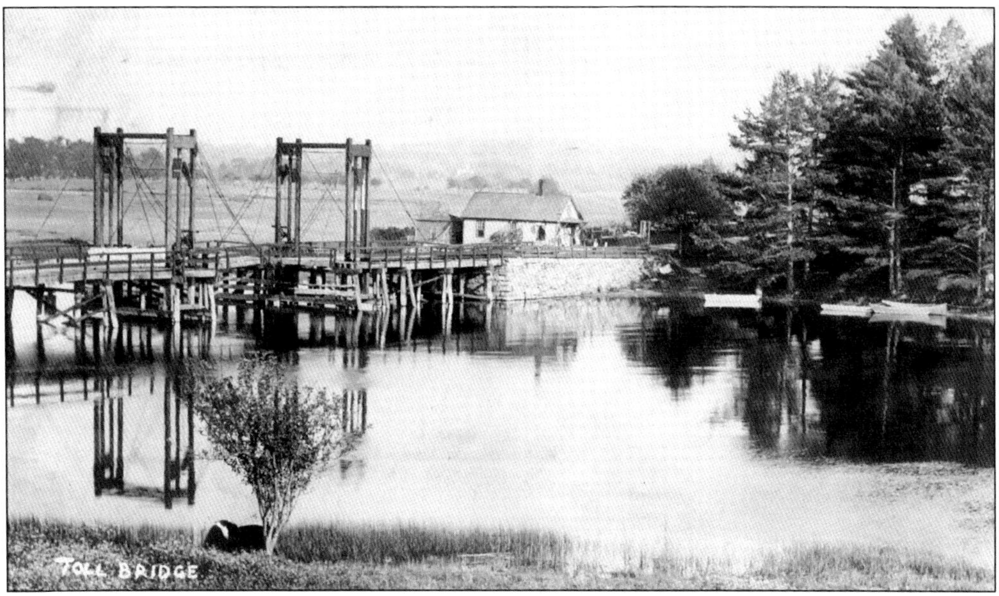

The old Squamscott Toll Bridge between Stratham and Newfields, this time from the Newfields side. It was considered a rite of passage for boys to dive off the towers. It was also a popular place to find horseshoe crabs. (SHS.)

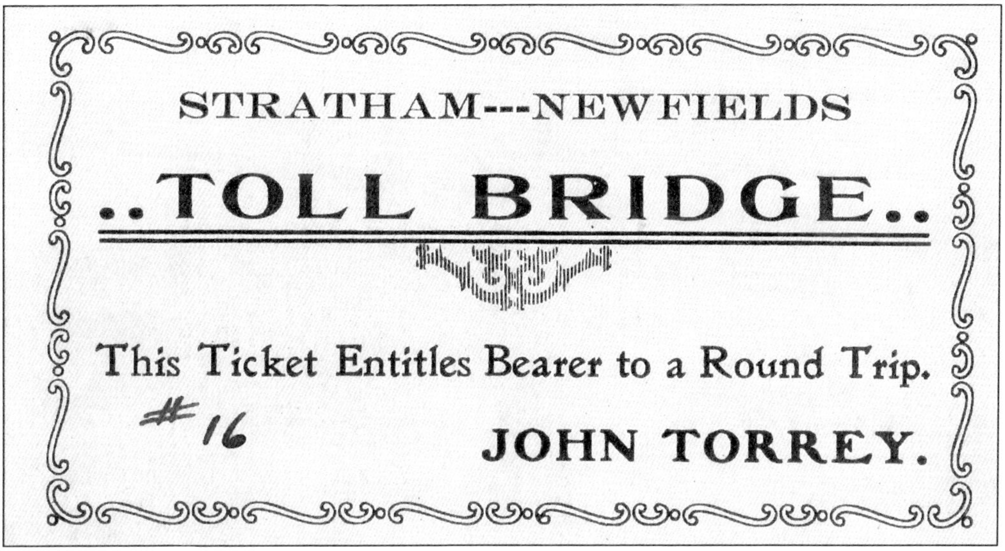
STRATHAM---NEWFIELDS

..TOLL BRIDGE..

This Ticket Entitles Bearer to a Round Trip.

#16 JOHN TORREY.

A ticket for free passage over the Stratham/Newfields toll bridge on the Squamscott River. While a state representative in 1906, J. Fred Emery succeeded in having the toll eliminated. H.F. Warden was the last toll collector. (SHS.)

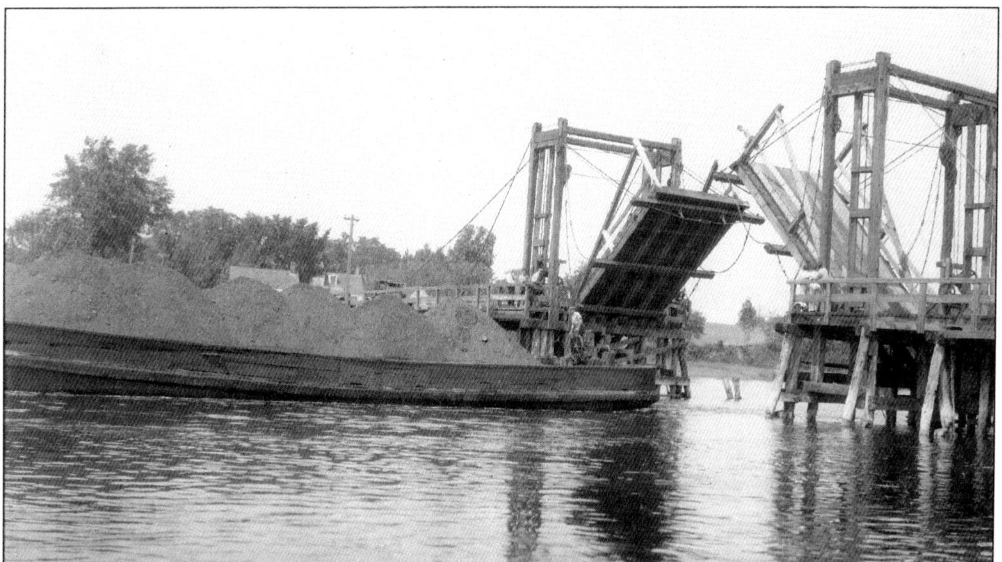

The old toll bridge on the Squamscott open for a coal barge. Although it could accommodate 4,000- to 5,000-ton ships, most vessels were 200 tons. (SHS.)

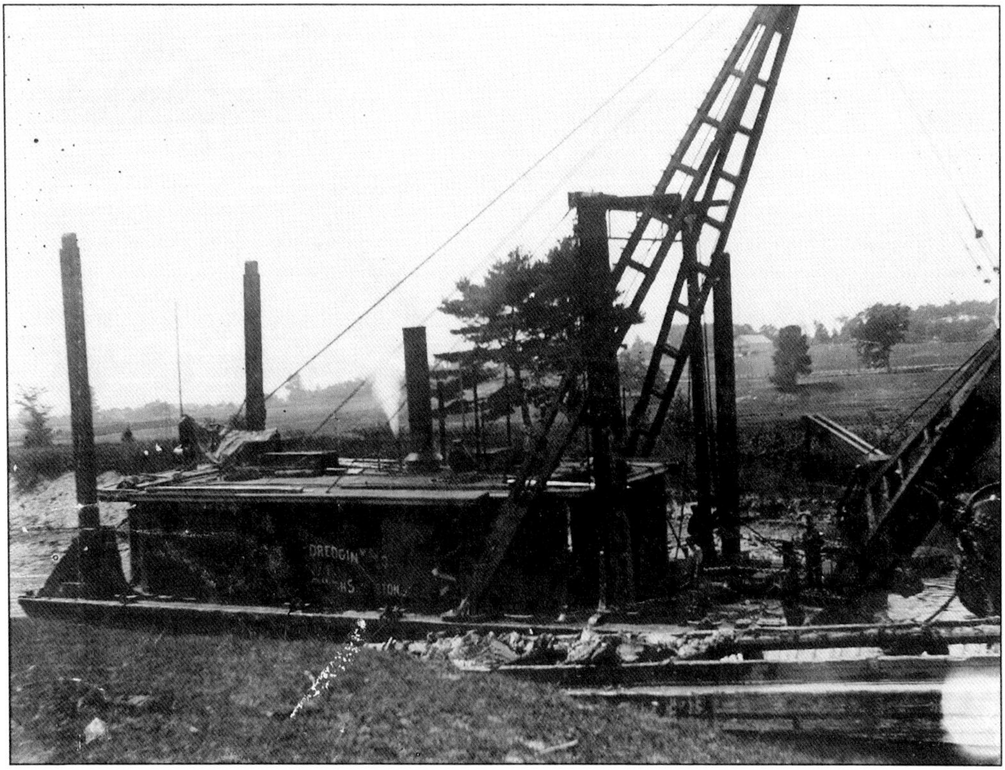

Dredging the river. In 1881 the U.S. Army Corps of Engineers dredged the Squamscott to deepen the channel, remove obstructions, and cut the roundabout on oxbow in the river. (SHS.)

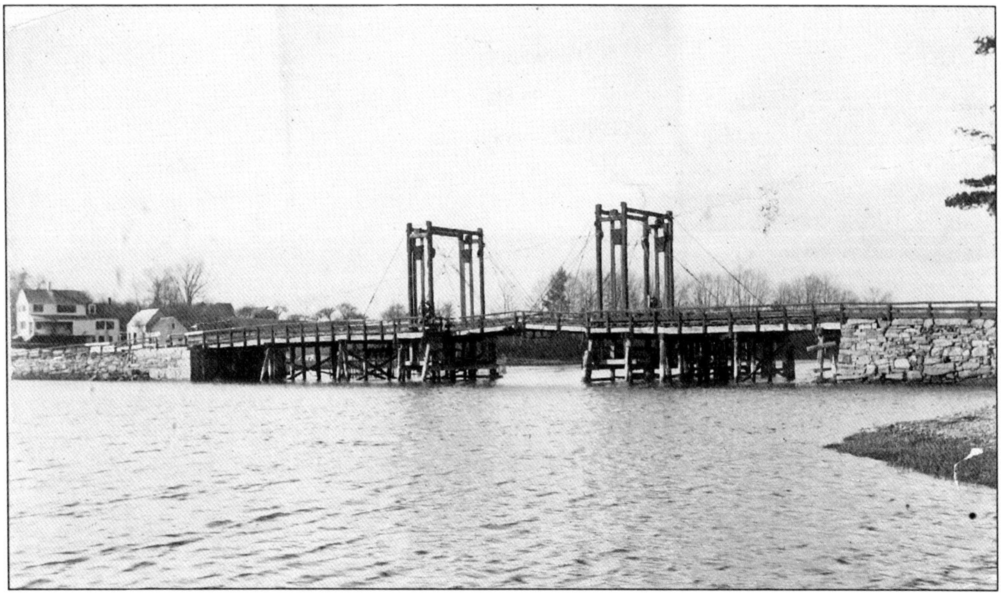

The old drawbridge on the Squamscott between Stratham and Newfields. There was extensive river traffic throughout all the tributaries to the Piscataqua from Colonial times to the early 20th century. (SHS.)

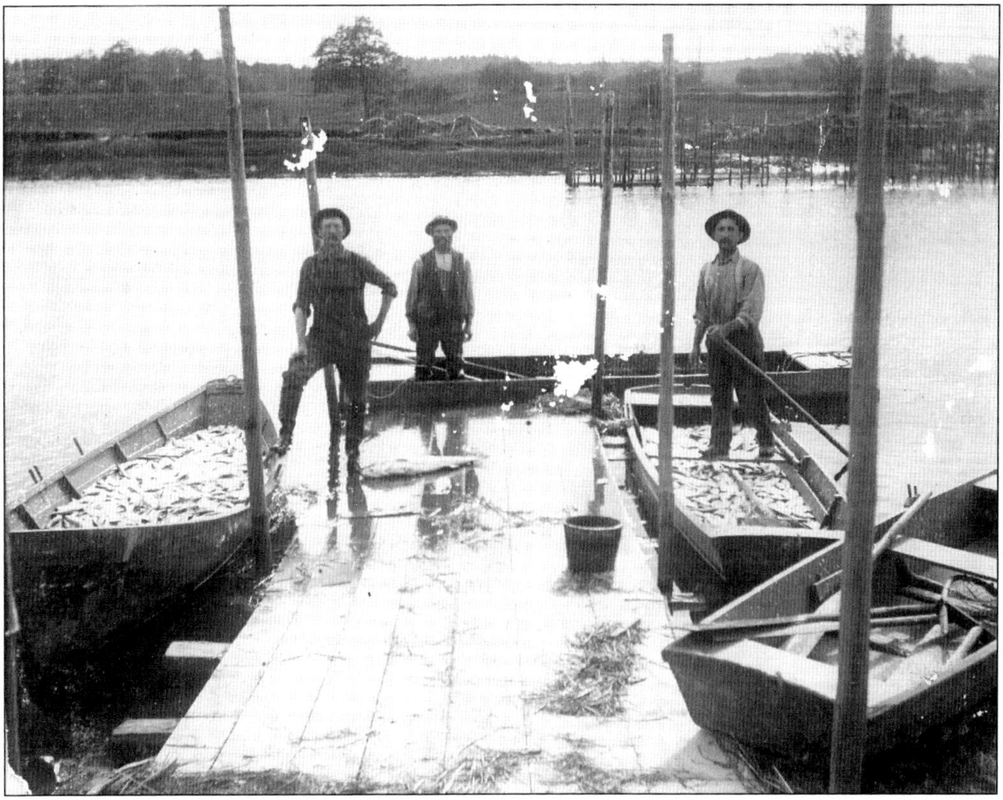

Nineteenth-century fishermen and their catch of Alewives on the Squamscott near the town landing. The Squamscott was teeming with eels and fish including bass, perch, smelts, and, in earlier times, salmon. There were also good clam beds. (SHS.)

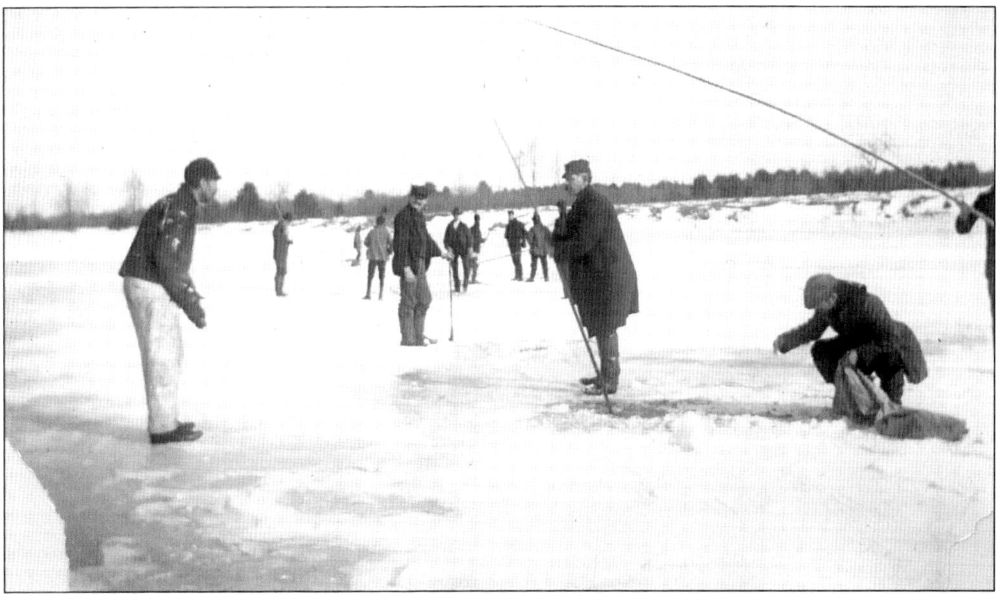

Ice fishing on the frozen Squamscott River in the late 19th century. The long poles were used to help the fishermen if they fell through the ice. (SHS.)

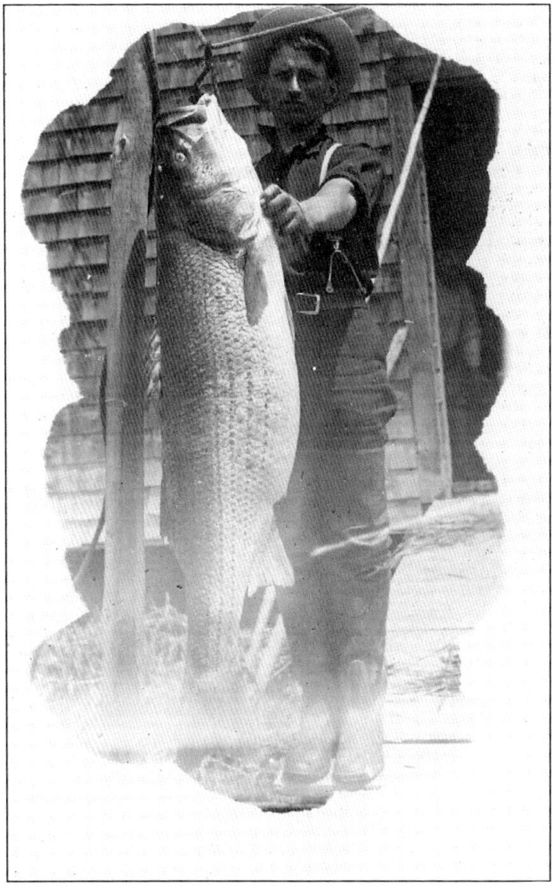

An 80-pound striped bass caught by Albert West, c. 1910. (SHS.)

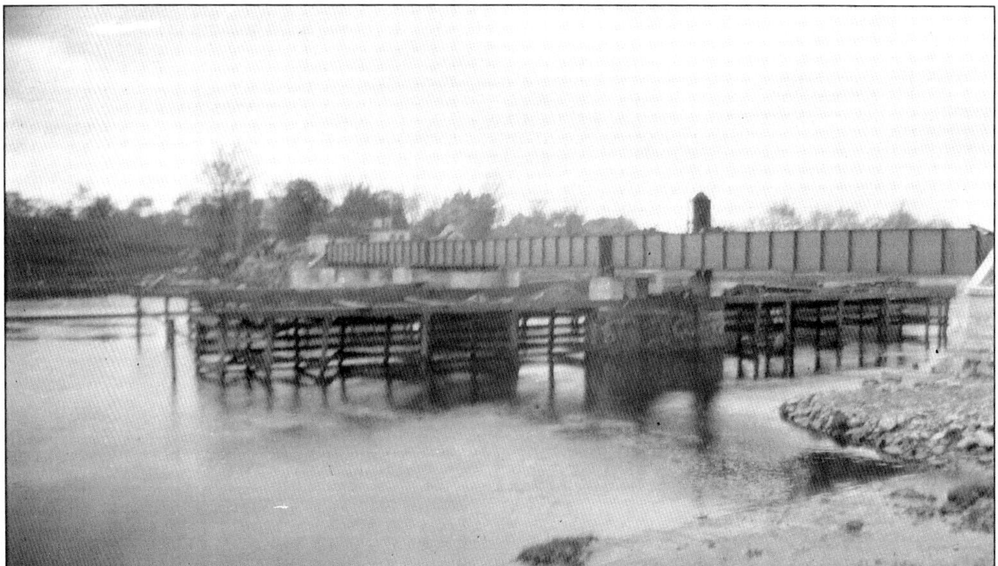

The swinging, also known as singing, bridge on the Squamscott. It replaced the drawbridge in the 1920s. (SHS.)

Seven

MILLS

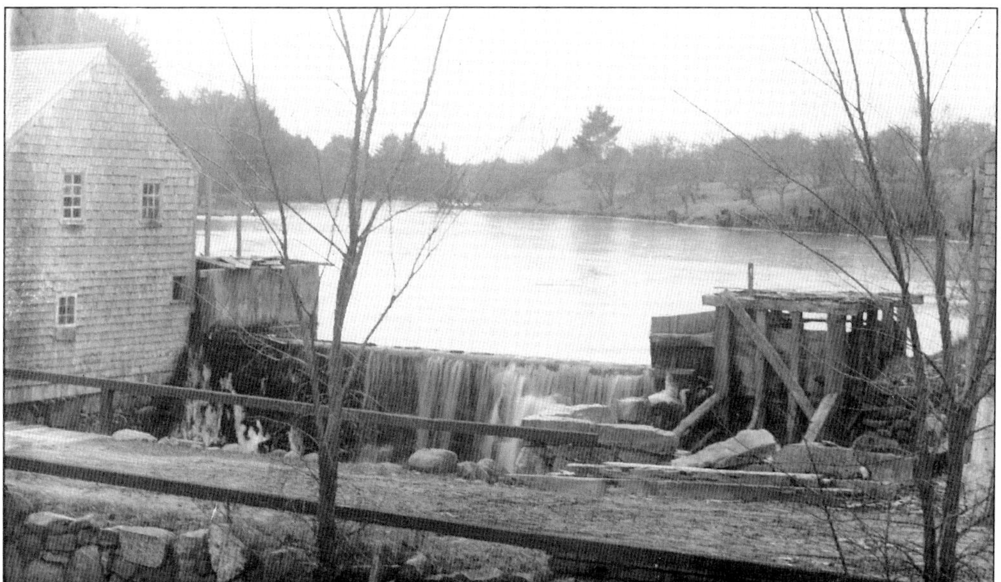

The Winnicutt Mill near the four corners intersection of Winnicutt and Union Roads. Union Road was once known as New Road and was not extended to and past the Winnicutt intersection until the 20th century. (SHS.)

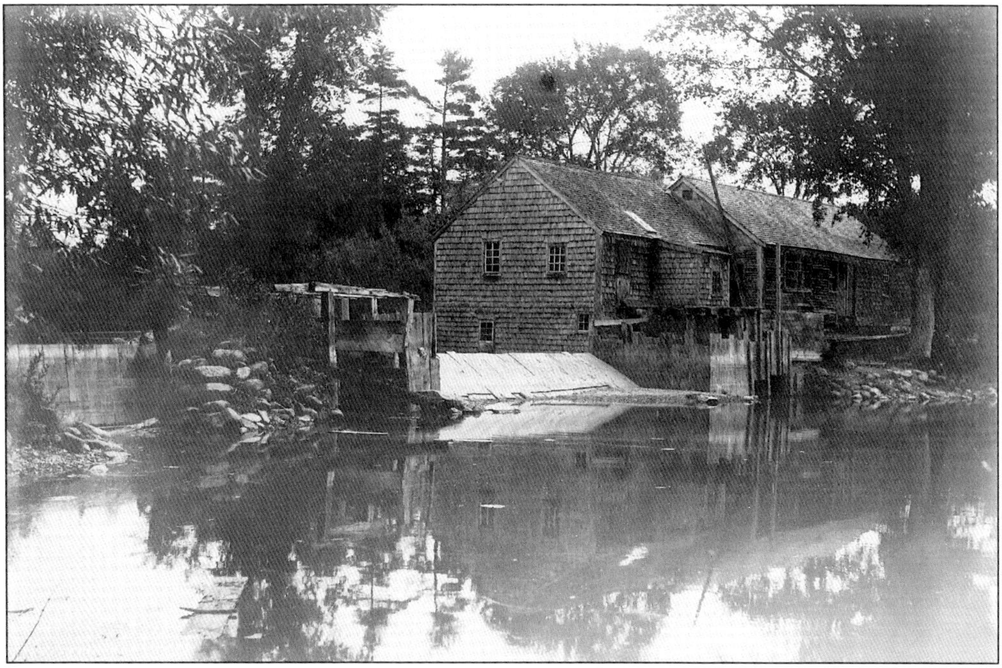

The Winnicutt Mill on the pond on the Winnicutt River. Barker Lane was constructed so that farmers bringing their products to the mill could avoid Jewell Hill, the steep hill at Union and Winnicutt. When the mill was taken down in 1962 detailed plans were made that are kept at the University of New Hampshire. (SHS.)

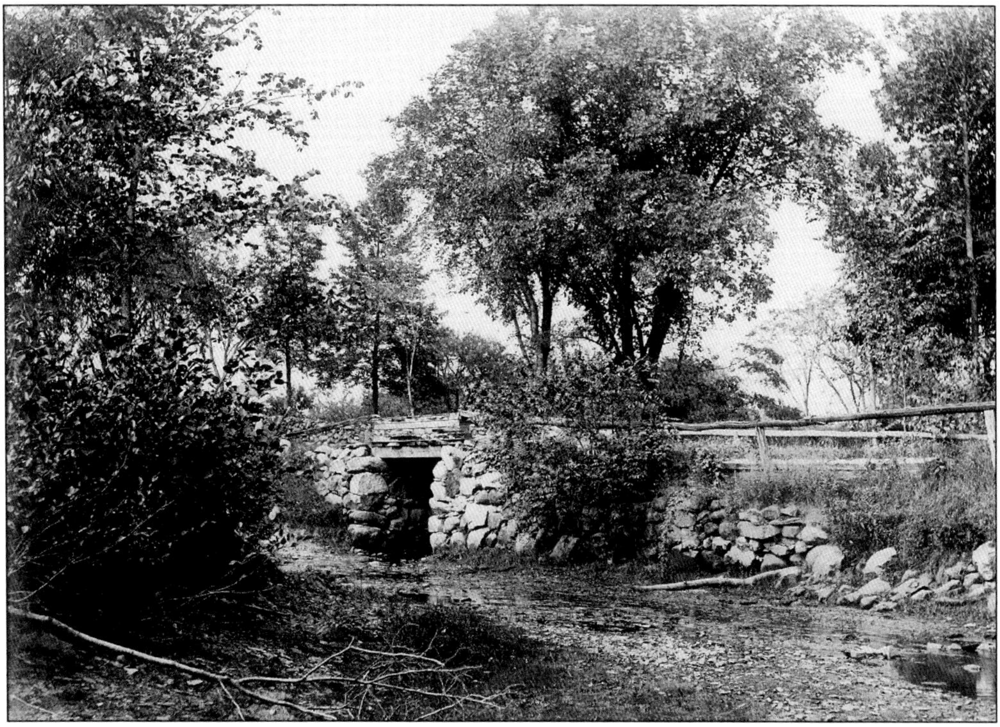

The old Winnicutt roadbed showing the bridge over the Winnicutt River. (SHS.)

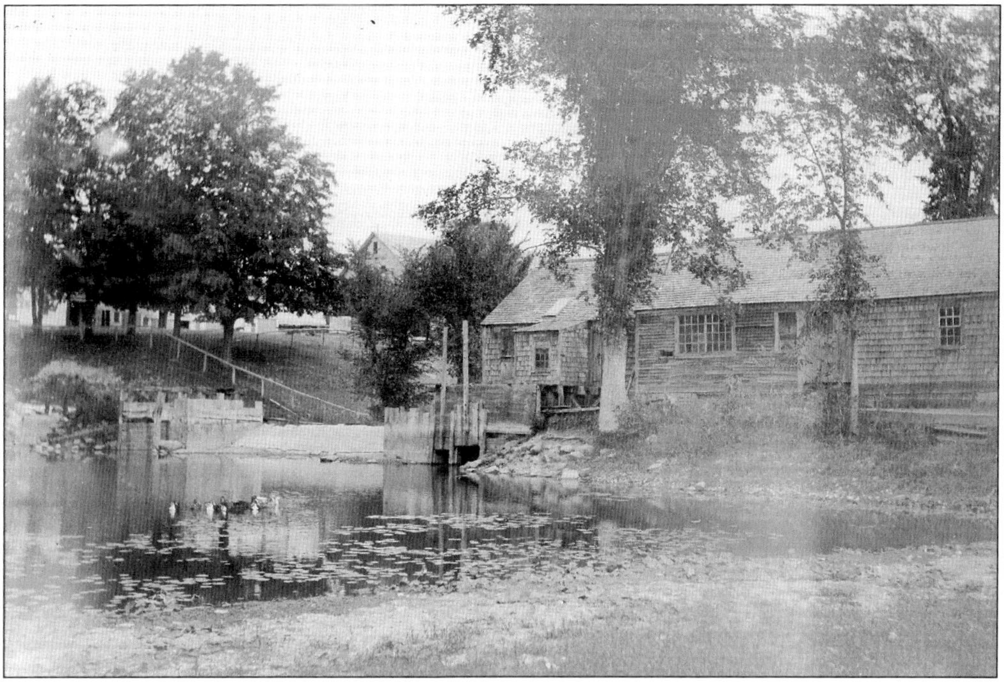

A view of the gristmill and pond on the Winnicutt. Fred Jewell's farm is on the hill on the left. (SHS.)

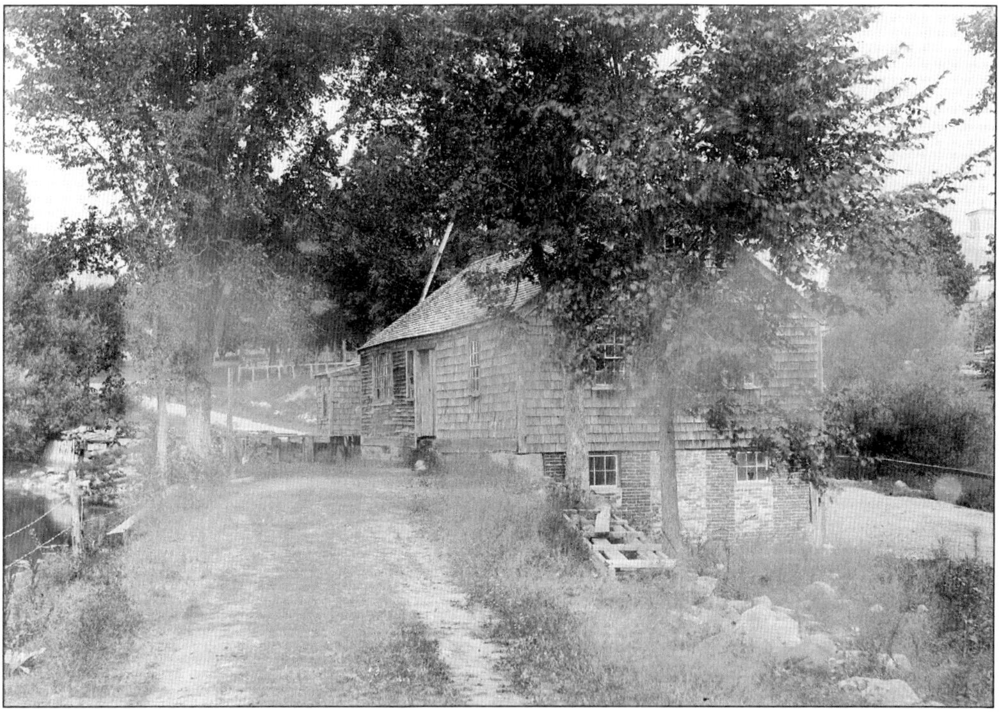

A view across the pond of the dam and mill at Mill Pond on Winnicutt Road. The dam controlled the water feeding the mills. A mile stretch included a starch mill, grain, corn, and wood mills. (SHS.)

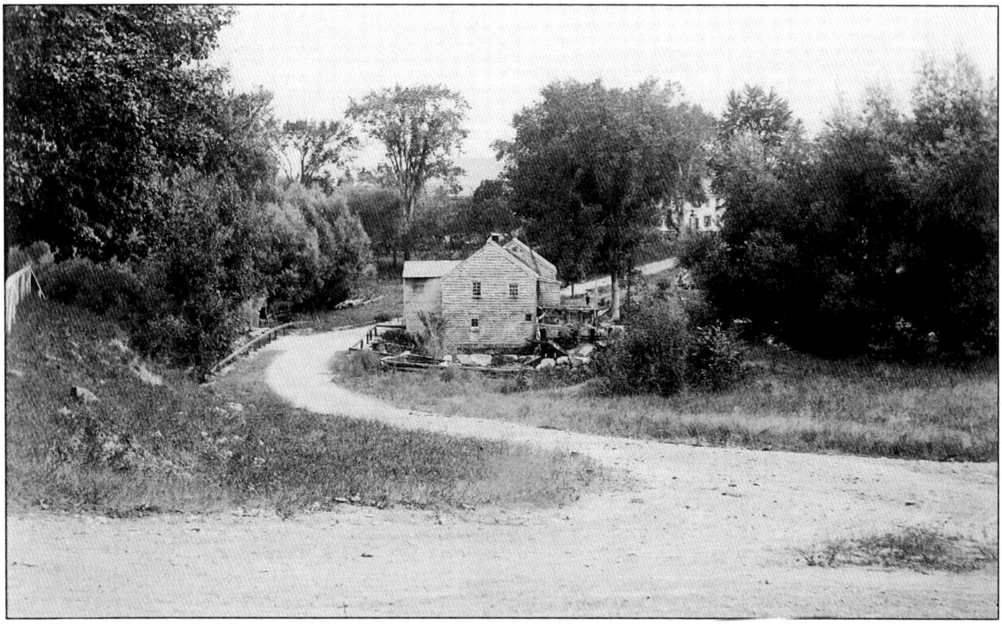

The Winnicutt gristmill and the Winnicutt bridge. There were mills on the Winnicutt from the 18th through mid-20th centuries. At one point eight mills lined the banks of the river. (SHS.)

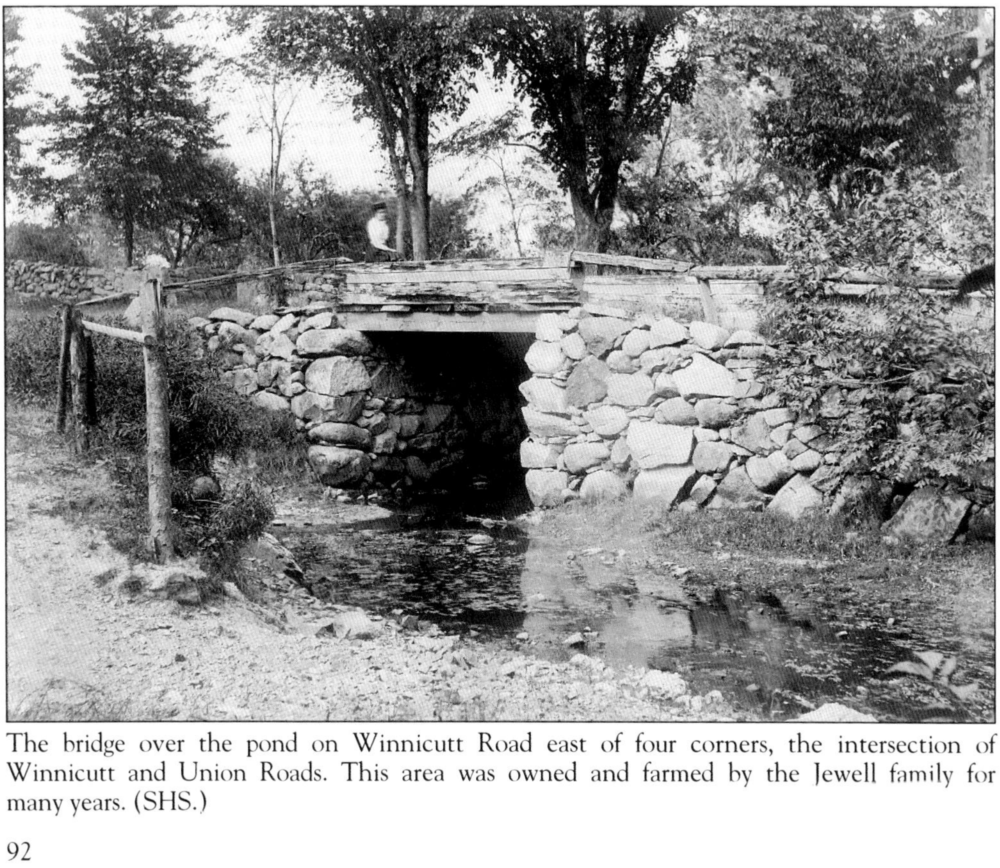

The bridge over the pond on Winnicutt Road east of four corners, the intersection of Winnicutt and Union Roads. This area was owned and farmed by the Jewell family for many years. (SHS.)

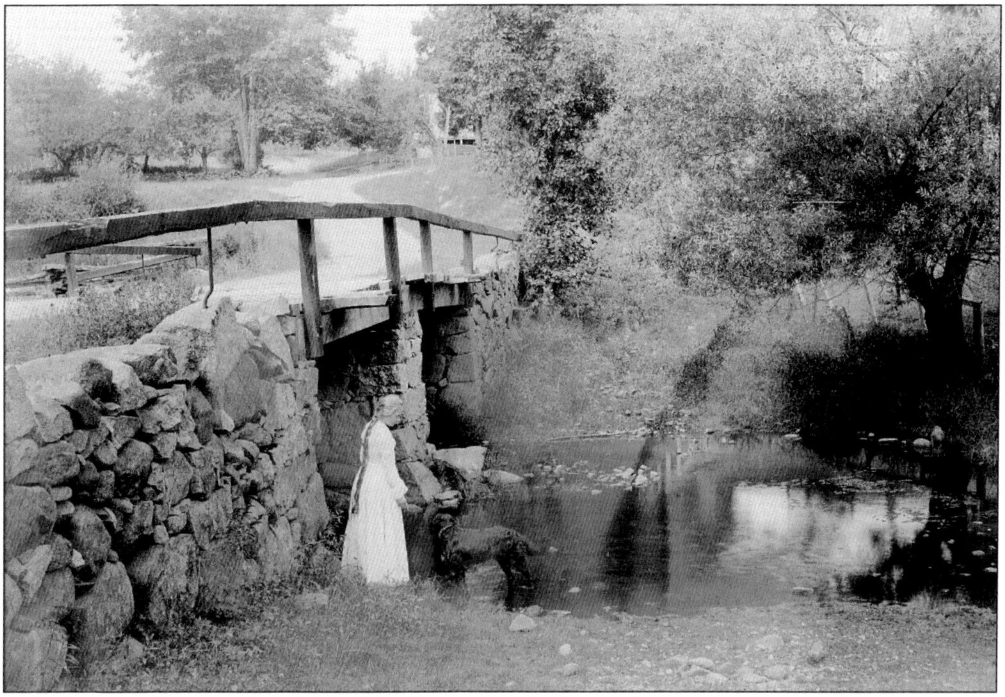

A view of the lower end of the Winnicutt River near the bridge between 163 and 173 Winnicutt Road. The woman is most likely a member of the Jewell family. Supposedly Winnicutt is a Native American word for "pretty river." (SHS.)

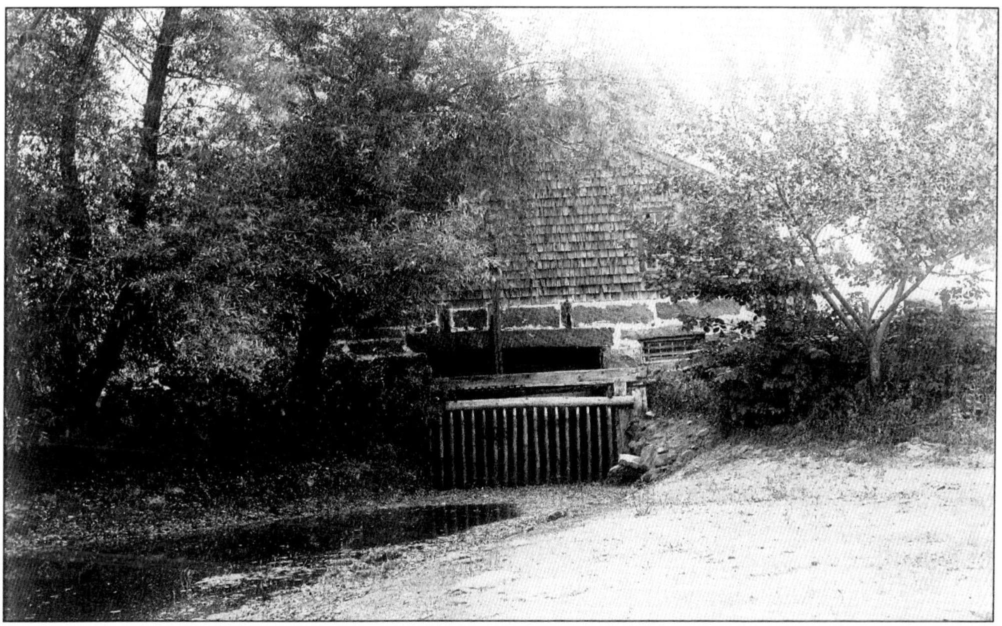

The gristmill and falls on the Winnicutt. (SHS.)

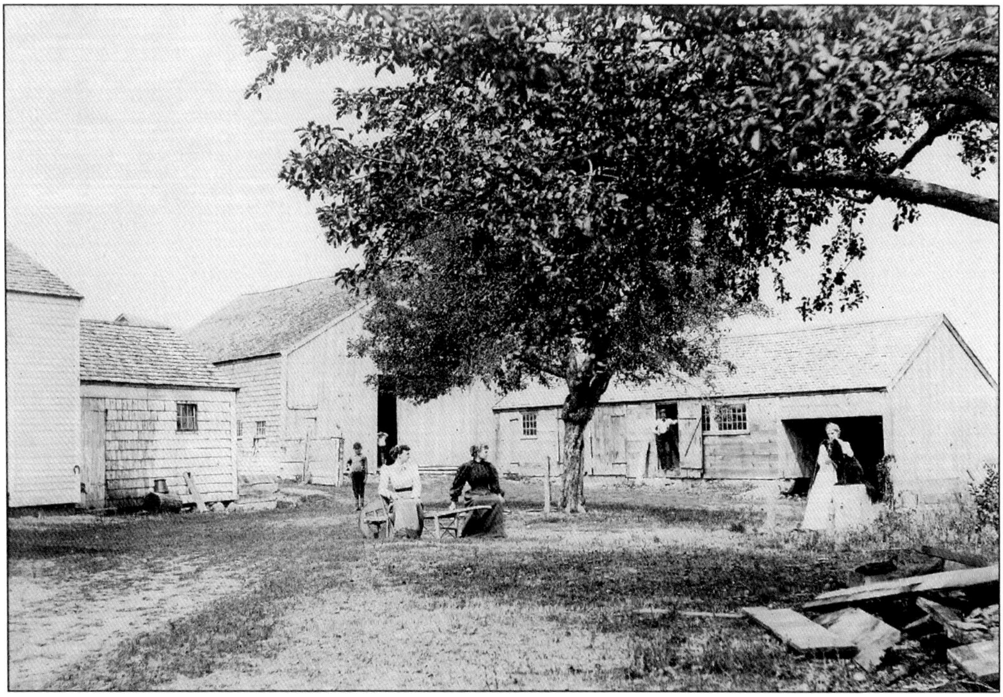

David Jewell's farm at 107 Winnicutt, across from Arthur Jewell's farm. These Jewell farms are further down Winnicutt heading toward the center of town. Two sisters, Harriett and Sadie Jewell (who grew up in Stratham and lived in Boston, where Harriett worked as a music teacher), summered in Stratham, where they sponsored band concerts on a pavilion in the field near 105 Winnicutt Road. (SHS.)

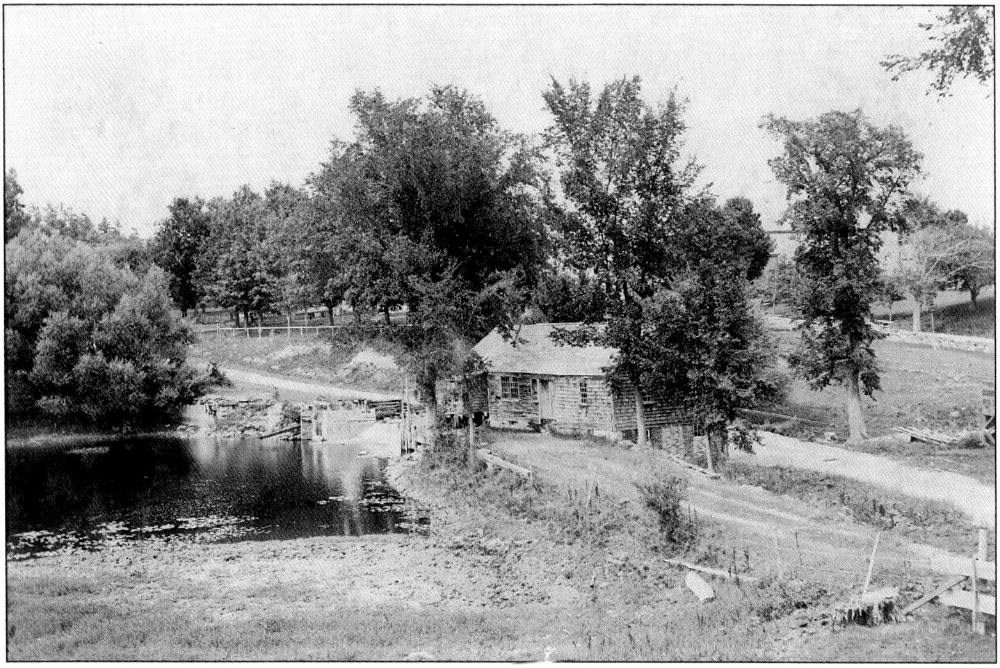

The gristmill on Fred Jewell's farm near four corners. (SHS.)

Farmer and dairyman Frank Herbert Barker (1873–1923), his wife, Laura May Snell Barker of Nova Scotia, and their daughter Flora, c. 1903, on their farm near the Winnicutt Pond. The Barkers eventually had six sons: Nelson, Ezra, Carmen, Chester Herbert, Levi Henry, Earl Leslie, and Donald. Herbert's mother, Hanna Jewell Barker, was the first holder of the Boston Post Cane, held by the eldest resident of the town. (BB.)

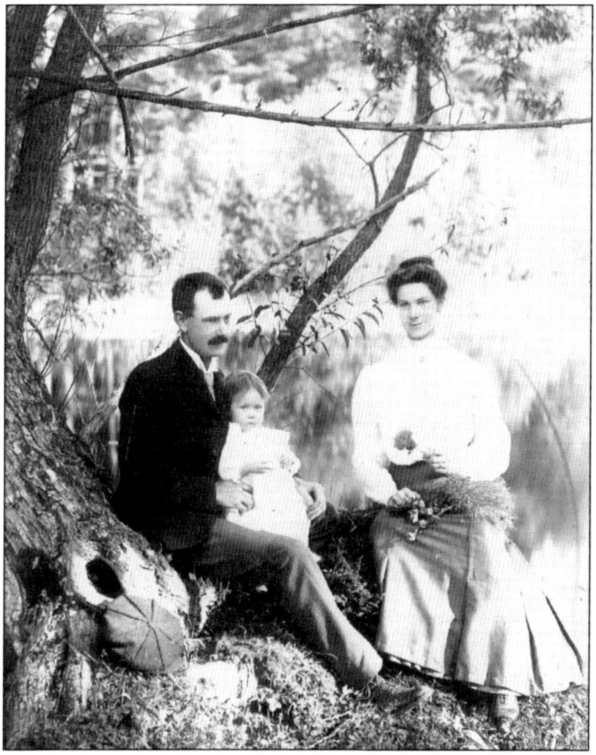

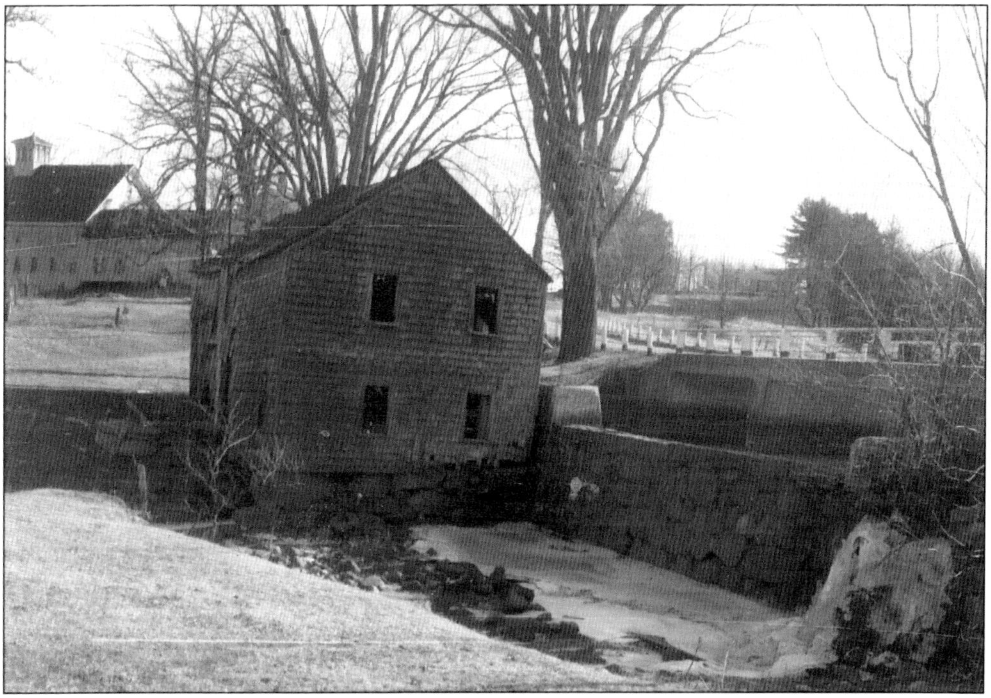

The dam on the Winnicutt looking from the old road bed that is several yards north and lower than the current road. This was Jewell farmland and a Jewell house and barn at 173 Winnicutt Road are on the left. (C and KP.)

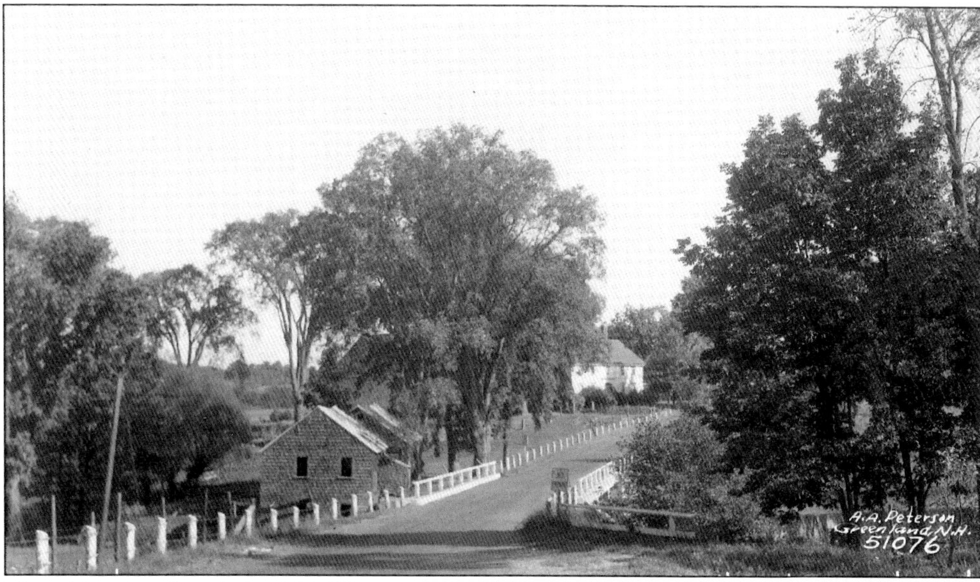

The old gristmill and the 173 Winnicutt Road home of George C. Jewell, built by his great-great-grandfather. (SHS.)

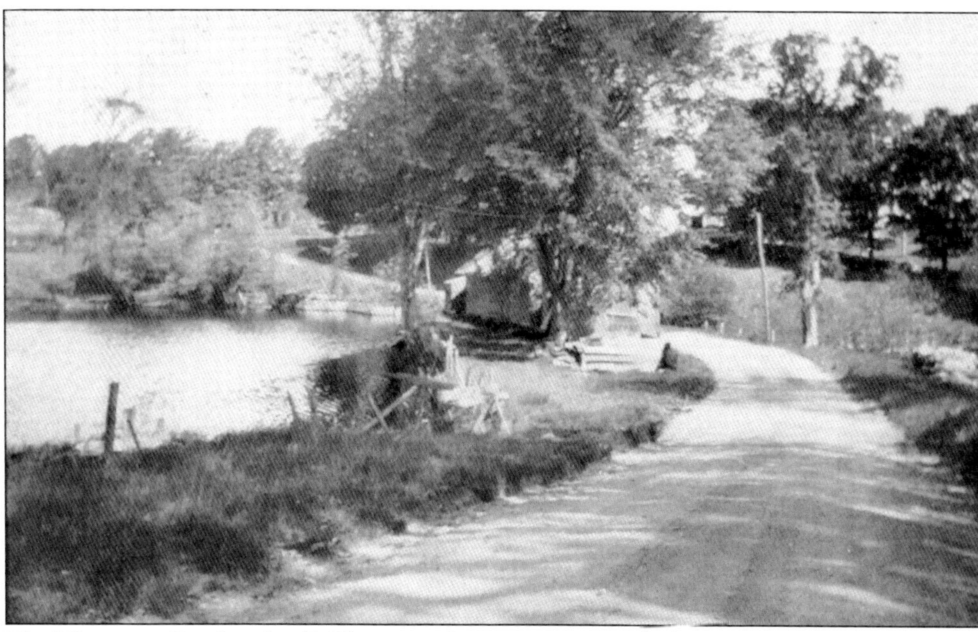

The Winnicutt Pond and mill. This was a favorite swimming hole. (SHS.)

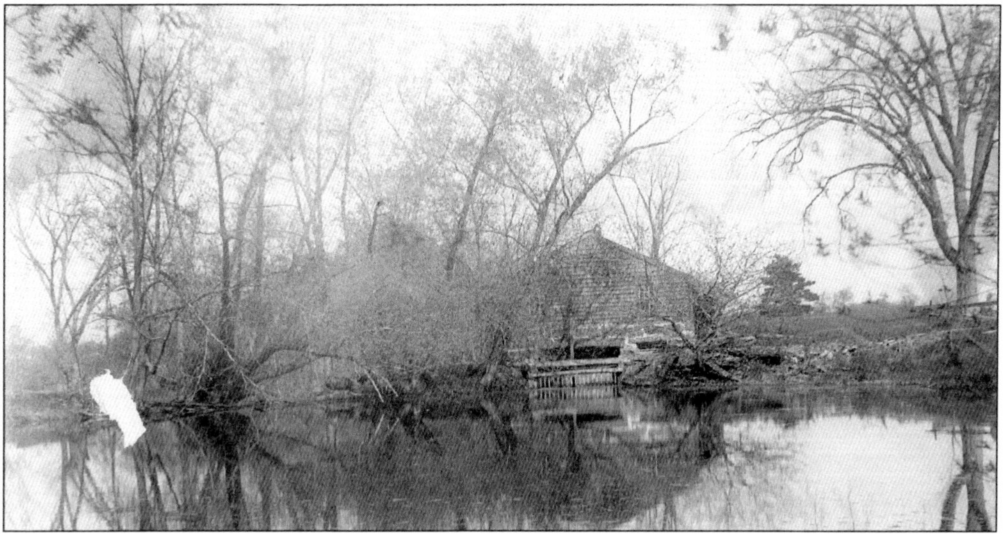

The Winnicutt Gristmill from across the pond. There was, at one point, an icehouse attached to the mill. (SHS.)

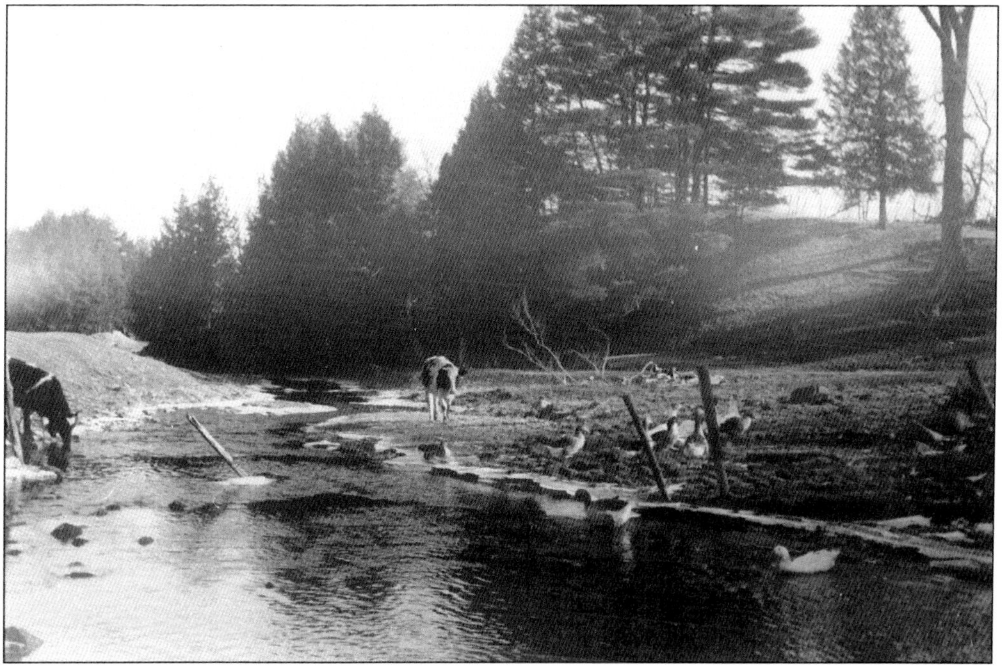

Two cows on the Winnicutt River as viewed from the bridge on Winnicutt Road. To the left is 163 Winnicutt and to the right 173. This was a popular goose pond. (LC.)

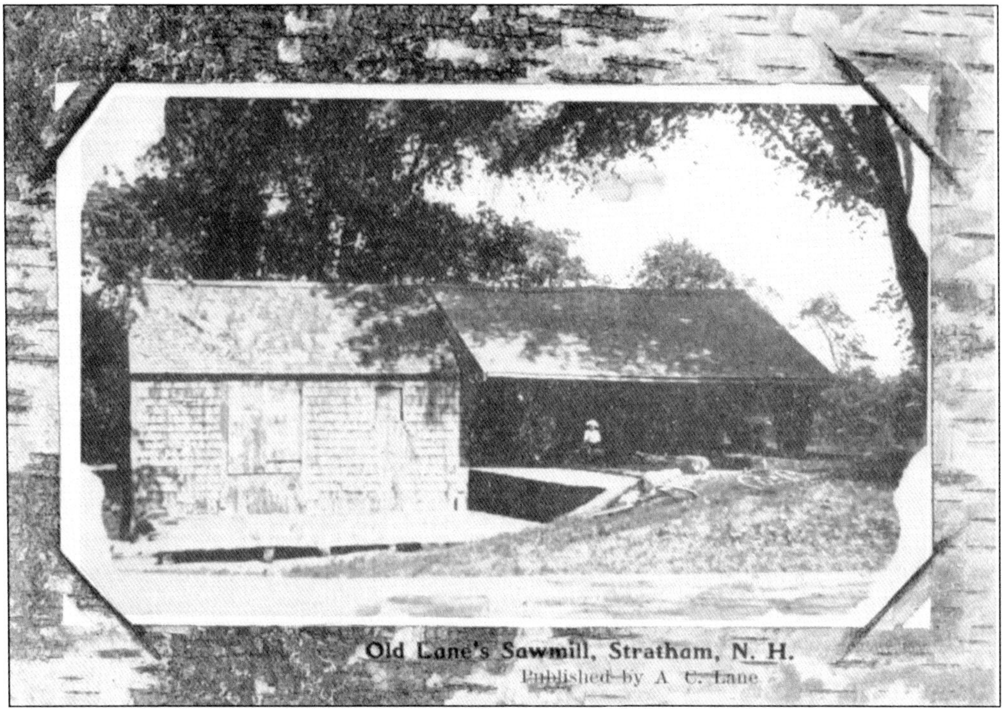

Old Lane's Sawmill at Mill Pond on Portsmouth Avenue, where the circle is now. (SHS.)

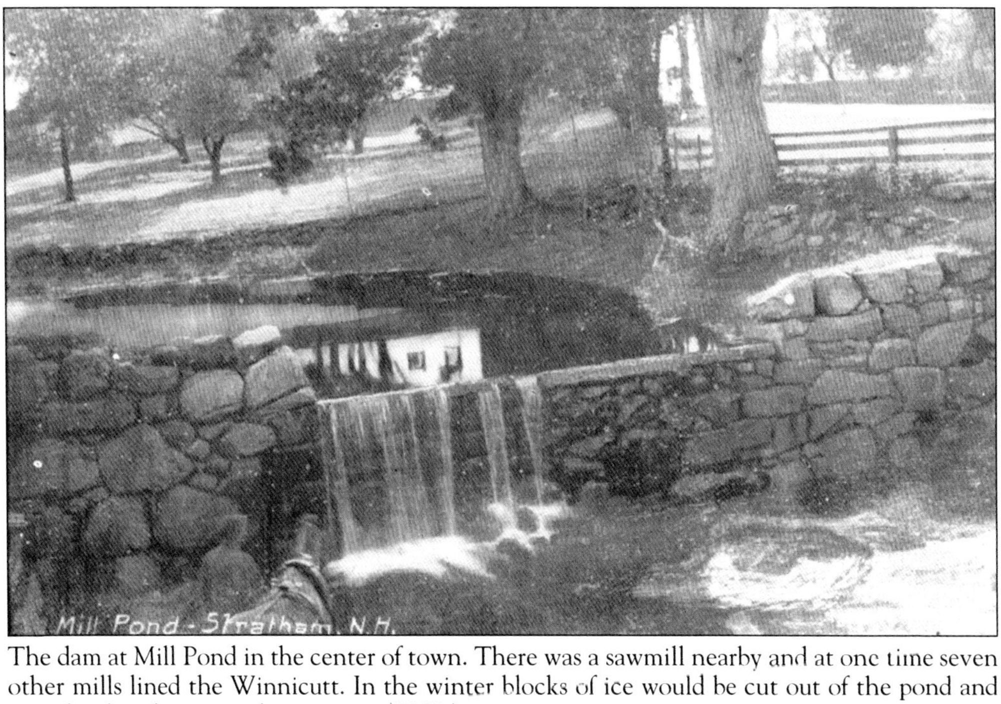

The dam at Mill Pond in the center of town. There was a sawmill nearby and at one time seven other mills lined the Winnicutt. In the winter blocks of ice would be cut out of the pond and stored in hay for use in the summer. (SHS.)

Eight

RELAXATION

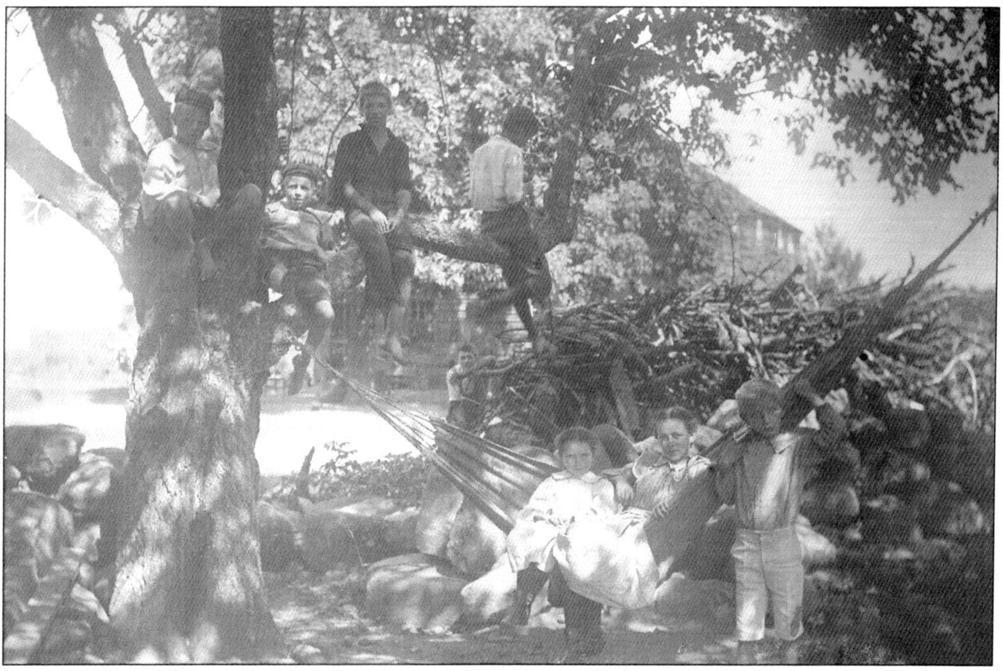

Gowen children and friends enjoy tree climbing and swinging in the 1890s. The old, long gone Hillside Farm barn is in the background. The children are Ben, Phil, Howard, Tytus, Rachel, Edna, and Shirley. The boy by the woodpile is unidentified. (HC.)

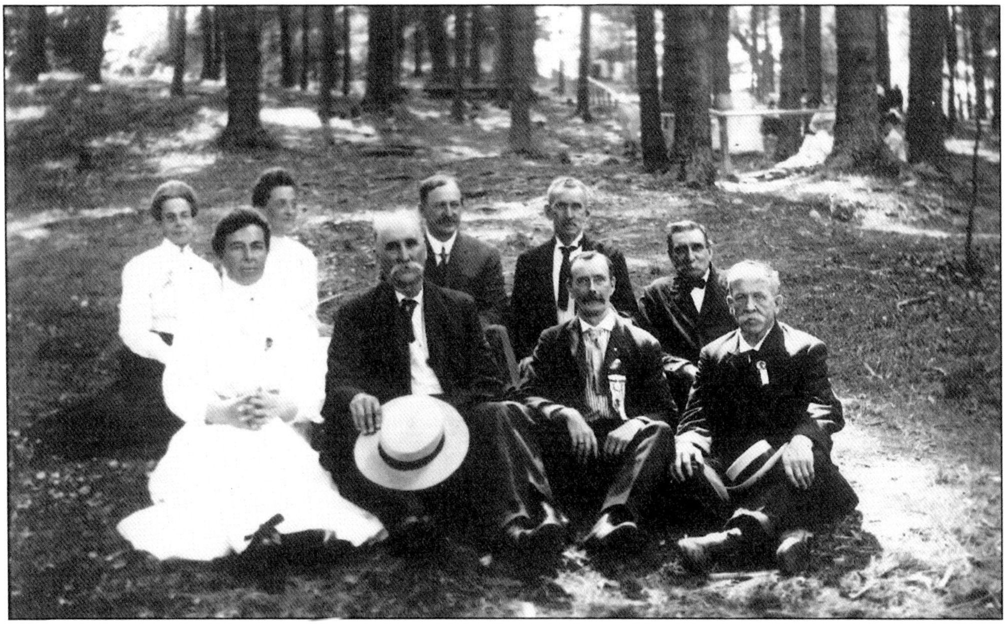

A picture postcard from Stratham Hill Park showing the planning committee for Old Home Day. Listed from left to right are as follows: (front row) Annie W. Scammon, Isaac Wiggin, and Fred Edwards; (back row) Mrs. J.T. Smart, two unidentified, Albert C. Lane, and unidentified. (SHS.)

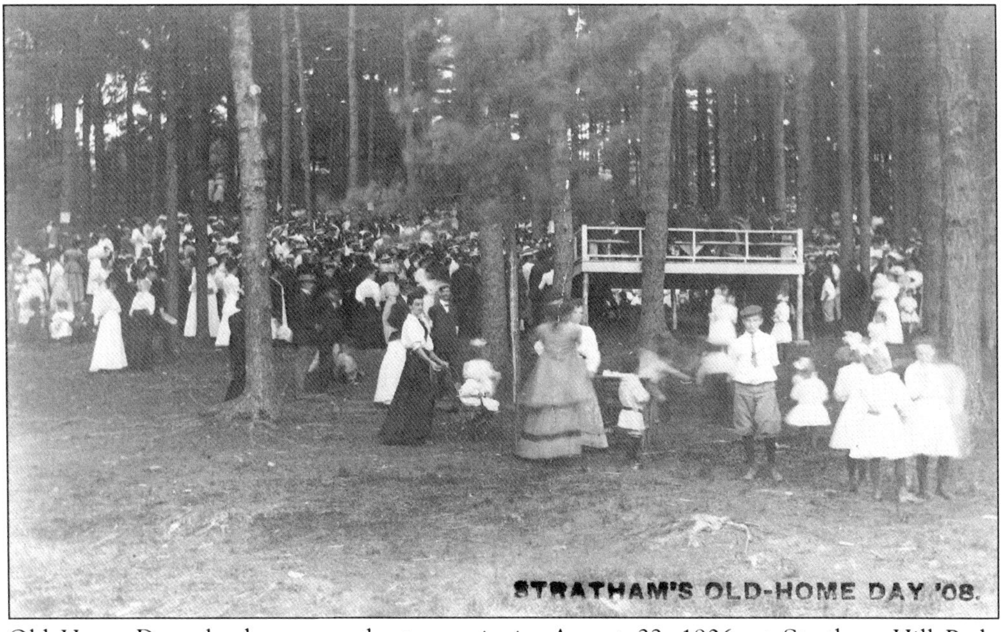

Old Home Day, also known as the town picnic, August 22, 1906, at Stratham Hill Park. Founded in 1904, Old Home Day was a popular summer festival for the entire town as well as natives who resided elsewhere. No longer held annually, the most recent Old Home Day was in 1983. (SHS.)

A playbill from the turn of the century. From the description of the cast it looks like quite a melodrama. (LB.)

THURSDAY EVENING, MAR. 24.

THE THREE ACT DRAMA

The Turn *of the* Tide

Will be presented at

TOWN HALL, . . STRATHAM, N. H.

Proceeds to be used to purchase dishes and other necessary articles for general use in the Hall.

CAST OF CHARACTERS:

JONAS ALDRICH, a fisherman of the coast, ... Irving L. Godfrey

CAPT. HUGH St. MORRIS, commander of the "Tidal Wave," . . . . J. Fred Emery

COL. ELLSWORTH, a wealthy shipowner, . . Asa C. Craig

HERMAN CLYDE, captain of the pirates. . Charles H. Craig

BOWIE KNIFE JACK, } Pirates, . . { Asa C. Craig
SLING SHOT RUBE, } { George C. Jewell

PEPPER, a colored individual, . . Frank H. Pearson

AUNT REBECCA, the fisherman's wife—a quiet body, ... Mrs. Hattie L. Brewster

SUSIE ALDRICH, the ocean waif, . Miss Alice G. Smart

LILLIAN LACEY, Clyde's deserted wife, ... Miss Elizabeth W. Wiggin

FRISKY, with no one to love, . Mrs. Grace K. Godfrey

ADMISSION, ... 15 Cents.
CHILDREN under 12, . . . 10 Cents.

ICE CREAM AND CAKE, 15 Cents.

Doors open at 7, commence at 8. If stormy, Friday Evening.

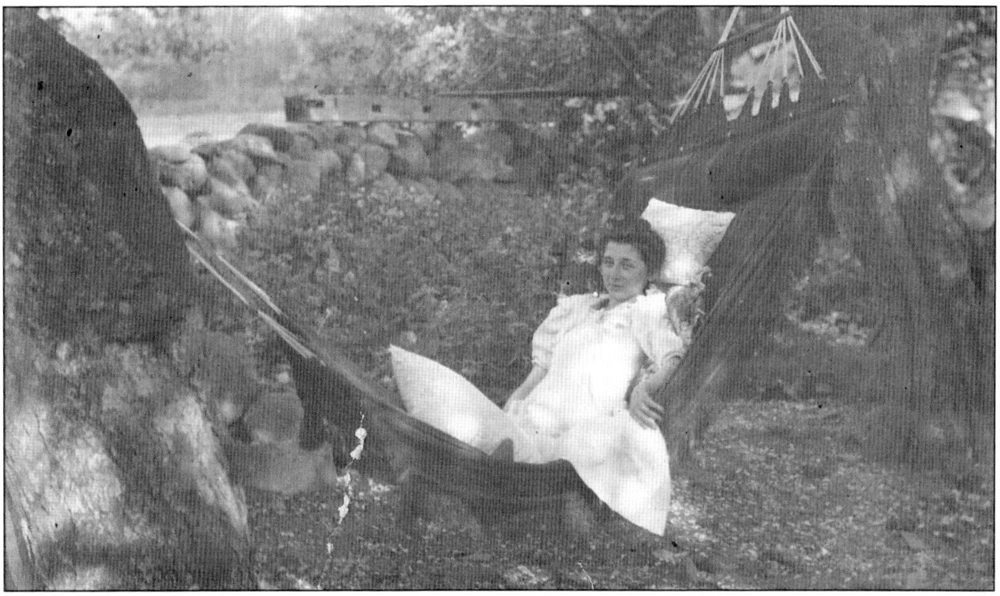

Bertha Gowen relaxing in the hammock on the Gowen Farm at 83 High Street. (HC.)

GYPSY FAIR.

If you are in search of a friend, or a jolly good time, do not fail to attend the Fair to be given in the

TOWN HALL, STRATHAM,

TUESDAY AND WEDNESDAY EVENINGS,

MAY 2d and 3d, 1893,

For the purpose of purchasing a Piano for the hall.

The committee have spared no pains to make this a grand success, having prepared a number of novelties that must be seen to be appreciated.

Come and see the Gypsy Bazar, Tuesday.
" " " " " Play, Wednesday.
" " " " " Costumes, Wednesday.
" " hear the Gypsy Music, } Both evenings.
" " eat a Gypsy Supper, }
" " have a Gypsy Dance, Wednesday.

Music by Hallinan's Orchestra.

ADMISSION 15 CENTS, SUPPER 20 CENTS.

There will be on sale at the various booths, Fancy Articles in great variety, both ornamental and useful. Also ICE CREAM, CAKE and CONFECTIONERY.

THE FISH POND,

Will please everybody.

Don't forget the 2d and 3d of May, 1893, Stratham Town Hall.

An early fund-raiser for the town hall. I wonder what a Gypsy supper is? (SHS.)

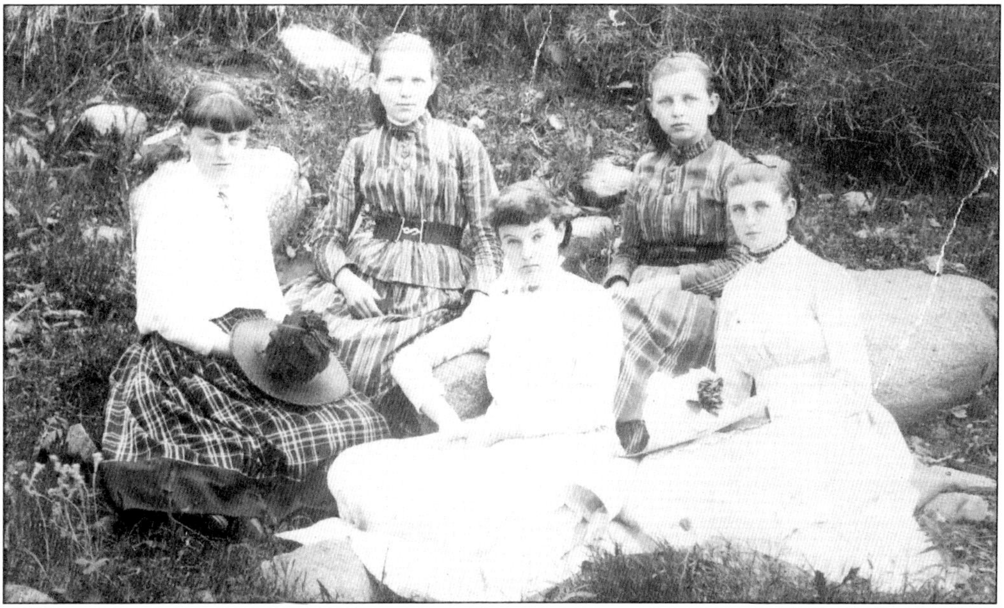

Late-19th-century young ladies Grace and Helen Gowen, Etta Chapman, Alice Jewell, and Nettie Thompson visiting. (SHS.)

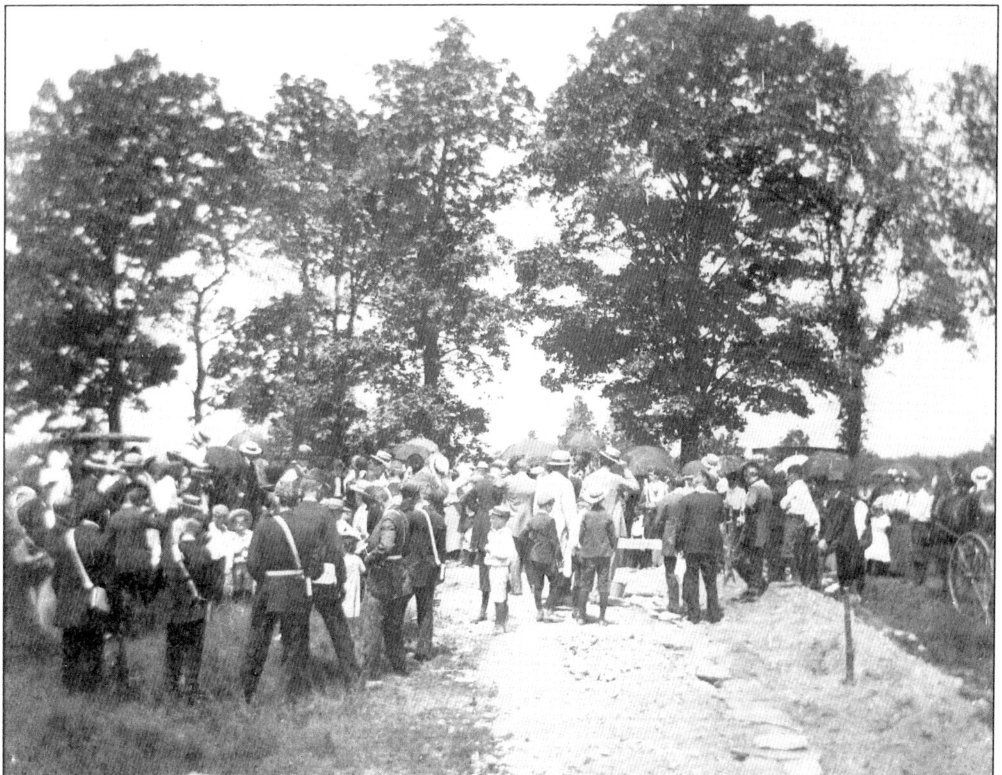

Uniformed men and parasoled ladies. They gather perhaps for a Memorial Day or Independence Day celebration, or even the 1916 town bicentennial. (BB.)

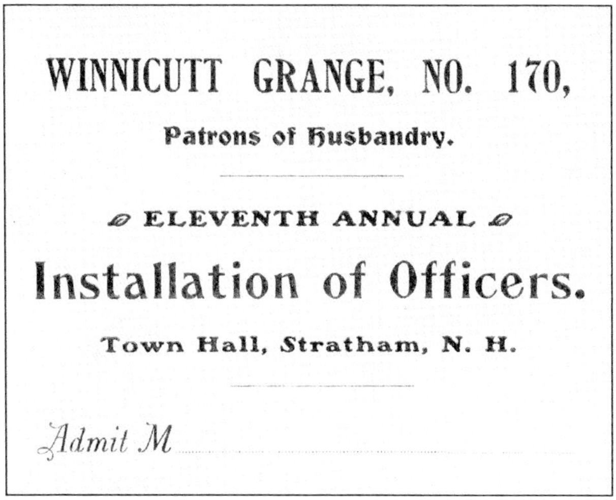

WINNICUTT GRANGE, NO. 170,

Patrons of Husbandry.

ELEVENTH ANNUAL

Installation of Officers.

Town Hall, Stratham, N. H.

Admit M

A ticket for the Grange installation of 1902. The Winniconic Grange #170 was organized in Stratham on February 7, 1892, and disbanded in November 1997. Founded to support and enhance agricultural efforts, the Grange was a vital part of the community and from 1919 supported numerous 4H youth groups including the Best Ever 4H Club for girls and Wee Little Farmers for boys. (SHS.)

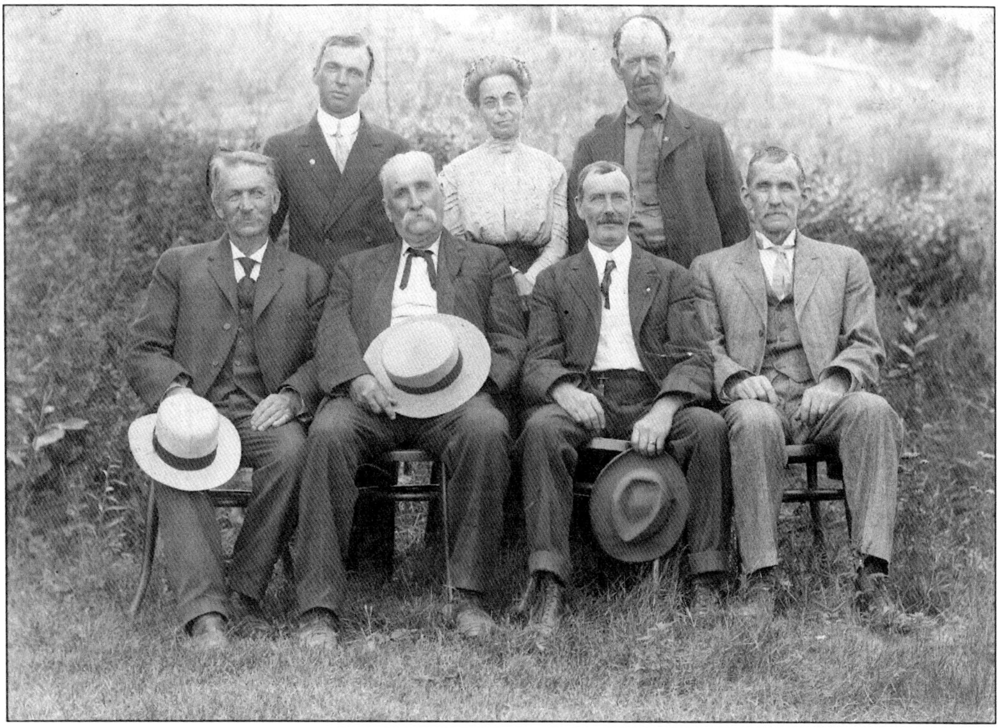

Stratham Old Home Day officers. Here they pose for newspaper pictures in August 1911. Listed from left to right are as follows: (front row) George E. Gowen, Isaac S. Wiggin, Fred N. Edmunds, and Albert C. Lane; (back row) Frank H. Pearson, Mrs. J.T. Smart, and Charles Grant. (SHS.)

James Scammon, a student a Brown University in Providence, Rhode Island, in 1868. He most likely attended Old Home Day in 1906, featured below. (SHS.)

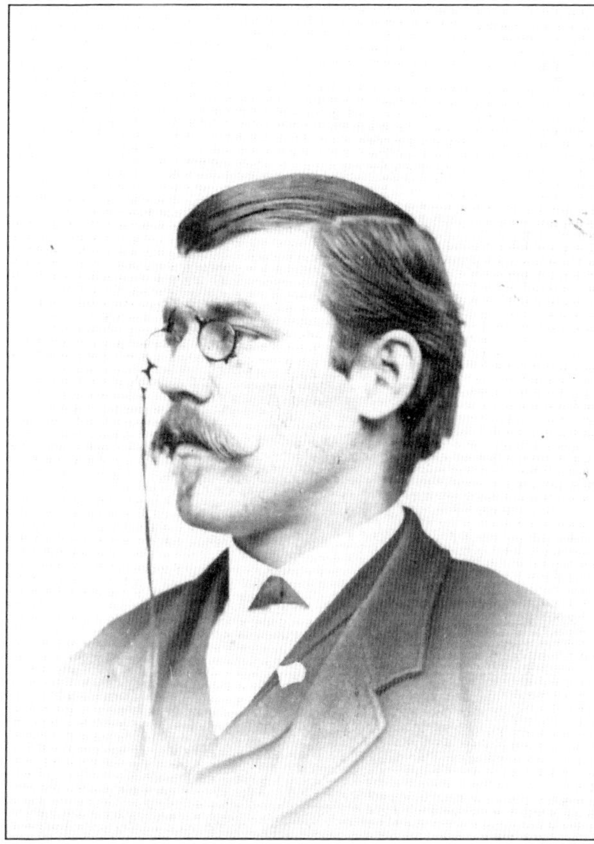

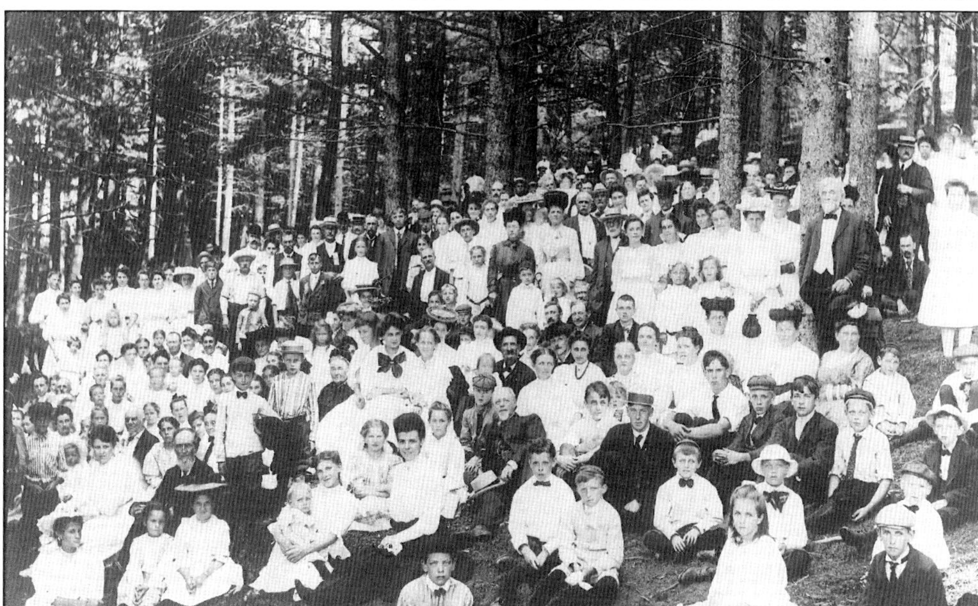

Old Home Day, August 1906. Celebrants pose on the hill at the park shortly after Stratham Hill Park was given to the town. (SHS.)

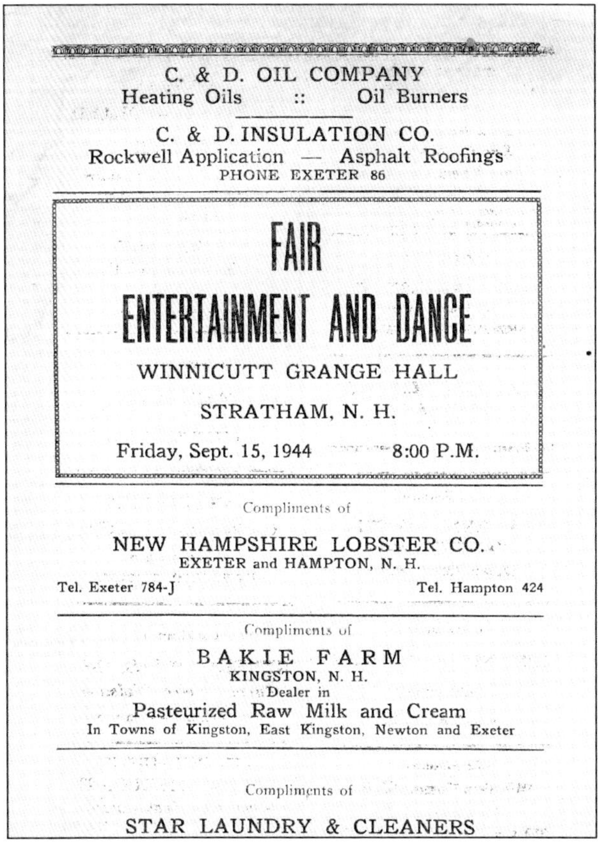

C. & D. OIL COMPANY
Heating Oils :: Oil Burners

C. & D. INSULATION CO.
Rockwell Application — Asphalt Roofings
PHONE EXETER 86

FAIR
ENTERTAINMENT AND DANCE
WINNICUTT GRANGE HALL
STRATHAM, N. H.
Friday, Sept. 15, 1944 8:00 P.M.

Compliments of
NEW HAMPSHIRE LOBSTER CO.
EXETER and HAMPTON, N. H.
Tel. Exeter 784-J Tel. Hampton 424

Compliments of
BAKIE FARM
KINGSTON, N. H.
Dealer in
Pasteurized Raw Milk and Cream
In Towns of Kingston, East Kingston, Newton and Exeter

Compliments of
STAR LAUNDRY & CLEANERS

A pamphlet for a Winnicutt Grange benefit in 1944. The pamphlet held advertisements from businesses in Exeter, Portsmouth, and Newburyport that supported the program. (SHS.)

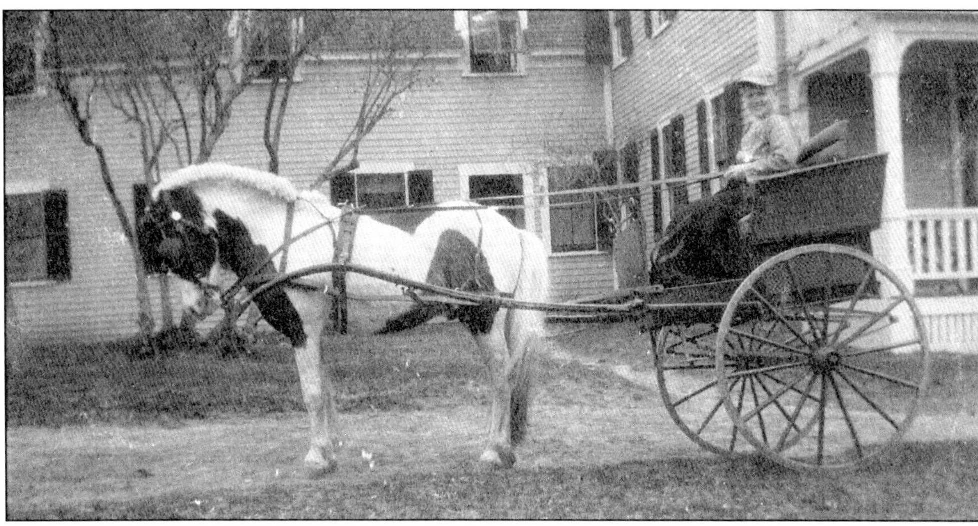

Mary Whitcomb in a carriage at the Riverside Stock Farm in 1915, when the farm was known for fine horses. At the site of the current Stuart Farm on College Lane, over the years the farm has been a major poultry and dairy farm. Dairy products from Stratham supplied the New Hampshire College Creamery in Durham as well as the Boston market. The dairy trucks started in Newington and came through Stratham on the way to Haverhill and further distribution, and like the mail, the dairy products went no matter what the weather. (SHS.)

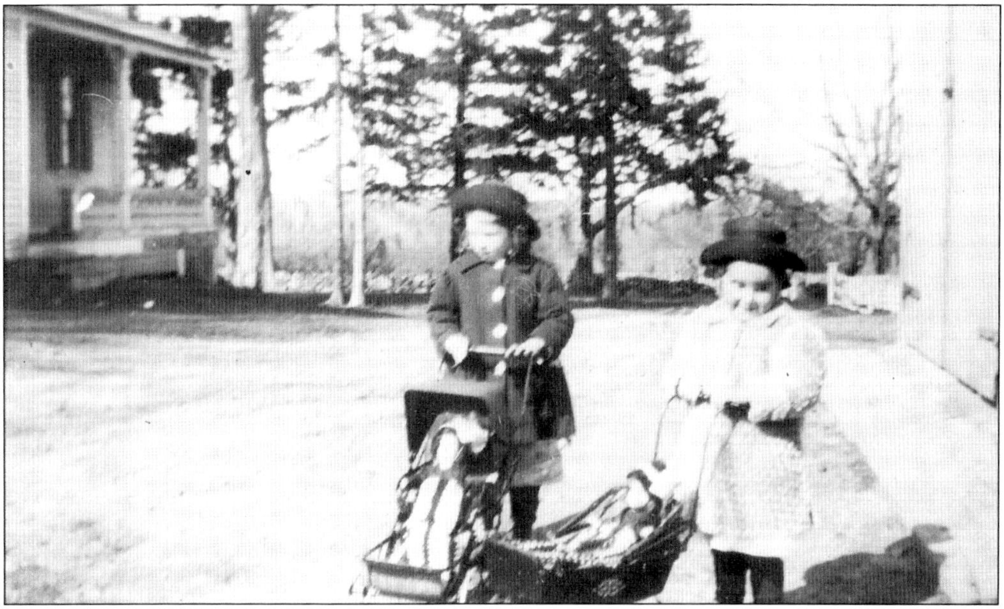

Mary and Jessia Chase and their dolls in the yard at the Chase Farm at 114 Bunker Hill Avenue, c. 1920. (HC.)

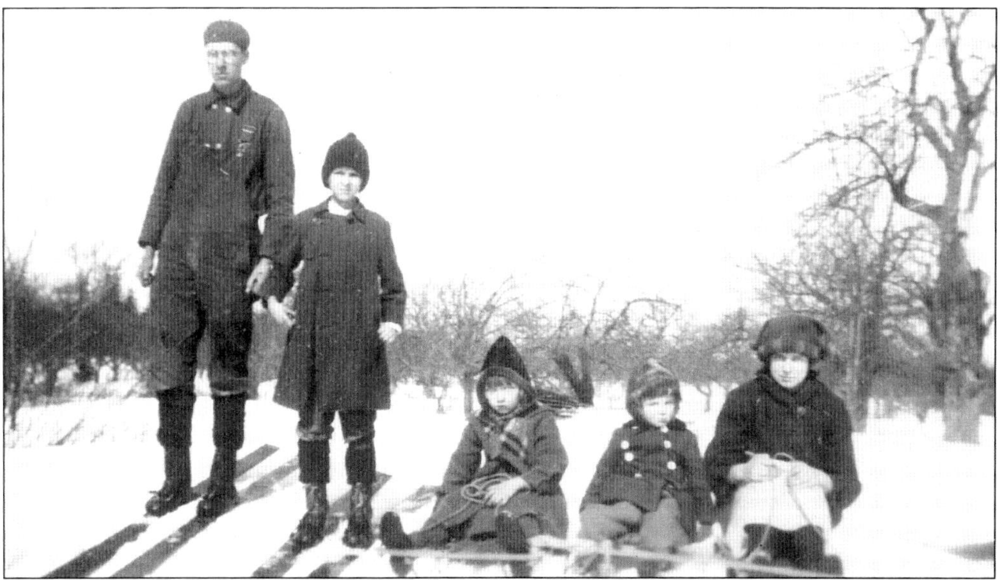

Paul, Harold, Florence, Helen, and Mary Chase. Here they are skiing and sledding at the Chase Farm, 114 Bunker Hill Avenue, in the 1920s. (HC.)

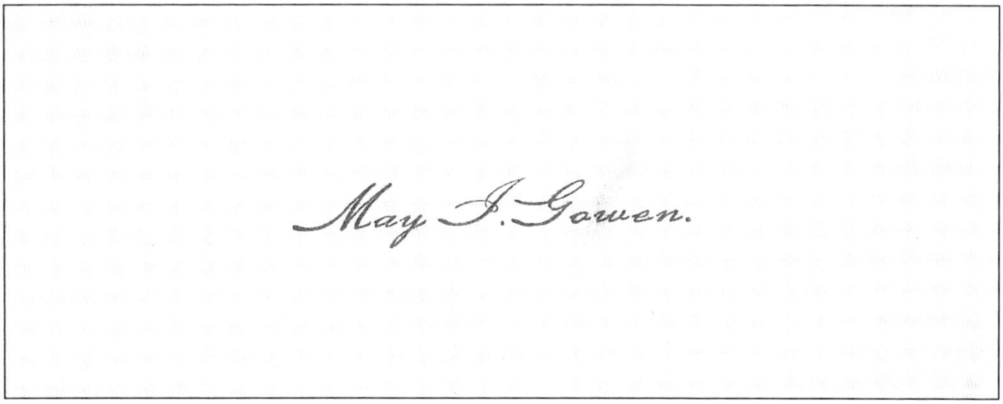

The gold-rimmed calling card of May Gowen from the early 20th century. Calling cards were left during visits to friends or family, whether one saw the visitee or not. (HC.)

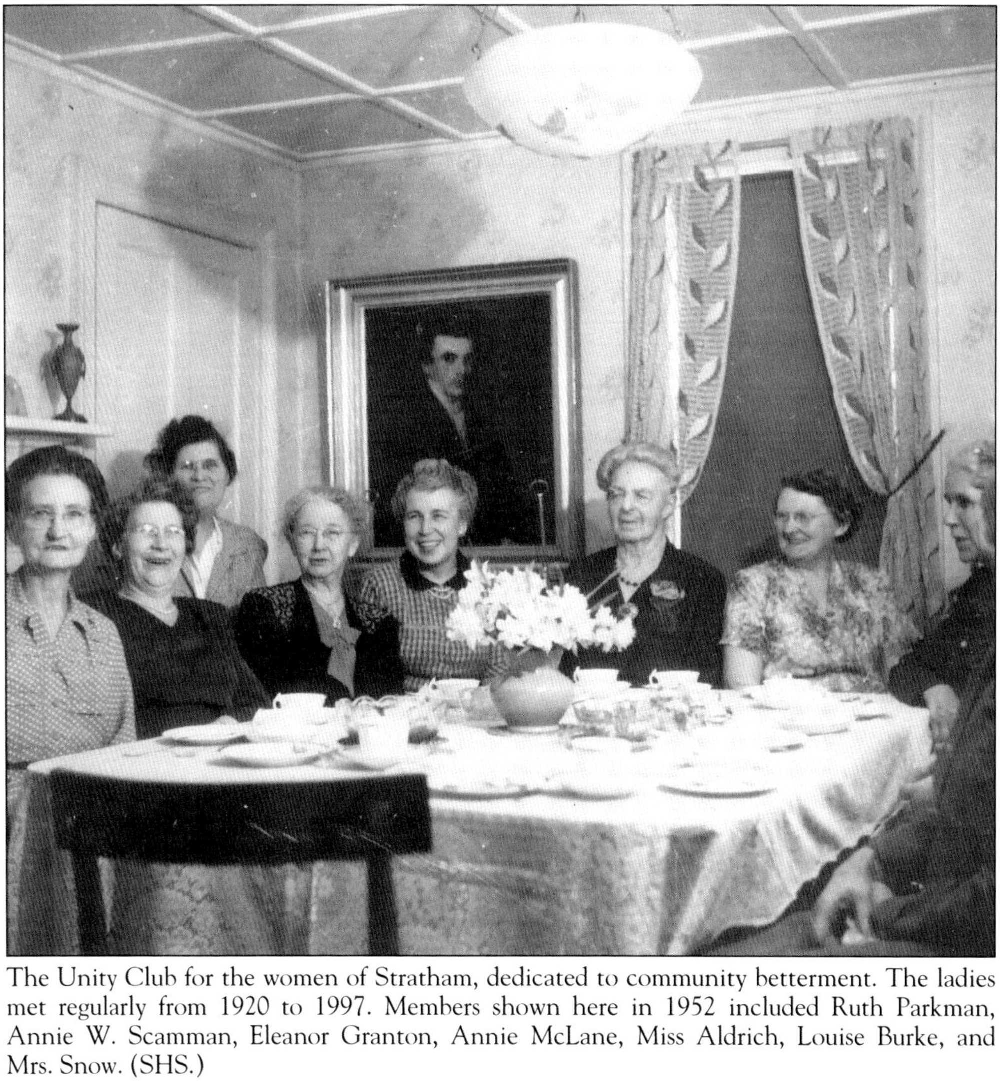
The Unity Club for the women of Stratham, dedicated to community betterment. The ladies met regularly from 1920 to 1997. Members shown here in 1952 included Ruth Parkman, Annie W. Scamman, Eleanor Granton, Annie McLane, Miss Aldrich, Louise Burke, and Mrs. Snow. (SHS.)

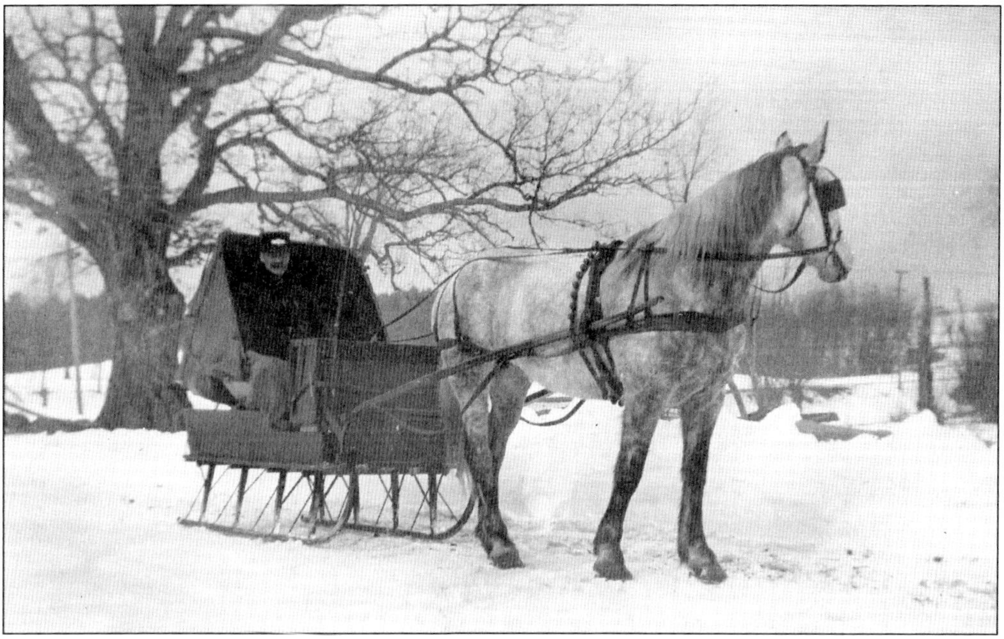

Out for a ride. A dapple-gray horse drawing a sleigh on Heights Road near Portsmouth Avenue, the intersection known as Parkman's Corner after the the Parkman family, longtime area residents. (SHS.)

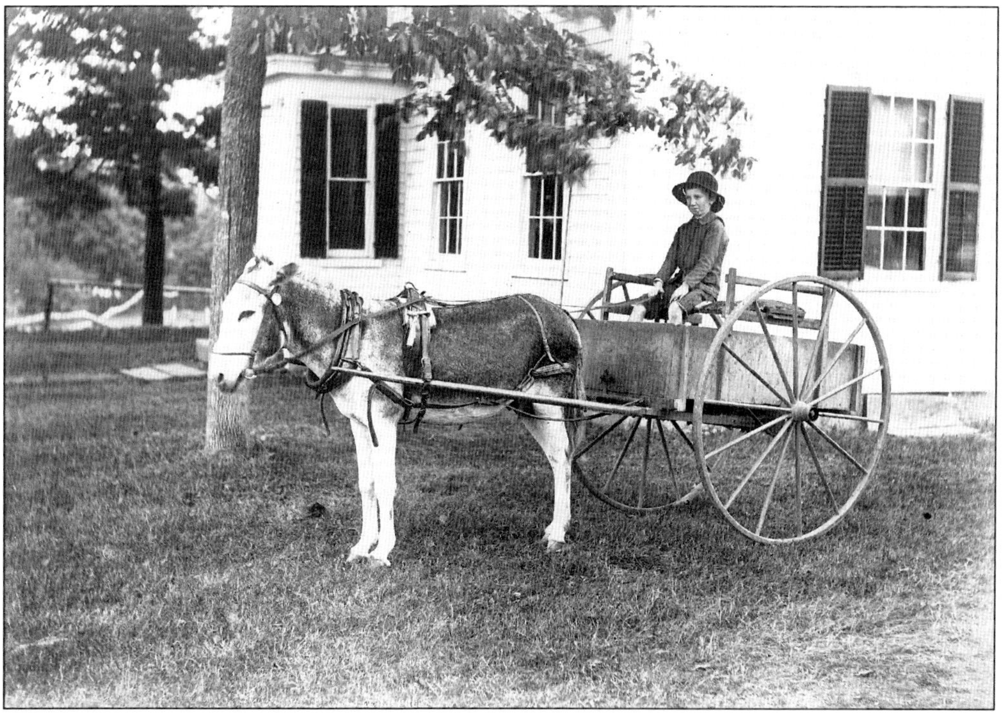

Arthur Jewell on a cart with a donkey on Winnicutt Road. (SHS.)

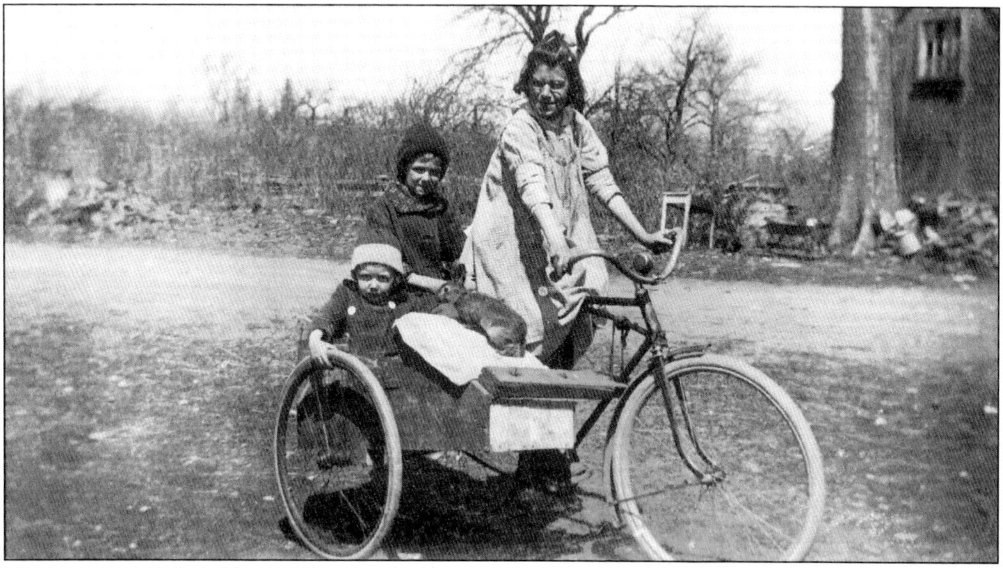

Florence and Helen Chase. The couple along with a friend ride a modified bicycle at the Chase Farm, 114 Bunker Hill Road, in the 1920s. (HC.)

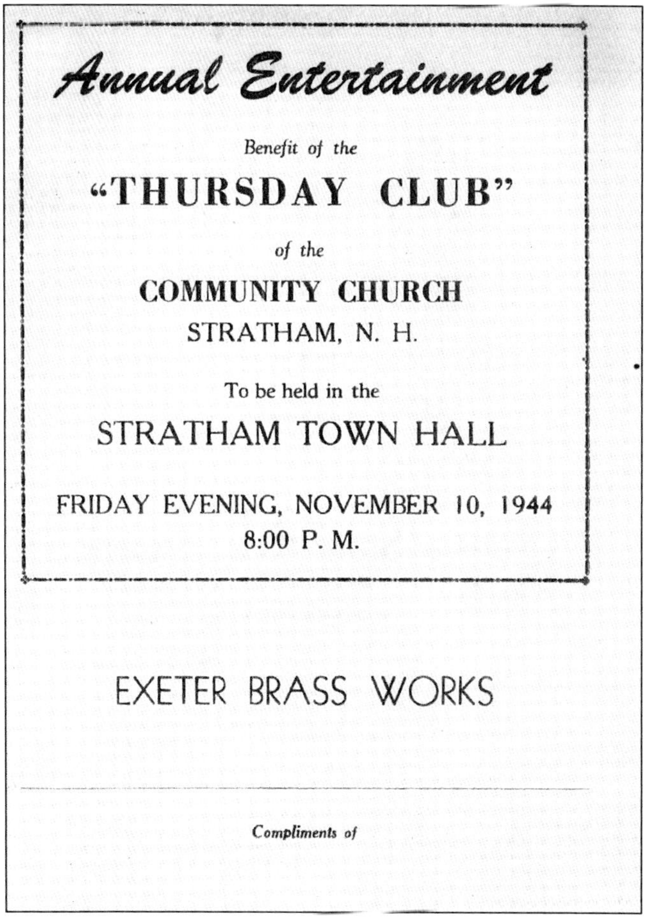

Annual Entertainment

Benefit of the

"THURSDAY CLUB"

of the

COMMUNITY CHURCH

STRATHAM, N. H.

To be held in the

STRATHAM TOWN HALL

FRIDAY EVENING, NOVEMBER 10, 1944

8:00 P. M.

EXETER BRASS WORKS

Compliments of

A flyer for a 1944 Thursday Club activity to benefit the Community church. The Thursday Club was a ladies club at the church; the program was sponsored by businesses throughout the area. (SHS.)

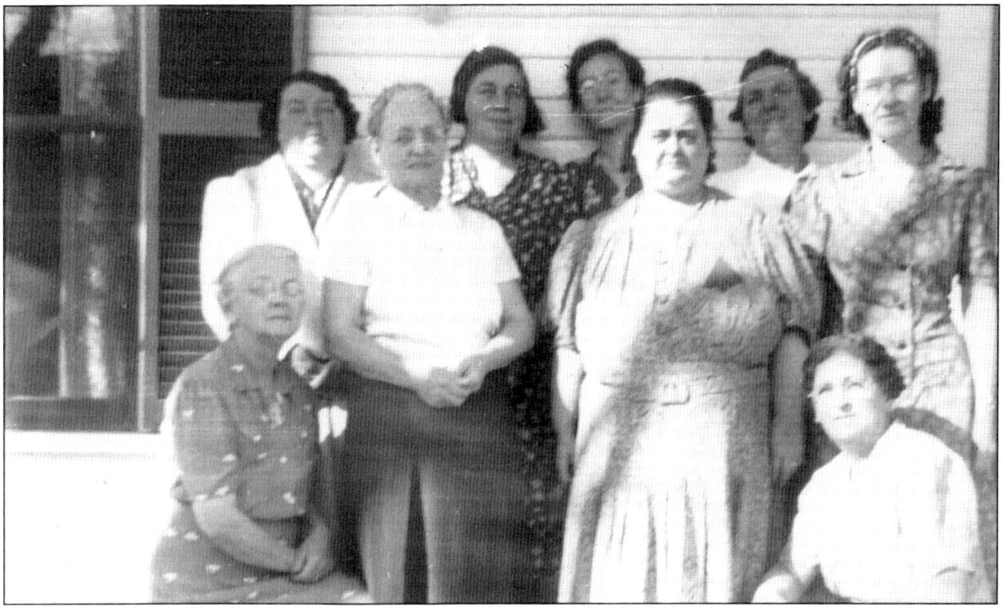

The Ladies Circle at the Baptist church in the 1930s or '40s. Listed from left to right are as follows: (front) Grace Pearson, Elizabeth Baker, Gladys Houghton, and Nellie Barker; (back row) Lillian Beals, Bertha Parks, Gladys Chapman, and Mary Gowen. (SHS.)

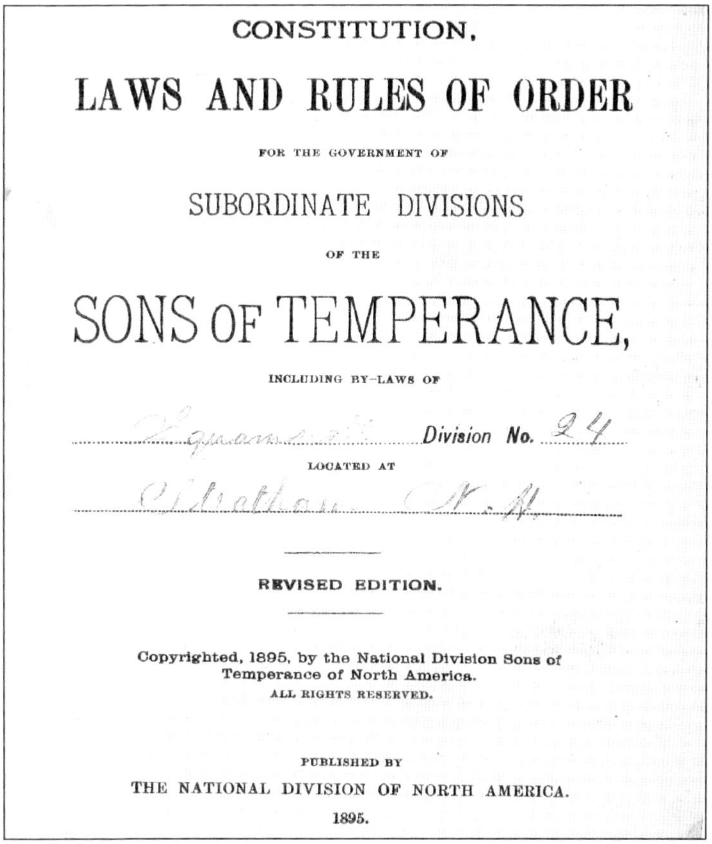

CONSTITUTION,

LAWS AND RULES OF ORDER

FOR THE GOVERNMENT OF

SUBORDINATE DIVISIONS

OF THE

SONS OF TEMPERANCE,

INCLUDING BY-LAWS OF

Squamscott Division No. 24

LOCATED AT

Stratham N.H.

REVISED EDITION.

Copyrighted, 1895, by the National Division Sons of Temperance of North America.
ALL RIGHTS RESERVED.

PUBLISHED BY
THE NATIONAL DIVISION OF NORTH AMERICA.
1895.

The front of the rule book for the local Sons of Temperance Chapter, c. 1895. Meetings were held on Friday evenings at eight o'clock and members were at least 14 years old and pledged "not to make, buy, sell or use, as a beverage, any spirituous or malt liquors, wine or cider." Initiation fees were $1 for males and 50¢ for females with quarterly dues of 25¢ for males and 15¢ for females. (SHS.)

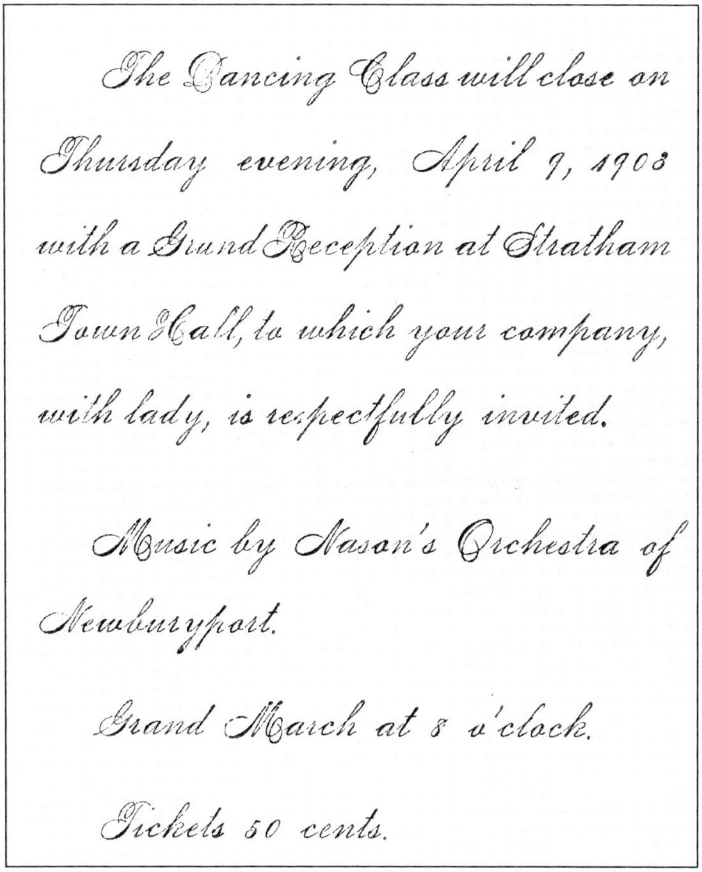

The Dancing Class will close on Thursday evening, April 9, 1908 with a Grand Reception at Stratham Town Hall, to which your company, with lady, is respectfully invited.

Music by Nason's Orchestra of Newburyport.

Grand March at 8 o'clock.

Tickets 50 cents.

Town festivities. In 1908, the dancing class invited dancers and spectators to a promenade at the town hall. (SHS.)

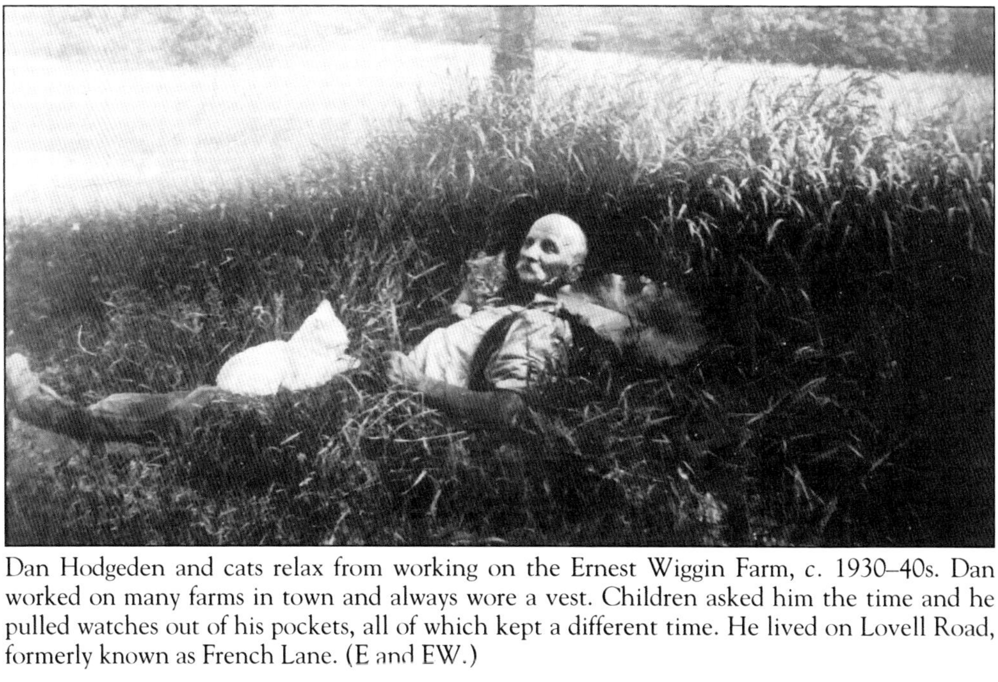

Dan Hodgeden and cats relax from working on the Ernest Wiggin Farm, c. 1930–40s. Dan worked on many farms in town and always wore a vest. Children asked him the time and he pulled watches out of his pockets, all of which kept a different time. He lived on Lovell Road, formerly known as French Lane. (E and EW.)

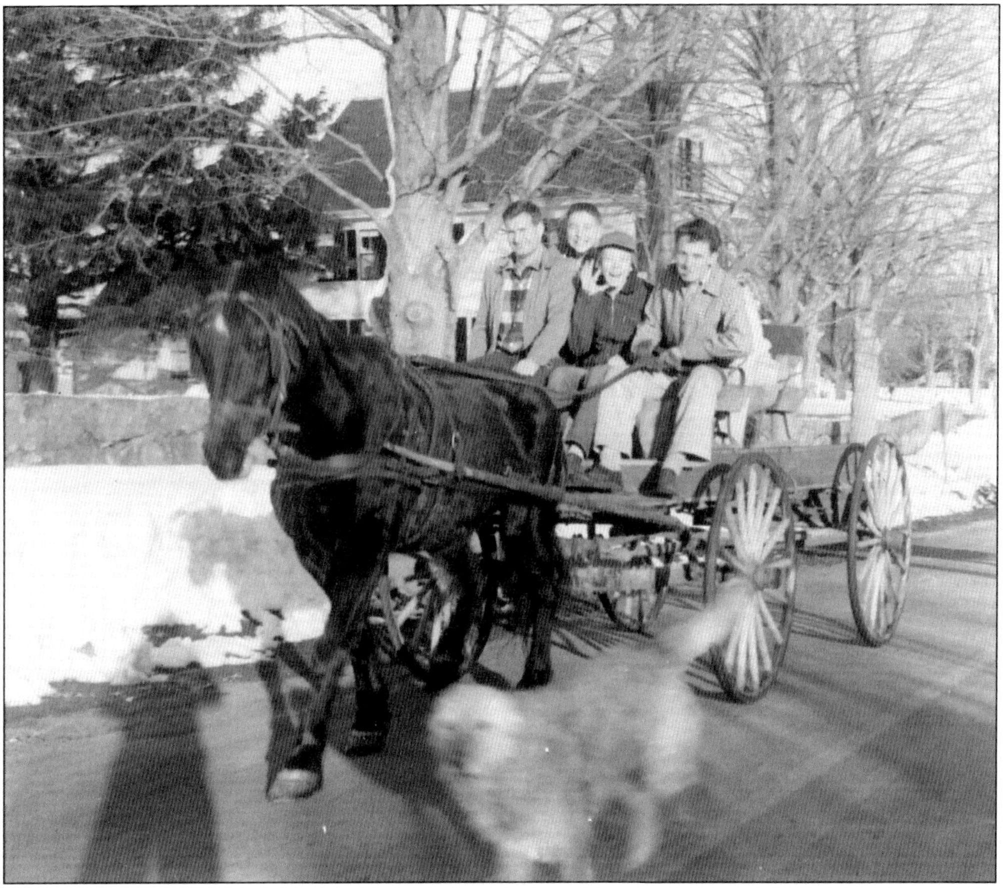

Jim and Charles Peabody Jr. and friends in a carriage on Portsmouth Avenue in the 1940s. Their horse's name was Beauty. (C and KP.)

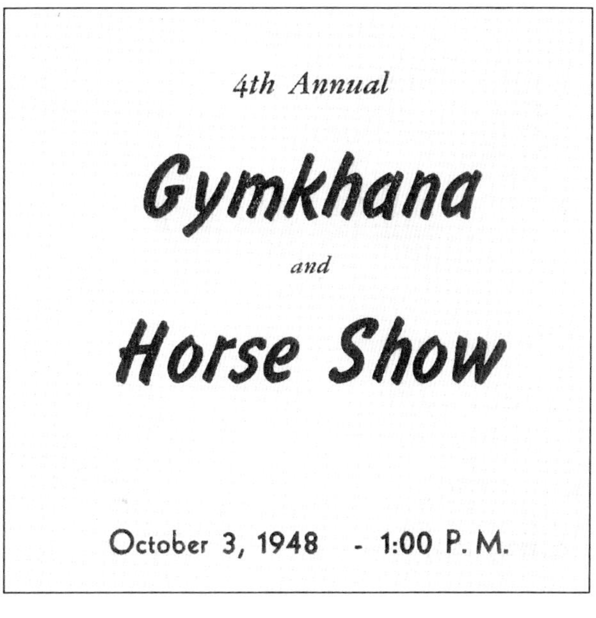

4th Annual

Gymkhana

and

Horse Show

October 3, 1948 - 1:00 P. M.

A pamphlet from a 1948 Parent Teacher Association fund-raiser. This horse show was for many years an annual event at the Goodrich Farm on Heights Road. (SHS.)

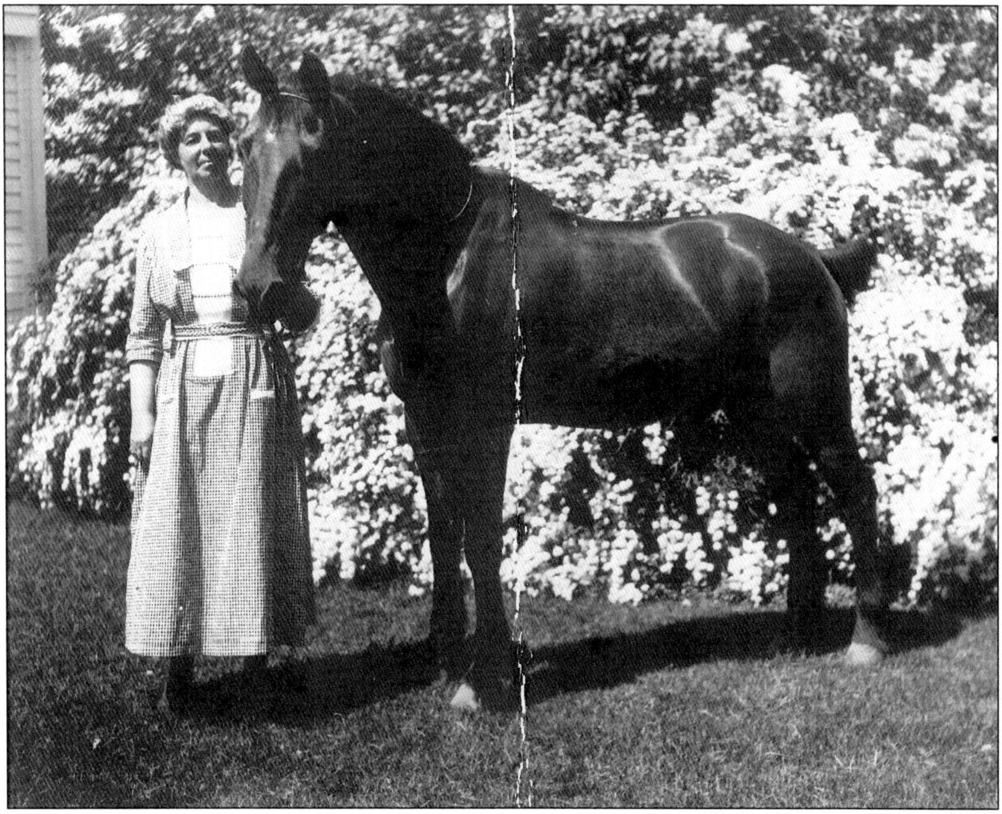

A formal portrait of Annie Wiggin Scammon and a bob-tailed horse. Married to distinguished state senate president Richard Scammon (1859–1917), Annie was relatively young when widowed and was active in town affairs for decades. The daughter of benefactor George Wiggin, she served as Wiggin Memorial Library trustee from 1907 to 1911 and 1916 to 1961. (SHS.)

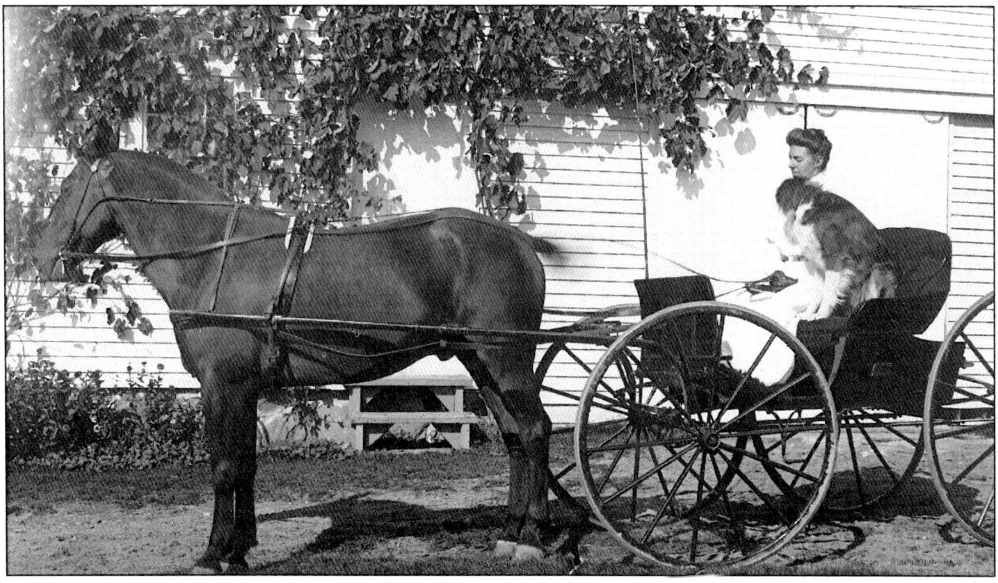

Annie Scamman and a canine friend in a buggy pulled by a bob-tailed horse. (SHS.)

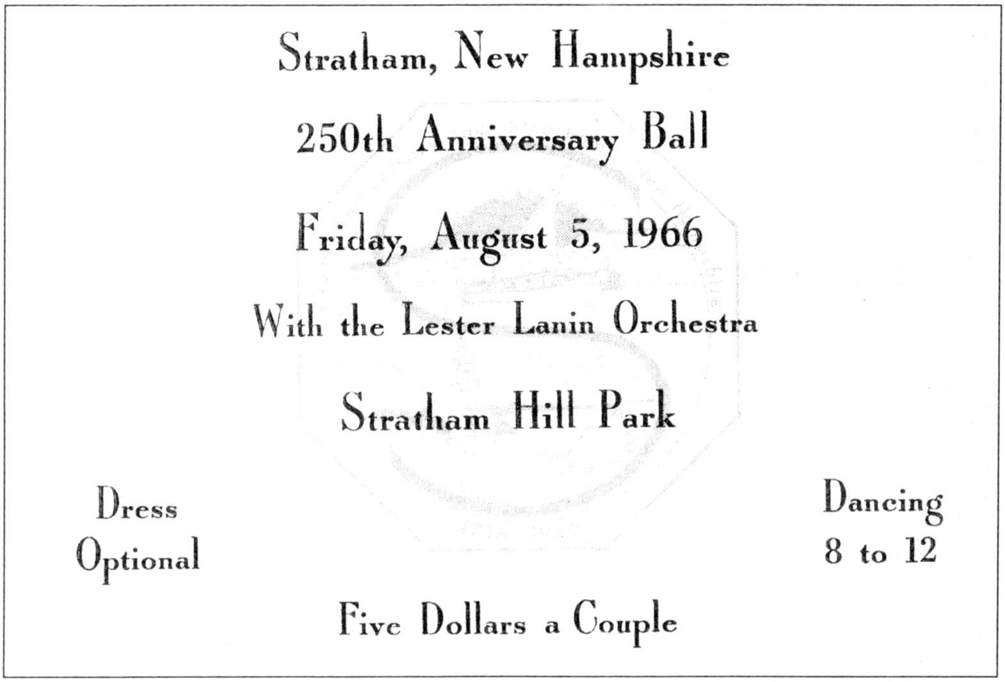

Stratham, New Hampshire

250th Anniversary Ball

Friday, August 5, 1966

With the Lester Lanin Orchestra

Stratham Hill Park

Dress Optional

Dancing 8 to 12

Five Dollars a Couple

An invitation to the largest dance ever held under canvas in New Hampshire, to that time. A highlight of the 250th celebration, over a thousand people attended. Gov. John W. King crowned Miss Sheila Scott of North Hampton queen of the celebration. Another celebratory event was the beard-growing contest—the winners were Bob Goodrich, Leland Goodrich, Carl Rogalski, Bob Haberland, and Charlie Nelson. (SHS.)

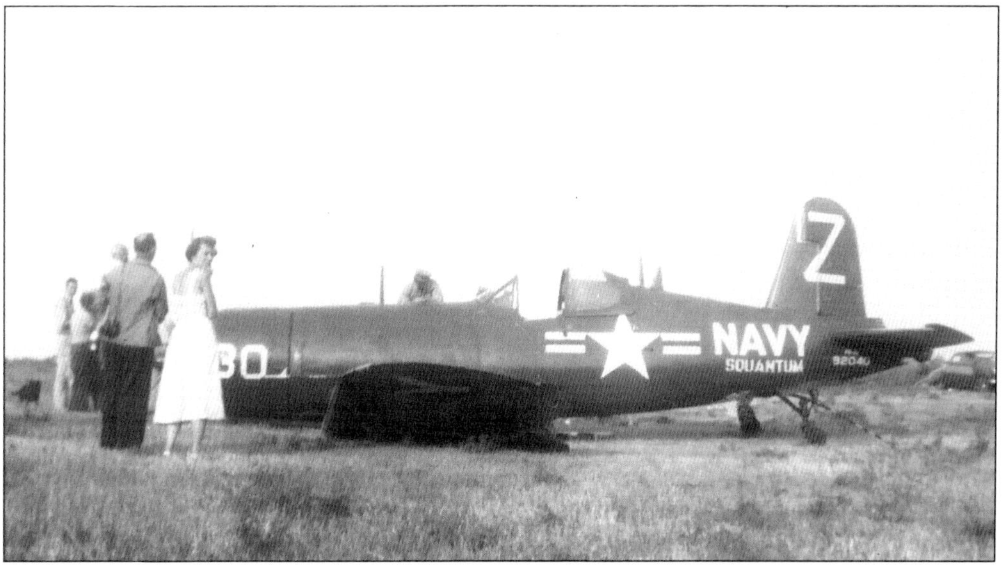

Just drop-by. In the 1950s Union Road residents were surprised to find a F4U Corsair from Squantum Naval Air Station in Massachusetts land on the Theophilus Smith Farm, near the site of Smith Farm Road. Betty Batchelder was among the interested viewers. During World War II a bomber had landed on the Whittaker Farm on High Street, near the current Whittaker Place. (E and EW.)

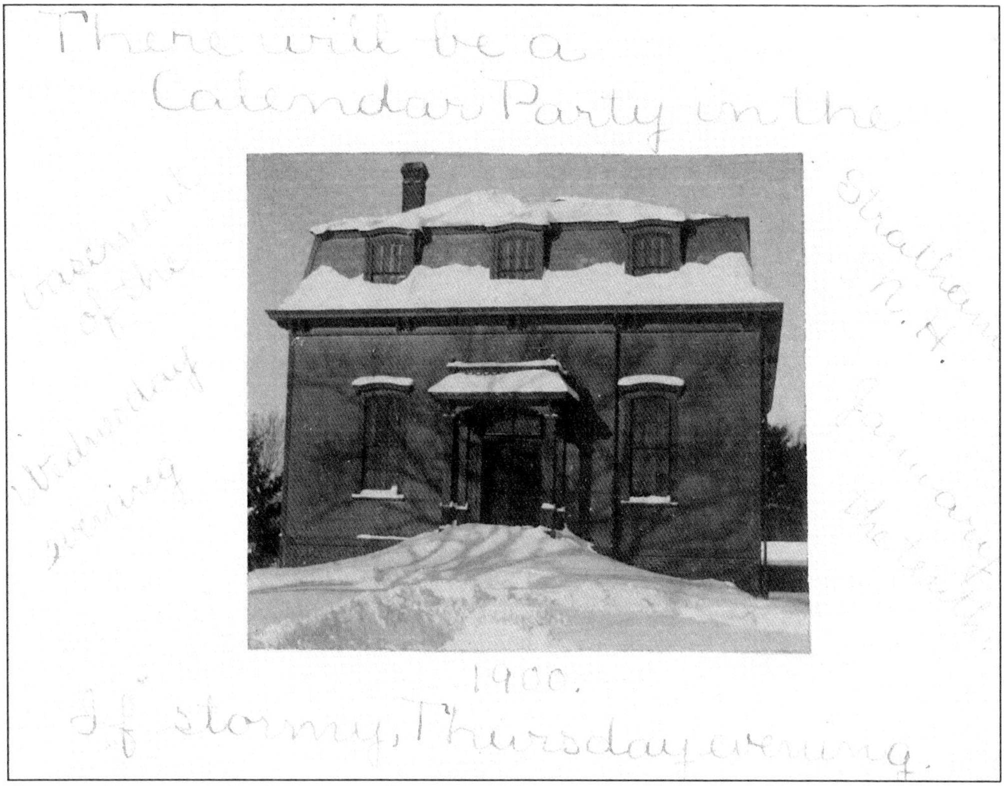

An invitation to a calendar party at the town hall in January 1900. In addition to housing town offices and the police department, the auditorium was used for town meetings, dances, parties, plays, recitals, and the annual auction to raise funds for the volunteer fire department. (SHS.)

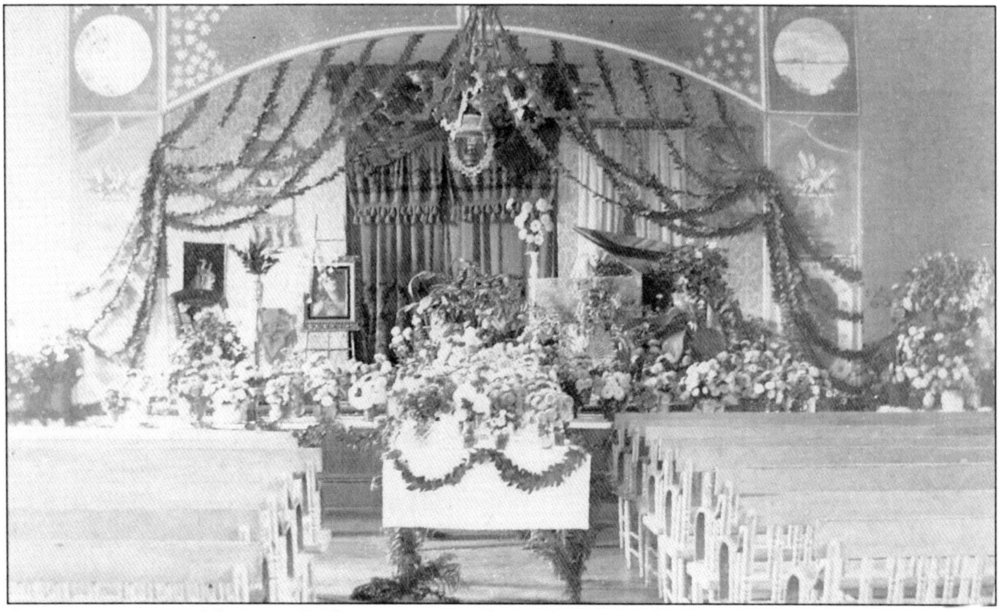

An interior view of the town hall c. 1900. It is shown here clearly decorated for a grand occasion, possibly a play, party, or Grange fair. (SHS.)

A playbill from the early 20th century. Generations of residents participated in community theatricals. (SHS.)

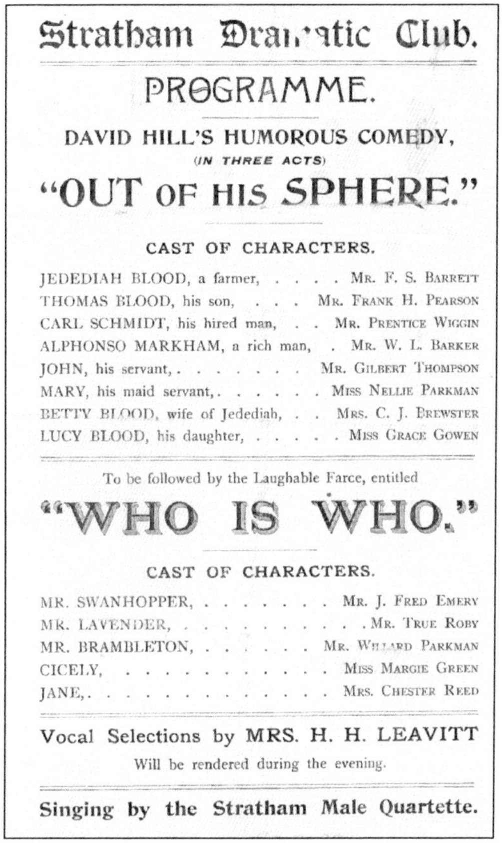

Stratham Dramatic Club.

PROGRAMME.

DAVID HILL'S HUMOROUS COMEDY,

(IN THREE ACTS)

"OUT OF HIS SPHERE."

CAST OF CHARACTERS.

JEDEDIAH BLOOD, a farmer, ... Mr. F. S. Barrett
THOMAS BLOOD, his son, . . . Mr. Frank H. Pearson
CARL SCHMIDT, his hired man, . . Mr. Prentice Wiggin
ALPHONSO MARKHAM, a rich man, . Mr. W. L. Barker
JOHN, his servant, ... Mr. Gilbert Thompson
MARY, his maid servant, ... Miss Nellie Parkman
BETTY BLOOD, wife of Jedediah, . . Mrs. C. J. Brewster
LUCY BLOOD, his daughter, ... Miss Grace Gowen

To be followed by the Laughable Farce, entitled

"WHO IS WHO."

CAST OF CHARACTERS.

MR. SWANHOPPER, ... Mr. J. Fred Emery
MR. LAVENDER, ... Mr. True Roby
MR. BRAMBLETON, ... Mr. Willard Parkman
CICELY, ... Miss Margie Green
JANE, ... Mrs. Chester Reed

Vocal Selections by MRS. H. H. LEAVITT

Will be rendered during the evening.

Singing by the Stratham Male Quartette.

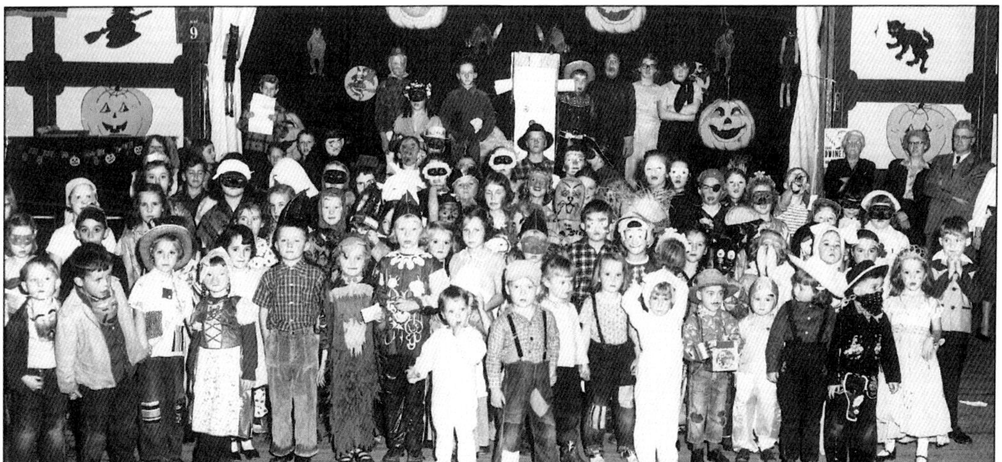

Halloween partygoers. The postwar baby boom hit Stratham and in the 1950s the Unity Club sponsored Halloween parties in the town hall. All the children received a grab bag with candy and apples. Among the costumed celebrants are Lucy Hutton, Martha Peabody, Charles Scamman, Caroline Saltonstall, Kent Saltonstall, Dottie French, Charles Peabody Jr., Ruth Peabody, Marlene Scamman, Laura Barker, William S. Berry, Gertrude Berry, Kathy Berry, Russell Stevens, Lester Carbonneau, Donna Goodrich, and Leslie Barker. Lauren Dixwill won the silver dollar prize with her bird costume. (LC.)

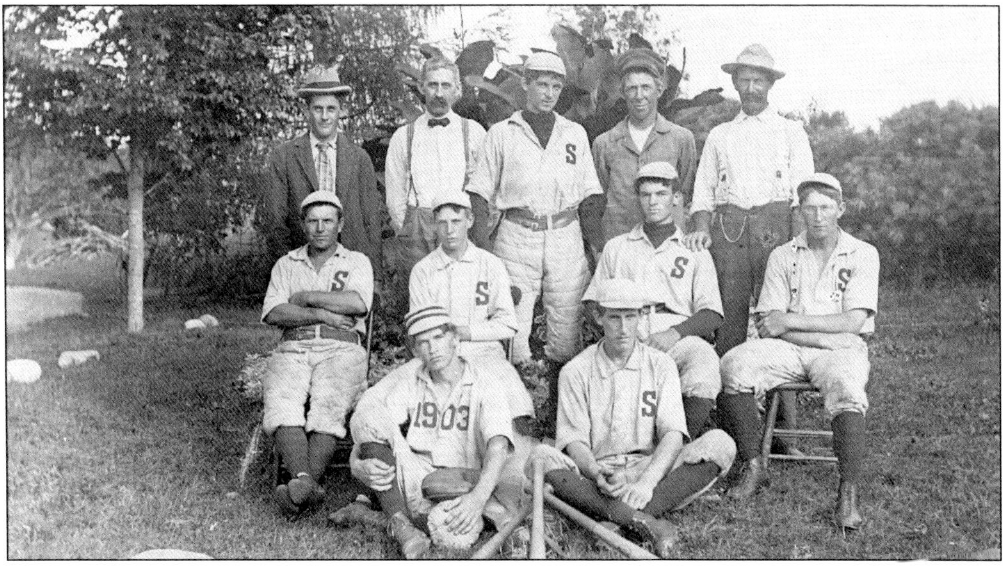

The Stratham men's baseball team in 1903. Listed from left to right are as follows: (front row) Ralph Gowen and Ralph Barker; (second row) George Jewell, Jimmy Nixon, and ? Batchelder; (back row) Ridgely Marsh, Charles Gear, Clarence Gowen, Harry Smith, and Charles Grant. (SHS.)

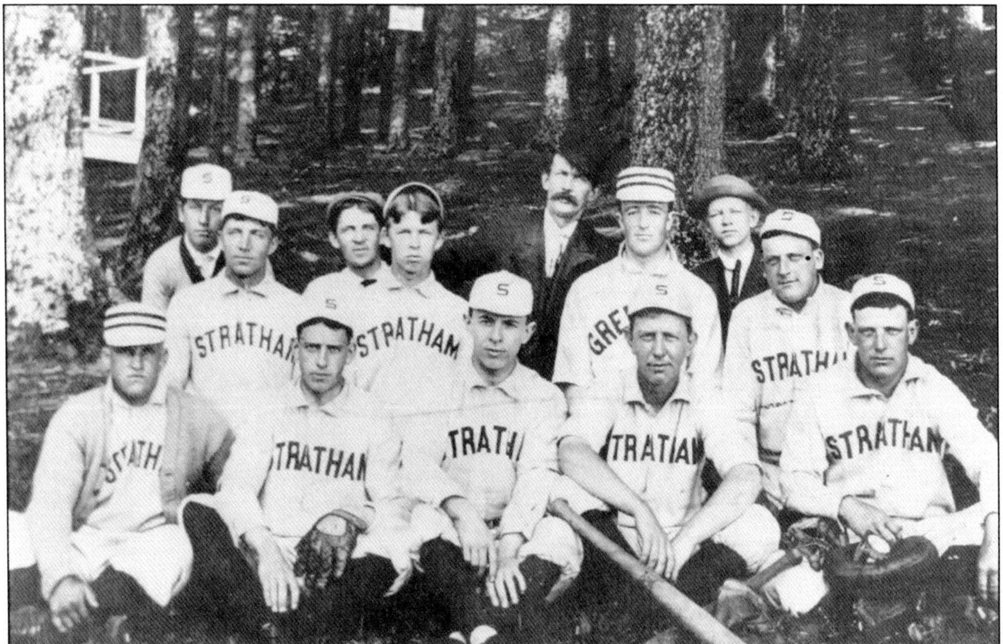

The famous 1908 Stratham baseball team. In 1916 they played the current team in a bicentennial exposition. Listed from left to right are as follows: (first row) Eddie Brackett from Greenland, A. Simpson from Newfields, Earle Stockbridge, Eddie Tuttle, and catcher George Jewell; (second row) R.H. Gowen, B.F. Gowen, A.R. Hatch from Greenland, and Percy Jewell; (third row) L. Brewster, umpire C.E. Gowen, manager Burt Burbank, and scorekeeper P.L. Gowen. (SHS.)

Dick Wiggin, Jim Scamman, and Ernie Wiggin in their Stratham baseball uniforms in the late 1940s. For decades Stratham fielded a men's baseball team in the Men's Great Bay League and played against Exeter, Newmarket, Hampton, etc. After 1961 they played softball. (E and EW.)

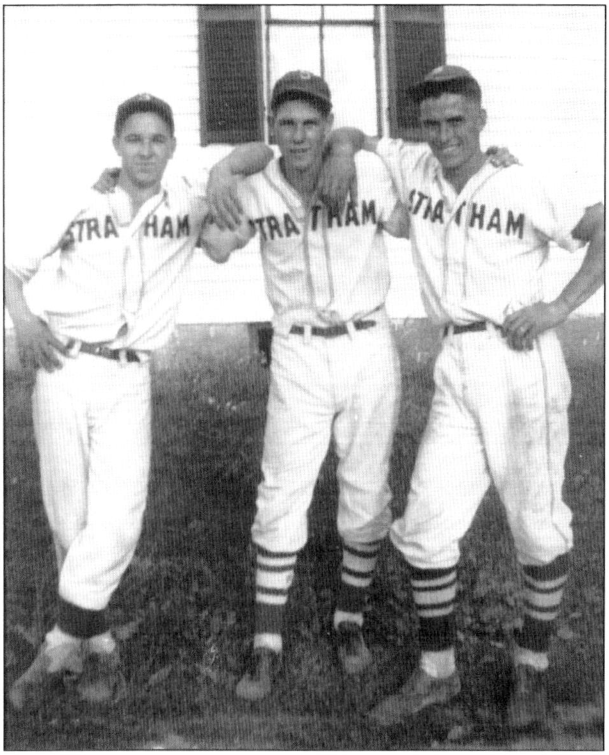

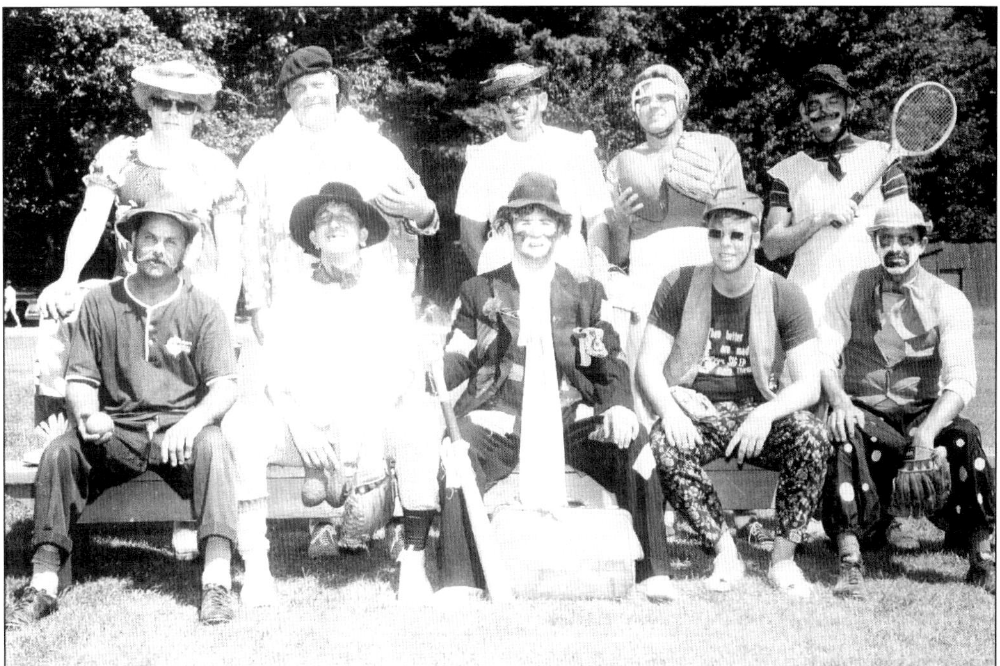

The Stratham men's baseball team. Here they are dressed theatrically in the early 1960s, probably for a game against Newmarket. Players included are Jim Scamman, Les Scamman, and Carl Rogalski. (SHS.)

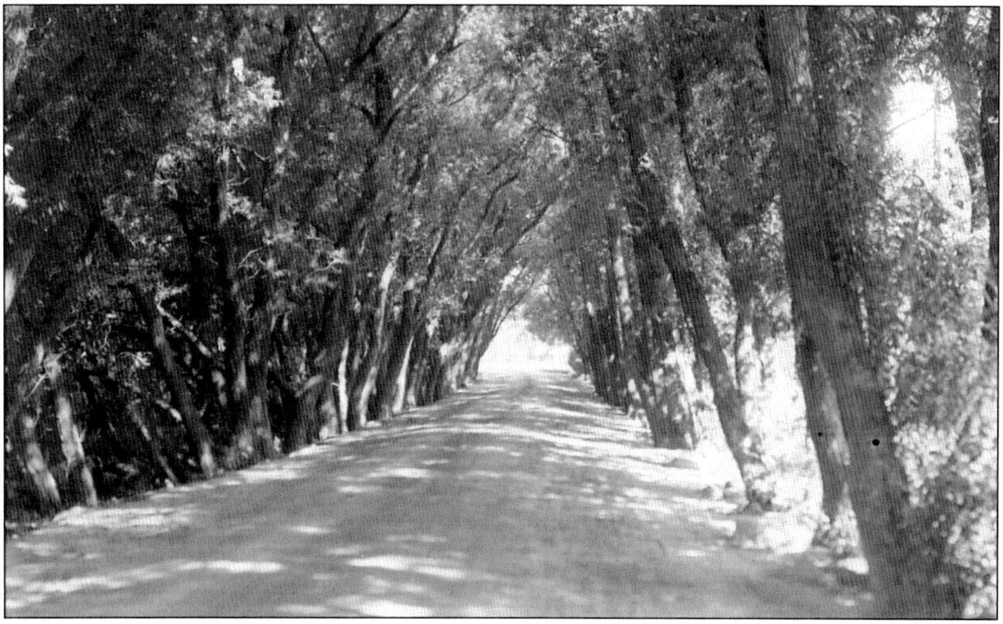

Maple, oak, elm, and black cherry trees along Union Road. They are located near the site of the current transfer station, before it was widened and paved. Horseback riding here was like riding through a tunnel. (SHS.)

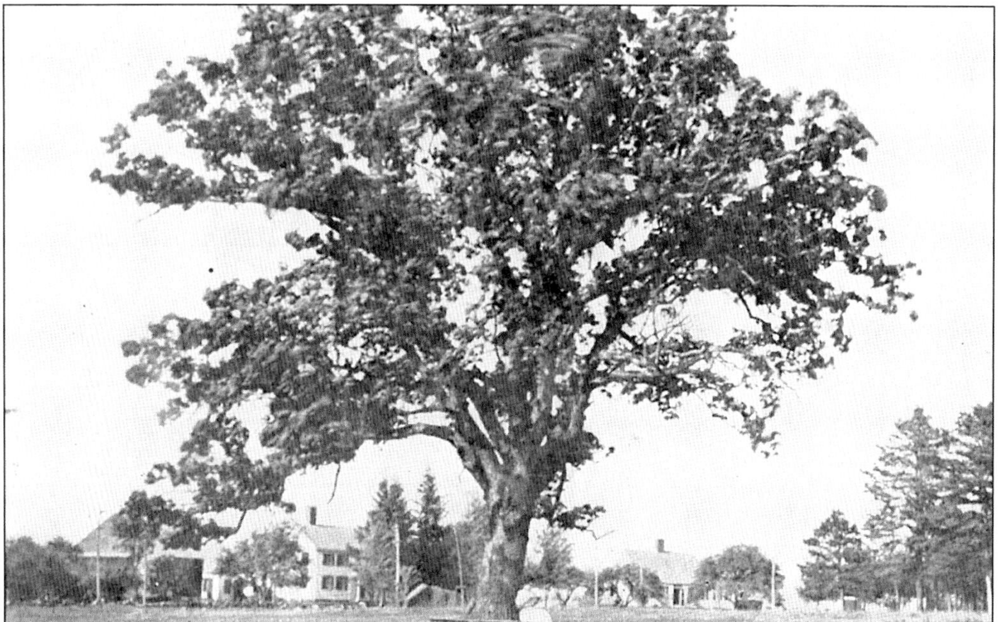

A postcard of the Century Oak at Stratham Hill Park *c.* 1910. The oak was where the parking lot is now. Ernest Wiggin's farm at #271 is on the left across Portsmouth Avenue. (SHS.)

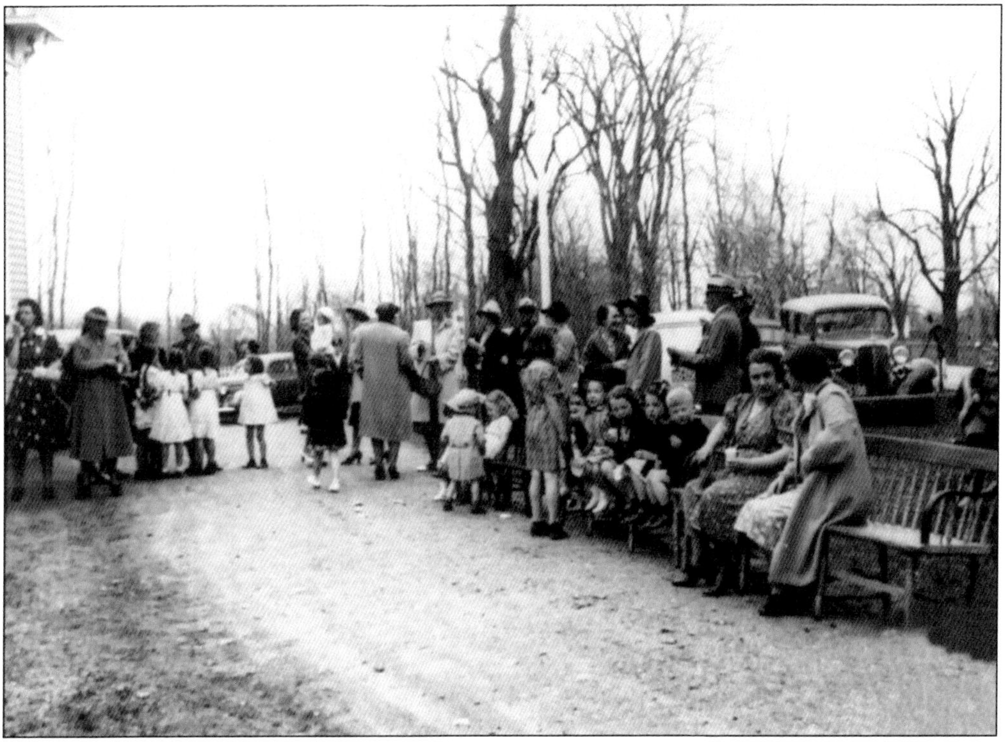

Students and parents outside the Stratham Hill School in May 1940. (SHS.)

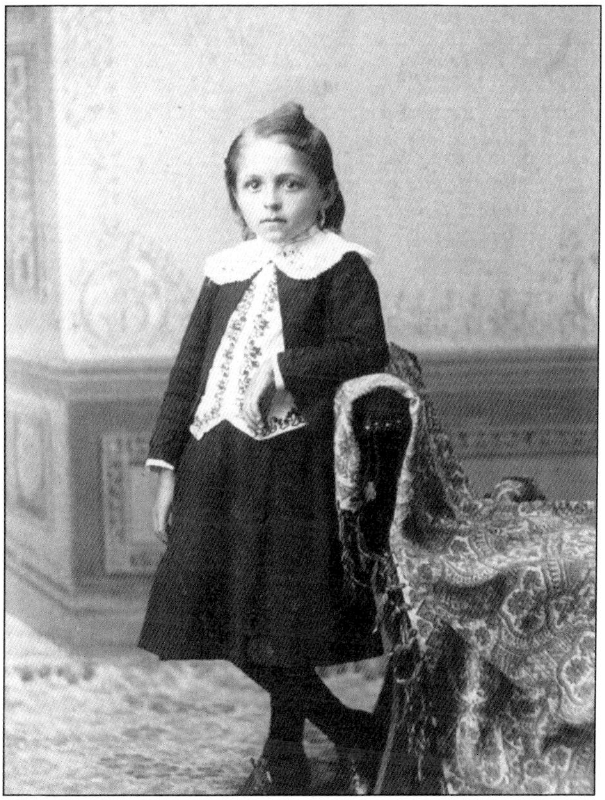

Ralph D. Parkman, about six years old, in the early 20th century. Parkman and his sister Ruth lived at the corner of Portsmouth Avenue and Plains Road, now known as Stratham Heights Road (the corner was known as Parkman's Corner). Thompsons Brook, the site of an early brickyard, runs nearby. He had a egg farm and was the town tax collector for many years. (SHS.)

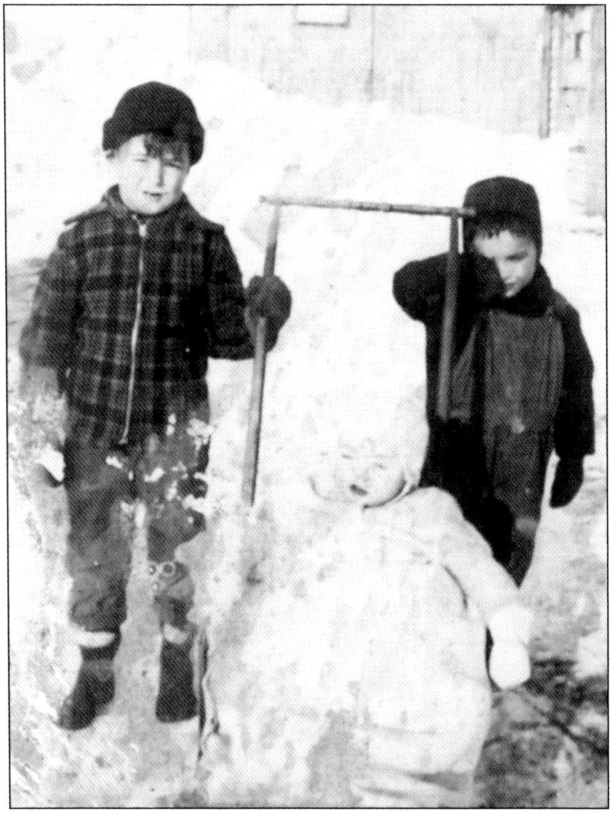

Francis and Dick Wiggin with Jody in the sled at Henry Jewell's farm at 273 Portsmouth Avenue, c. 1930. (E and EW.)

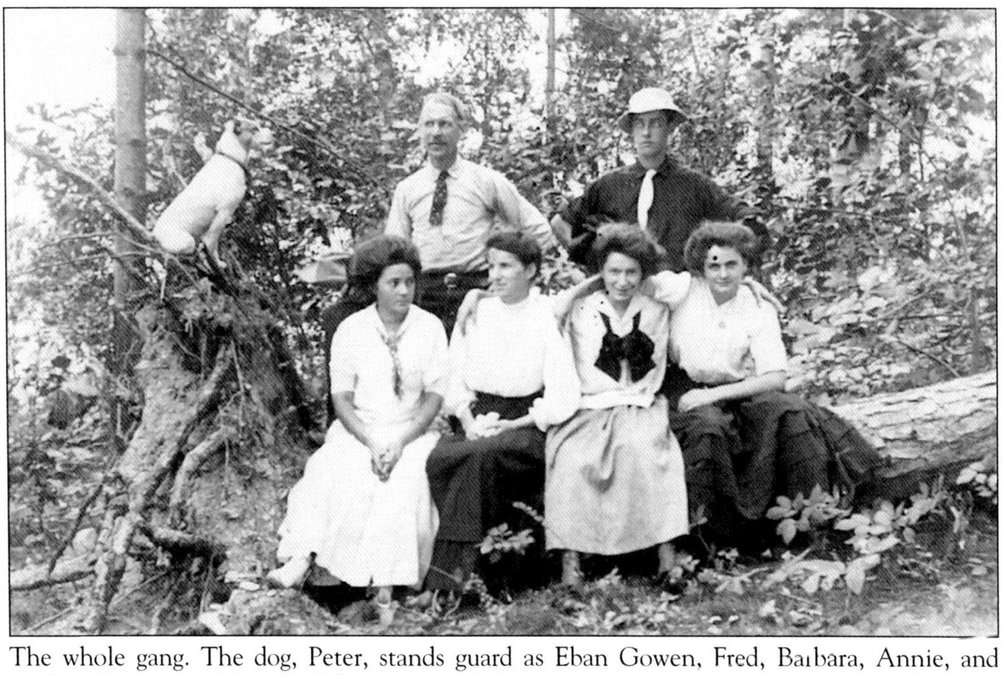

The whole gang. The dog, Peter, stands guard as Eban Gowen, Fred, Barbara, Annie, and Pauline Severance, Dorothy Whitcomb, and Connie Emerson, a summer visitor to the Elms from Boston, enjoy a holiday, c. 1916. (SHS.)

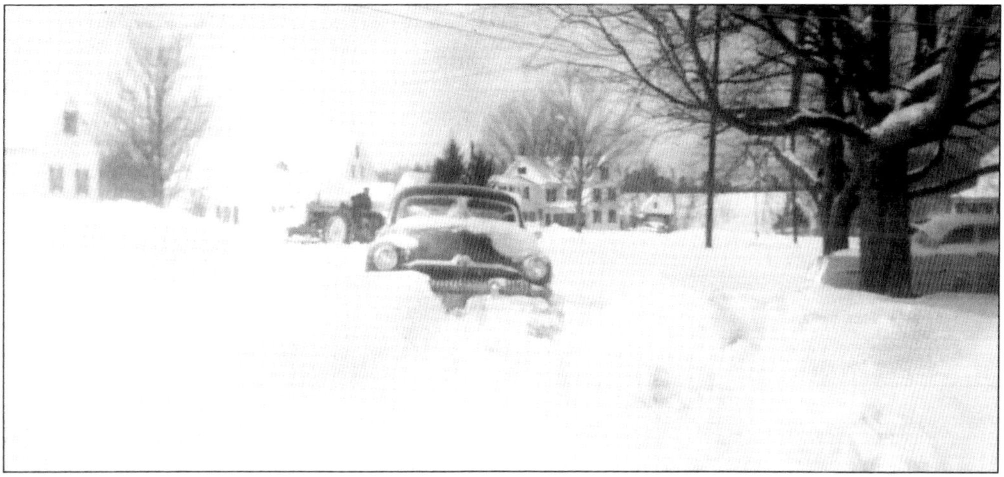

A view from Wiggin's Variety Store, 157 Portsmouth Avenue, looking toward the circle during the blizzard of March 17–19, 1957. That's Flossie Wiggin's car. The old Christian church is on the left and Mildred Parker's house is on the right. (E and EW.)

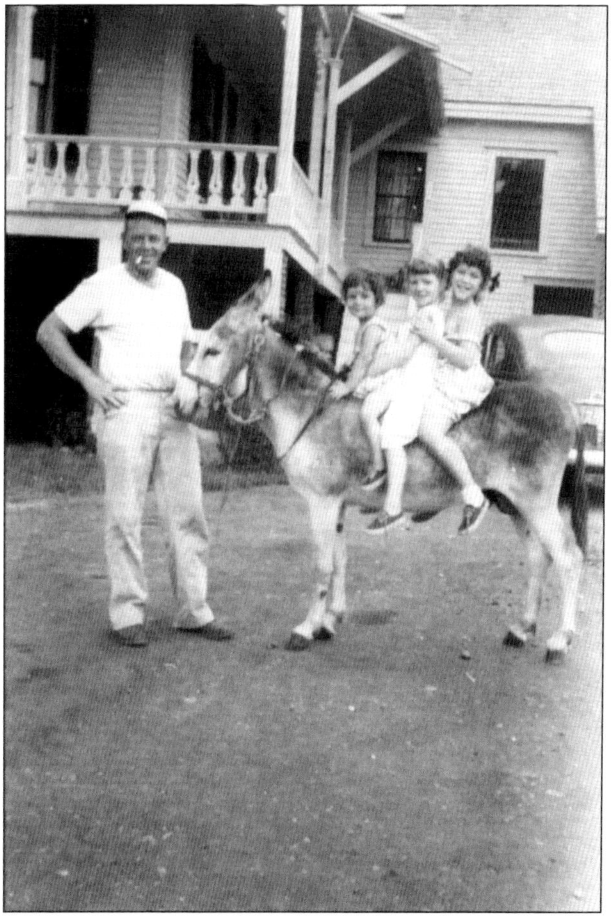

John Hutton with daughters Joyce, Lucy, and Nancy on a donkey at their farm at 163 Winnicutt Road, c. 1958. (LC.)

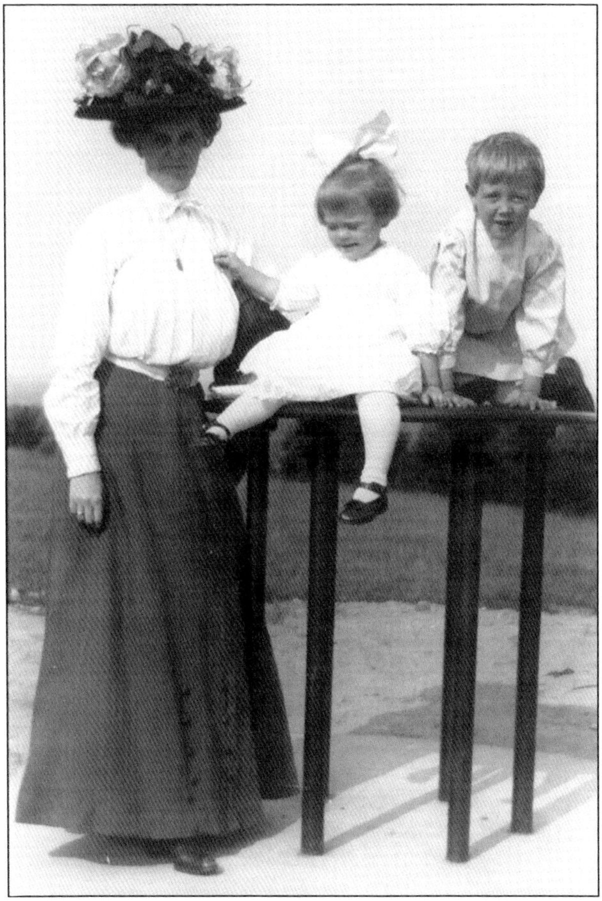

Verne Clough Higgins, her two-and-a-half-year-old daughter Ella, and her four-year-old son John on the top of Stratham Hill Park in 1910. (TS.)

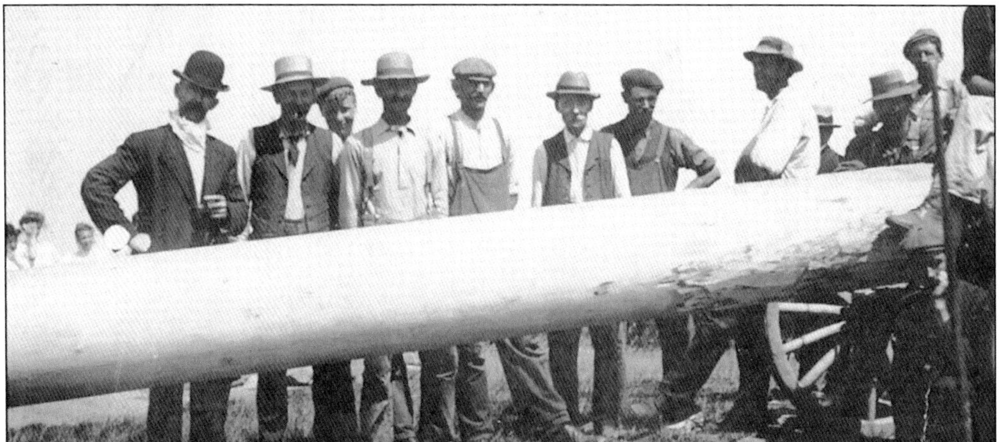

Raising the flagpole at Stratham Hill Park on Old Home Day, August 1908. Shown here are Bert Burbank, George E. Gowen, Eddie Tuttle, Arthur Jewell, Melvin Stickney, Levi Prentiss Wiggin, J.C. Piper, and Gilbert Thompson. The old growth pine mast was cut from Mrs. Josiah B. Wiggin's lot and shaped by a spar maker from the Portsmouth Naval Shipyard. Ralph Laighton, a Portsmouth bank president who had lived in Stratham, donated the flag. (SHS.)

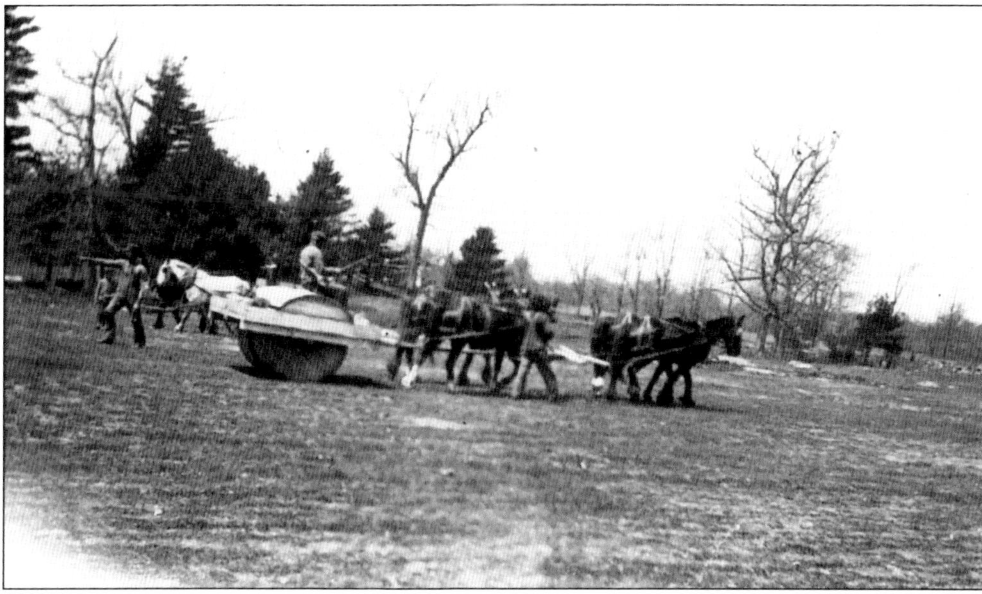

Rolling the ballfield at the Stratham Hill Park, probably around the turn of the century. The ball was also used to roll snow and clear roads throughout town. This ballfield is on the site of the parking lot. (SHS.)

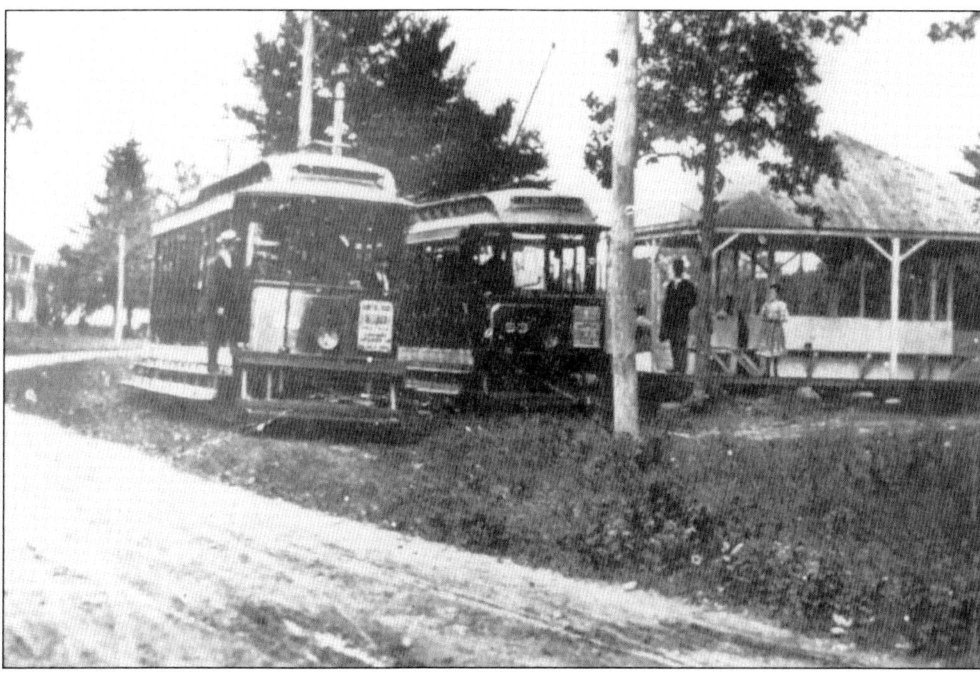

A trolley stops at the Stratham Hill Park. Electric trolley service between Exeter and Portsmouth served Stratham from 1902 to 1913. The town cut down Ayers Hill to make it easier to build the trolley and mandated that all public and private crossings be planked. There were proposals for trolley service on College and Winnicutt Roads that were never pursued. (SHS.)

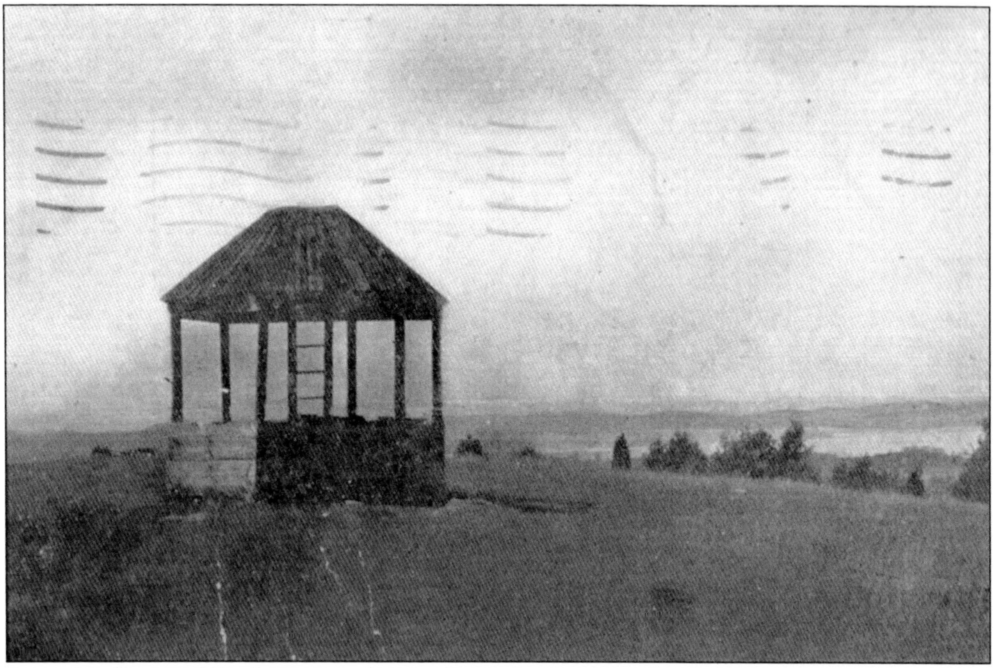

Atop Stratham Hill looking toward Great Bay, *c.* 1900. (SHS.)

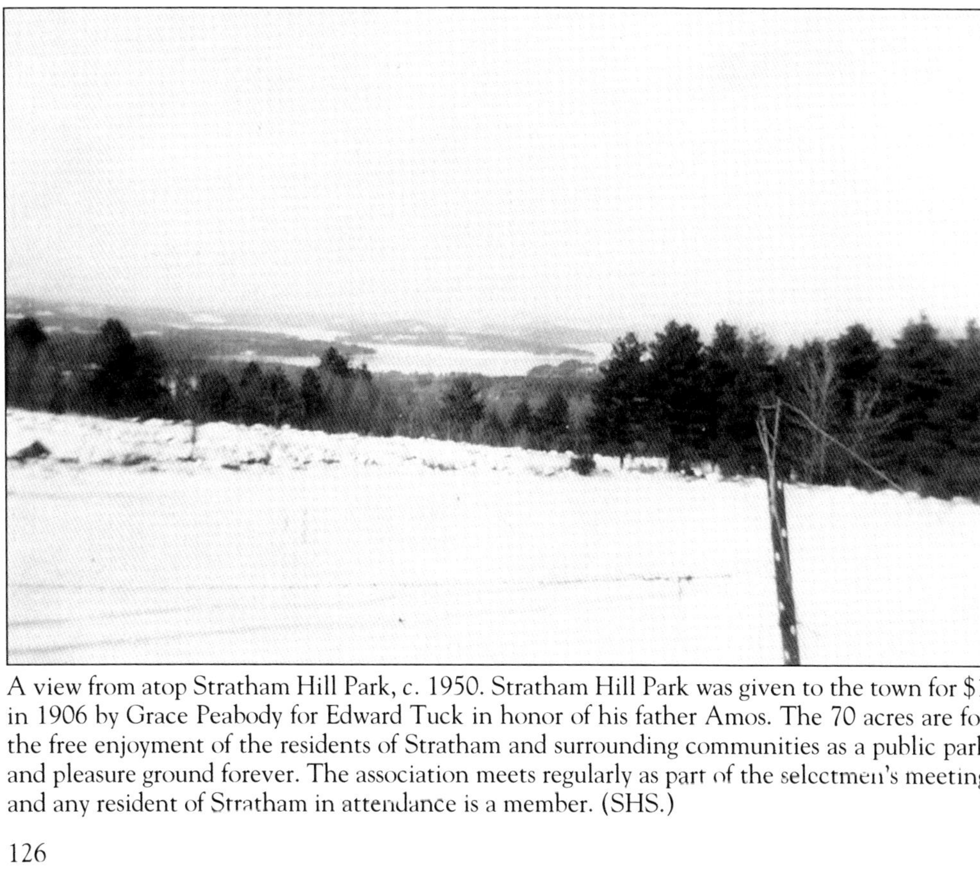

A view from atop Stratham Hill Park, *c.* 1950. Stratham Hill Park was given to the town for $1 in 1906 by Grace Peabody for Edward Tuck in honor of his father Amos. The 70 acres are for the free enjoyment of the residents of Stratham and surrounding communities as a public park and pleasure ground forever. The association meets regularly as part of the selectmen's meeting and any resident of Stratham in attendance is a member. (SHS.)

The fire lookout atop Stratham Hill Park. The elevation, at 288 feet, is the highest point in the area. In 1931 the State of New Hampshire Forest Fire Service erected a steel lookout station. Clayton Eastman was the last to man the tower in the early 1970s. (SHS.)

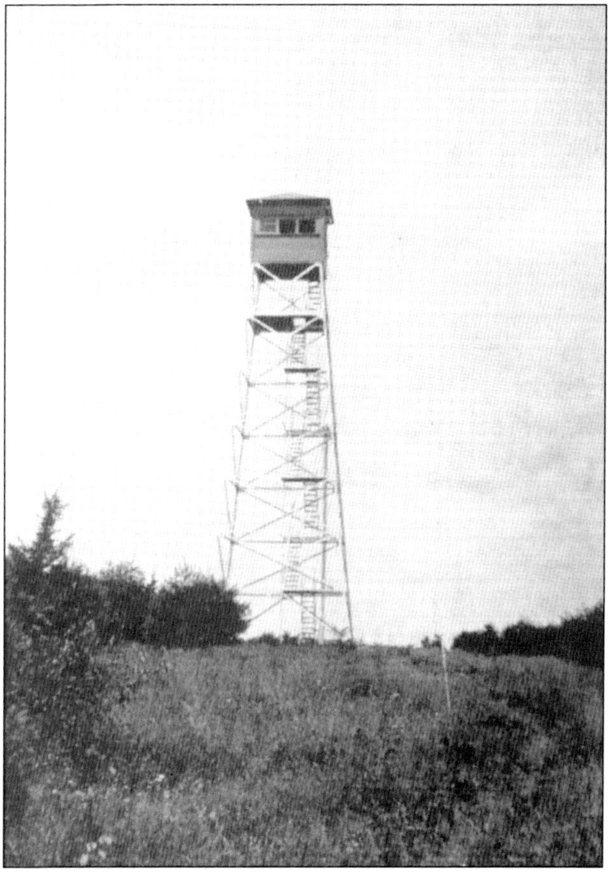

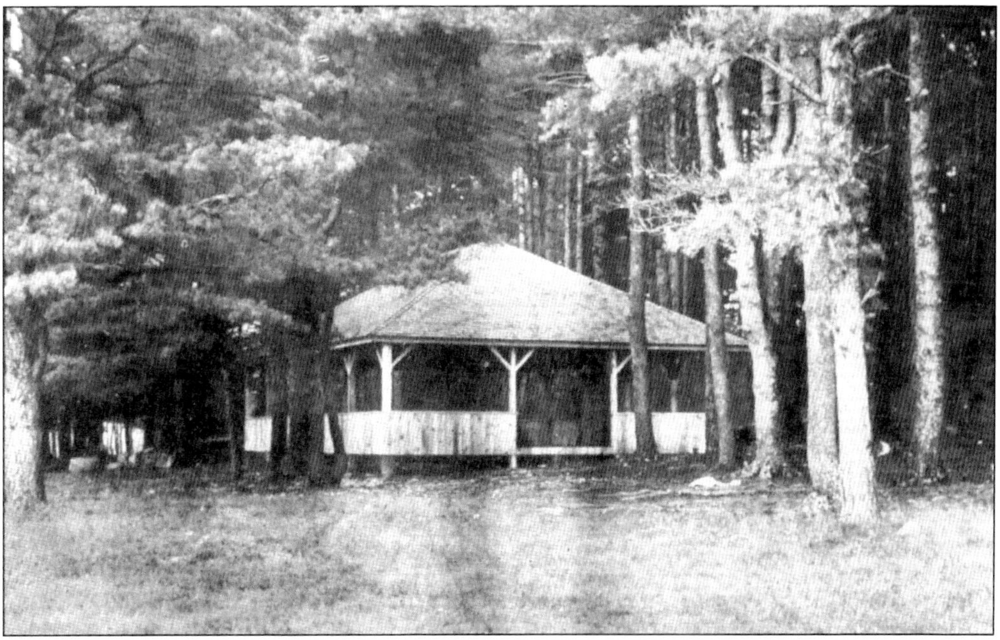

The old pavilion at Stratham Hill Park. It was crushed during a storm in 1990. (D and SS.)

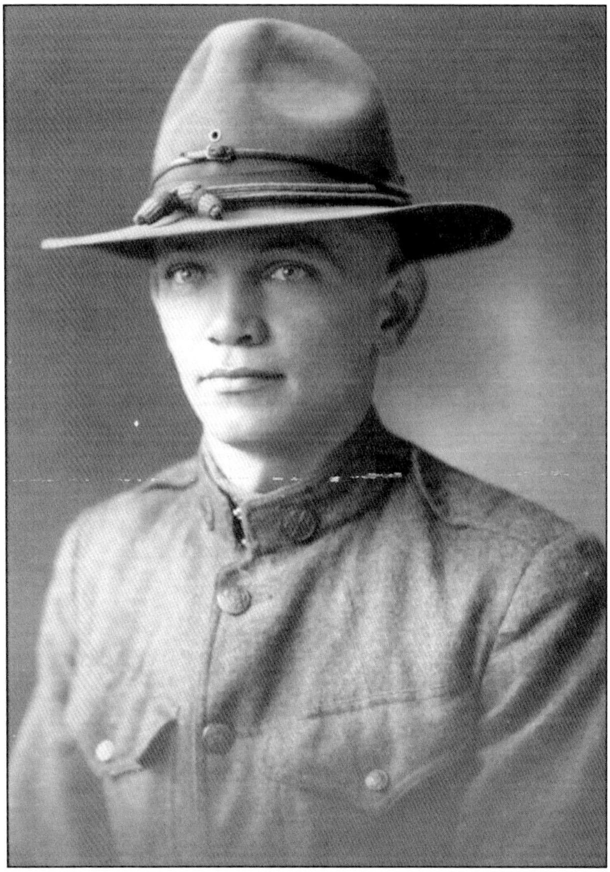

Shirley W. Gowen in his World War I uniform. (HC.)

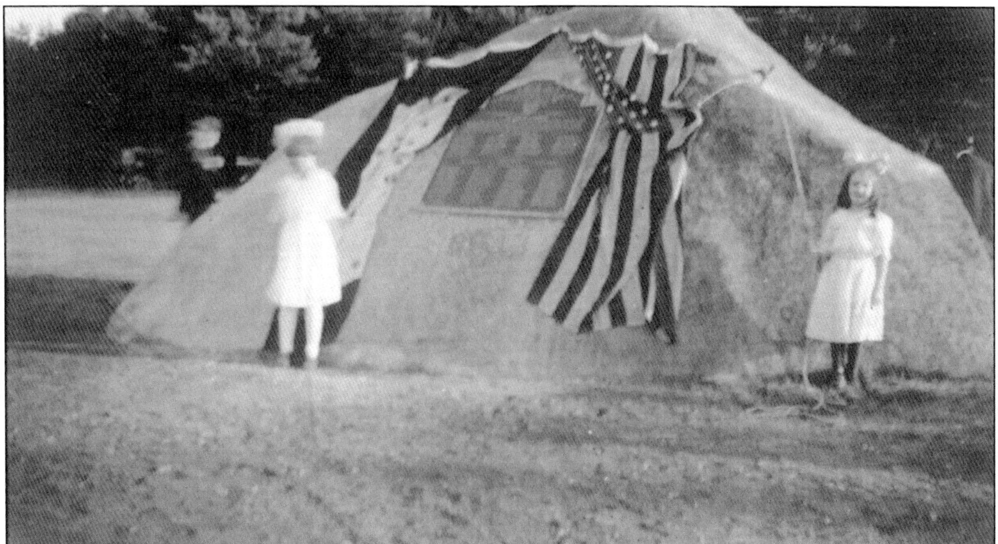

Nan Pearson and Murial Dining, granddaughters of Civil War Veterans, at the Civil War and Great War Memorials at the Stratham Hill Park in 1920. Nan was also a niece of Shirley Gowen. (SHS.)